JOURNAL FOR THE STUDY OF THE OLD TESTAMENT
SUPPLEMENT SERIES
355

Sheffield Academic Press
A Continuum imprint

The Lord of the Dreams

A Semantic and Literary Analysis of Genesis 37–50

Ron Pirson

Journal for the Study of the Old Testament
Supplement Series 355

Copyright © 2002 Sheffield Academic Press
A Continuum imprint

Published by Sheffield Academic Press Ltd
The Tower Building, 11 York Road, London SE1 7NX
370 Lexington Avenue, New York NY 10017-6550

www.continuumbooks.com

British Library Cataloguing-in-Publication Data
A catalogue record for this book is available from the British Library

Typeset by Sheffield Academic Press
Printed on acid-free paper in Great Britain by Bookcraft Ltd, Midsomer Norton, Bath

ISBN 0-8264-6209-X

Ron Pirson

To Wim Weren

He is beyond the shadow of your doubt and mine
He is no man's opinion—he is truth divine
16 Horsepower, 'Splinters' (*Secret South*, 2000)

CONTENTS

ABBREVIATIONS

AB	Anchor Bible
ABD	David Noel Freedman (ed.), *The Anchor Bible Dictionary* (New York: Doubleday, 1992)
BDB	Francis Brown, S.R. Driver and Charles A. Briggs, *A Hebrew and English Lexicon of the Old Testament* (Oxford: Clarendon Press, 1907)
Bib	*Biblica*
BibInt	*Biblical Interpretation: A Journal of Contemporary Approaches*
BKAT	Biblischer Kommentar: Altes Testament
BN	*Biblische Notizen*
BR	*Bible Review*
BZAW	Beihefte zur *ZAW*
CBQ	*Catholic Biblical Quarterly*
CBQMS	*Catholic Biblical Quarterly*, Monograph Series
DCH	D.J.A. Clines (ed.), *The Dictionary of Classical Hebrew* (Sheffield: Sheffield Academic Press, 1993–).
ExpTim	*Expository Times*
GKC	*Gesenius' Hebrew Grammar* (ed. E. Kautzsch, revised and trans. A.E. Cowley; Oxford: Clarendon Press, 1910)
HALAT	Ludwig Koehler *et al.* (eds.), *Hebräisches und aramäisches Lexikon zum Alten Testament* (5 vols.; Leiden: E.J. Brill, 1967–1995)
HUCA	*Hebrew Union College Annual*
IBS	*Irish Biblical Studies*
ICC	International Critical Commentary
Int	*Interpretation*
JBL	*Journal of Biblical Literature*
JNES	*Journal of Near Eastern Studies*
JSOT	*Journal for the Study of the Old Testament*
JSOTSup	*Journal for the Study of the Old Testament*, Supplement Series
JSS	*Journal of Semitic Studies*
KB	Ludwig Koehler and Walter Baumgartner (eds.), *Lexicon in Veteris Testamenti libros* (Leiden: E.J. Brill, 1953)
KJV	King James Version
NICOT	New International Commentary on the Old Testament

NIDOTE	Willem A. VanGemeren (ed.), *New International Dictionary of Old Testament Theology and Exegesis* (5 vols.; Grand Rapids: Zondervan, 1997)
NIV	New International Version
NRSV	New Revised Standard Version
OTL	Old Testament Library
OTS	*Oudtestamentische Studiën*
RB	*Revue biblique*
SANT	Studien zum Alten und Neuen Testament
SBLDS	SBL Dissertation Series
TBü	Theologische Bücherei
ThWAT	G.J. Botterweck and H. Ringgren (eds.), *Theologisches Wörterbuch zum Alten Testament* (Stuttgart: W. Kohlhammer, 1970–)
VT	*Vetus Testamentum*
VTSup	*Vetus Testamentum*, Supplements
WBC	Word Biblical Commentary
ZAH	*Zeitschrift für Althebraistik*
ZAW	*Zeitschrift für die alttestamentliche Wissenschaft*

PREFACE

From 1994 onwards the Theological Faculty of Tilburg gave me the opportunity to write my PhD thesis on the story of Joseph and his brothers, which I finished in the Spring of 1999. This study is a revision and expansion of the second part of this unpublished doctoral dissertation, which I defended on 24 September 1999 at Tilburg University, the Netherlands.

Here I want to express my gratitude to Professor Ellen van Wolde, who supervised my project on Gen. 37–50. It has been and still is very stimulating for me to work in the same department as her. I also want to thank Professors T. Muraoka from Leiden University and David Clines from Sheffield University for their advice and support while I was doing this research, and for their presence when I had to defend my thesis.

Yet, there are some more people I want to thank. These are my fellow-researchers at the Theological Faculty of Tilburg with whom I shared a room while we were all working on our theses: Harald van Veghel, Door Brouns-Wewerinke and Yvonne van den Akker-Savelsbergh. Apart from those colleagues in Tilburg I also mention the attendants of Professor Muraoka's seminars on Biblical Hebrew: Martin Baasten, Michael Malessa, Wido van Peursen and Max Rogland. Those sessions in Leiden between 1995 and 2000 were quite inspiring and encouraging.

Finally, I thank Petra, to whom I owe more than I can ever return.

INTRODUCTION

It is a truth universally acknowledged that pride and misunderstanding often give rise to conflict and alienation among people, and sometimes even result in murder. All these ingredients are present in Gen. 37, the opening chapter of the so-called 'Story of Joseph'.

Genesis 37–50 actually presents the tale in which several of Jacob's sons enter the spotlight. Therefore it is better to stick to the narrator's designation of this tale as the story of the *toledot* of Jacob (37.2). There are, of course, the oldest and youngest sons, Reuben and Benjamin. They, however, play only a minor part, for Joseph and Judah are most prominent. At the beginning of the tale, the former is his father's favourite. He appears to be heading for the top position in the family, but in the end he will disappear from his relatives. The most prominent position in Israel is going to be taken by Judah. He is the one from whom the kingship of David will eventually come forth. How did this come to be? Why did Joseph fall from his elevated status? Why is there in the biblical account no tribe of Joseph in the promised land and is his territory given to Ephraim and Manasseh?

Although this study is based on synchronic analyses, this does not imply that the results of diachronic studies on Gen. 37–50 are neglected. The tale of the 12 brothers has given rise to a substantial number of historical critical studies, because the 'Joseph-cycle'—and especially its opening chapter —is considered an outstanding example of a conflation of various sources.[1] To mention but two textual phenomena in Gen. 37 that point to distinct traditions: there is a doubling of the brother who tries to prevent Joseph's

---

1.   For a chronological overview of historical critical studies of the story of Gen. 37–50, see C. Paap, *Die Josephsgeschichte, Genesis 37–50: Bestimmungen ihrer literarischen Gattung in der zweiten Hälfte des 20. Jahrhunderts* (Europäische Hochschulschriften, 23, Theologie, 534; Frankfurt am Main: Peter Lang, 1995), esp. pp. 9-87 and 123-163. Also cf. L. Schmidt, *Literarische Studien zur Josephsgeschichte* (BZAW, 167; Berlin: W. de Gruyter, 1986), 127-41; R. de Hoop, *Genesis 49 in its Literary and Historical Context* (Leiden: E.J. Brill, 1998), 366-450.

murder, and both Midianites and Ishmaelites are involved in Joseph's sale. Moreover, in the entire story the narrative flow is suddenly interrupted by the intrusion of Gen. 38, the story of Tamar and Judah—not to mention the death-bed episode in Gen. 48 and the old tribal sayings in Gen. 49, which are not considered an integral part of the Joseph story.

It may be true that, with regard to the 'traditional' sources (Elohist, Yahwist, Priestly source), as Donner wrote a quarter of a century ago, the 'Kriterien der Pentateuchquellenscheidung versagen an Gen. 37–50' ('criteria of Pentateuchal source-criticism fail concerning Gen. 37–50').[2] Yet, this does not imply that historical critical investigations should be no longer executed. Indeed, since Donner's statement quite a few new studies concentrating on historical critical issues have been published,[3] and—with regard to the development of the texts—studies like these on Gen. 37–50 need to be and will undoubtedly be prosecuted,[4] and the same is applicable to studies in which the biblical accounts are related to the *Umwelt* of the Bible.[5] The present study, as was indicated above, shall not pursue this

2.   H. Donner, *Die literarische Gestalt der alttestamentlichen Josephsgeschichte* (Heidelberg: Carl Winter/Universitätsverlag, 1976), 24. Also cf. H.-C. Schmitt, 'Die Hintergründe der "neuesten Pentateuchkritik" und der literarische Befund der Josefsgeschichte Gen 37-50', *ZAW* 98 (1985), 161-79; L. Ruppert, 'Die Aporie der gegenwärtigen Pentateuchdiskussion und die Joseferzählung der Genesis', *BZ* 29 (1985), 31-48; *idem*, 'Zur neueren Diskussion um die Josefsgeschichte der Genesis', *BZ* 33 (1989), 92-97.

3.   E.g. H. Seebass, *Geschichtliche Zeit und theonome Tradition in der Joseph-Erzählung* (Gütersloh: Gütersloher Verlagshaus/Gerd Mohn, 1978); Schmidt, *Literarische Studien zur Josephsgeschichte*; J. Scharbert, *Ich bin Joseph euer Bruder. Die Erzählung von Joseph und seinen Brüdern wie sie nicht in der Bibel steht* (St Ottilien: EOS Verlag Erzabtei, 1988); W. Dietrich, *Die Josephserzählung als Novelle und Geschichtsschreibung: zugleich ein Beitrag zur Pentateuchfrage* (Biblisch-Theologische Studien, 14; Neukirchen–Vluyn: Neukirchener Verlag, 1989); N. Kekebus, *Die Josepherzählung: Literarkritische und redaktionsgeschichtliche Untersuchungen zu Genesis 37-50* (Internationale Hochschulschriften; Münster: Waxmann, 1990).

4.   Especially so since the publication of Philip Davies' *In Search of 'Ancient Israel'* (JSOTSup, 148; Sheffield: Sheffield Academic Press, 1992).

5.   With regard to Gen. 37–50 cf. J. Vergote, *Joseph en Egypte: Genèse chap. 37–50 à la lumière des études Egyptologiques récentes* (Orientalia et Biblica Lovaniensia, 3; Leuven: Publications Universitaires/Instituut voor Oriëntalisme, 1959); T.L. Thompson, 'The Joseph and Moses Narratives', in J.H. Hayes and J.M. Miller (eds.), *Israelite and Judean History* (OTL; London: SCM Press, 1977), 149-212; D.B. Redford, *A Study of the Biblical Story of Joseph (Genesis 37-50)* (VTSup, 20; Leiden: E.J. Brill, 1970); *idem*, *Egypt, Canaan and Israel in Ancient Times* (Princeton, NJ: Princeton University Press, 1992).

path. The results of the historical-critical studies, however, are taken into account—especially in the case of those passages that are often designated as not belonging to the story of the brothers.[6] I will show that these texts or the seemingly alien elements, can actually be accounted for on a narrative level.

The purpose of this study is to find an answer to the questions posed above: Why is Joseph hardly ever mentioned outside Genesis? Why does Joseph not receive a portion of the land promised to his ancestors? And how did he come to lose his special position to Judah?

It will become clear that I consider the reader to play a prominent part in the process of attaching meaning to the text.[7] Yet, this process of interpretation is not restricted to the reader only: she or he is for a substantial part steered by the Hebrew language and the context in which the text at issue is to be found. So, attributing meaning to a text, or interpreting a text is a complex process between text, reader, and a number of circumstances which influence the interpretative process.[8] Moreover, a reader's perception of a text changes as the text is read a second time, a third, a fourth, and so on. Every subsequent reading offers new insights and information that add to a different understanding of this particular text or book. In this

6.   I subscribe to Lamprecht's remark on the method employed in his doctoral dissertation: 'Hierdie studie gaan van die oortuiging uit dat die twee heersende benaderings, te wete die historiese en sinchroniese, komplementêr tot mekaar in Ou-Testamentiese navorsing gebruik moet word... Dit beteken dat sinchroniese benaderings van ter sake resultate van die histories-kritiese benadering sal kennis neem en omgekeerd. Die implikasie van hierdie keuse is dat nòg die historisme, nòg 'n a-historiese benadering aanvaardbaar is' (J.J. Lamprecht, 'Karakterisering in Gen 37-50' [unpublished PhD dissertation, University of Stellenbosch, 1990], 5).

7.   Although the biblical texts create a world of their own—these texts nevertheless refer to the world outside the texts (cf. Gen. 32.32: 'therefore to this day the children of Israel do not eat the tendon attached to the socket of the hip...'), and consequently do have a historical and theological significance. The act of reading brings a reader into the world of the text, after which this reader must relate this textual world to his or her own. Cf. T. Longman, III: 'It is necessary to integrate literary analysis with the study of history and the text's ideology (theology). They are all aspects of the text's act of communication' ('Literary Approaches and Interpretation', in *NIDOTE*, 103-24 [113]). On the going together of diachronic and synchronic analyses, see V.P. Long, *The Reign and Rejection of King Saul: A Case for Literary and Theological Coherence* (SBLDS, 118; Atlanta, GA: Scholars Press, 1989), esp. 7-20.

8.   Cf. E. van Wolde, 'Semantics and (Ana)Logic', in *idem, Words become Worlds: Semantic Studies of Genesis 1–11* (Leiden: E.J. Brill, 1994), 149-59.

study I take the position of a reader who considers Gen. 37–50 to be a unity (not a single verse is excluded), who has read those chapters more than once. This reader has found several interesting and intriguing phenomena, which he would like to present to others interested in Gen. 37–50.

The first chapter deals with a description of the way in which the semantic data derived from Gen. 37–50 are dealt with, and how these contribute to a literary analysis of those chapters. The remainder of this study is devoted to semantic and literary analyses of the tale of Joseph and his brothers. In the second chapter the children of Jacob are focussed upon as they are to be found prior to Gen. 37 and in the opening verses of the tale of the brothers (37.2-4). In Chapter 3 the centre of attention will be Joseph's dreams, whereas in Chapter 4 Joseph's sale to Egypt is dealt with. Chapter 5 is about Judah's and Joseph's departure from their family; and in Chapter 6 I will consider the brothers' journeys into Egypt and especially Judah's speech to the Egyptian vizier and how all this affects Joseph. In the final chapter I make some observations based on the farewell-accounts in Gen. 48–50. I will mention some topics of further research in the Epilogue; these may be pursued with regard to the historical circumstances in which the present text of Gen. 37–50 may have had its final redaction.

The investigations into Gen. 37–50 that I present here will result in an answer to the question why Joseph has disappeared from Israel's literary history.

Chapter 1

MEANING IN CONTEXT

1. *Introduction*

In 'Parallels', an episode of the television series *Star Trek: The Next Generation*, Lieutenant Worf is returning in a shuttle to the starship Enterprise. However, before reaching his ship something has gone wrong. Due to a state of 'quantum flux' Worf begins to jump between different 'quantum realities': he appears to be travelling from one universe to the next, never being at home anywhere, whereas the people inhabiting the different universes are not aware of Worf's fluctuating from one quantum state to another. This episode is based on the 'quantum measurement theory' in quantum-mechanics, a concept which is rather illogical to ordinary common sense:

> one of the most remarkable features of quantum mechanics is that objects observed to have some property cannot be said to have had that property the instant before the observation. The observation process can change the character of the physical system under consideration. The quantum mechanical wavefunction of a system describes completely the configuration of this system at any one time, and this wavefunction evolves according to deterministic laws of physics. However, what makes things seem so screwy is that this wavefunction can encompass two or more mutually exclusive configurations at the same time.[1]

1.   L.M. Krauss, *The Physics of Star Trek* (New York: Basic Books, 1995), 151. Cf. S. Hawking, *A Brief History of Time: From the Big Bang to Black Holes* (Toronto: Bantam Books, 1988); *idem*, *Black Holes and Baby Universes and Other Essays* (New York: Bantam Books, 1993). In quantum mechanic theory it is accepted that the observer has a determining influence on that which is observed, which is illustrated by the paradox of Schrödinger's cat: 'Imagine a box, inside of which is a cat. Inside the box, aimed at the cat, is a gun, which is hooked up to a radioactive source. The radioactive source has a certain quantum mechanical probability of decaying at any given time. When this source decays, the gun will fire and kill the cat. Is the wavefunction describing the cat, before I open the box, a linear superposition of a live cat and a dead

Every single quantum particle can have all possible histories—as long as it does not contradict physical laws—or as Lieutenant-Commander Data in the Star Trek episode says: 'All things which can occur, do occur'. As a kind of analogy—although less extreme—words or texts can have several possible histories; or, in this case, interpretations. These interpretations are always dependent on the reader, yet they cannot be random interpretations.

'Can an interpretation ever lay definitive claim to correctness?' starts Paul Armstrong's *Conflicting Readings*,[2] a book in which a plea is made for multiple and even conflicting interpretations of literary works. So, if there are conflicting readings, these ought to be founded on solid assumptions and have to be coherent and verifiable by others. Although literary criticism is a rational enterprise, the interpretation of a text can probably never be entirely conclusive or correct, which implies that interpreting a text is always tantamount to giving an interpretation that is as valid as possible. It is this question of interpretation that I will deal with in this first chapter.

2. *Meaning and Interpretation*

The most basic requirement for attaching meaning to a text and interpreting a text is the reader of the text in question. The text itself functions in a process of communication. To interpret it, is to try to discover the message that is communicated to the reader via the text.

This chapter then, is about the scholarly reader and the way she or he is able to attach meaning to a text and come to an interpretation of the text. The influence of the reader cannot be overestimated when one is talking about establishing meaning and interpretation. There are, of course, many possible readers: Western European readers will perceive a text differently from someone from South-Eastern Asia, and a twenty-first-century reader

cat?' (Krauss, *The Physics of Star Trek*, 152). With regard to the observer determining the observation one might also think of the Gestaltpsychology's principle 'the whole is different from the sum of its parts'—although in another way than is the case in quantum mechanics: '*Gestalt* is a word that has no exact English translation, though "form", "configuration" or "pattern" comes close. The word helps to emphasize that the whole affects the way in which the parts are perceived; perception acts to draw the sensory data together into a holistic pattern, or *Gestalt*' (R.L. Atkinson, R.C. Atkinson and E.R. Hilgard, *Introduction to Psychology* [New York: Harcourt Brace Jovanovich, 8th edn, 1981], 138).

2.　P.B. Armstrong, *Conflicting Readings: Variety and Validity in Interpretation* (Chapel Hill: University of North Carolina Press, 1990), 1.

will interpret a text in a different way than a fourteenth-century reader would have done, or a reader from the first century BC or a reader who—since that is the text to be dealt with in this book—is a contemporary of the author/editor of Gen. 37–50.[3] Many more circumstances affect the way a text is read and understood. As van Wolde remarks: 'A reader of a text attach[es] meaning to the linguistic signs by connecting them to the language code and also by relating these signs within the text both to each other as to his or her own knowledge or experience'.[4] A reader, therefore has to acquire both knowledge of the language, and knowledge of the cultural situation in which the text was written.

In this study I understand this reader to be someone who has read Gen. 37–50 many times, which means she or he can take the perspective of the whole story. Beginning, middle, and end coincide as it were. So, the reader remembers both the textual past and the textual future. She or he is able to see and study two fields of attention at once: one related to a limited moment or episode inside the story, and another encompassing the entire story.[5]

Since a text consists both of linguistic elements and of literary patterns, a textual analysis requires both a linguistic and a literary component. In my opinion a thorough study of a text's syntax and the words constituting it is necessary to come to a sound and reliable interpretation. The grammatical signs steer the reader through the text and mark the units that constitute the text. Moreover, the syntactic data indicate how to read a text—for example, which parts of the text are by the narrator and which are discursive texts.[6]

---

3.   In the case of biblical texts it is clear that the language and (historical) context of the biblical text enter into dialogue with the language and situational context of the present-day reader.

4.   Van Wolde, 'Semantics and (Ana)Logic', 156.

5.   The implication is that I do not present the reading of an 'implied reader'—it is too easy for a biblical scholar to have the implied reader read all kinds of things into the text which the scholar actually read her- or himself.

6.   See for an illustration of this E. van Wolde, 'Who Guides Whom? Embeddedness and Perspective in Biblical Hebrew and in 1 Kings 3.16-28', *JBL* 114 (1995), 623-42. This kind of syntactic application was inspired by Harald Weinrich's theory of the temporal value of verb forms, which he presented in his book *Tempus: Besprochene und erzählte Welt* (Sprache und Literatur, 16; Stuttgart: W. Kohlhammer, 4th edn, 1985), which was first published in 1964. Schneider's grammar of Hebrew, as well as Talstra's and Niccacci's studies are influenced by Weinrich's study. In my doctoral

. Apart from those syntactic analyses, semantic analyses of individual words are of major importance. While the meaning of a word is dependent on its position within a specific language system it is also determined by the context in which it occurs. The context of a word is not restricted to the level of the sentence in which the individual words appear, but goes beyond the sentence. Therefore I consider the entire textual unity in which a word occurs to be the scope of the examination of that particular word.[7] It is not possible to study all words extensively. In the following analyses a number of words are selected because of their importance with regard to existing studies on Gen. 37–50, and also because of the importance the present writer ascribes to them, in order to come to a coherent interpretation of Gen. 37–50.

Since words have a range of possible meanings, a dictionary alone is not enough to tell what a word means. Words are sensitive to context: 'In any sentence, a word's precise meaning is established by its interaction with other words, all of them "continually modifying" each other'.[8] The process of discerning meaning is dependent on the context in which a word or verse is found.[9] Therefore I will frequently refer to this context. The problem then, of course, is: What is 'context'?, and 'How large a context must we establish in order to interpret a text correctly?'[10]

---

dissertation of 1999 I applied Weinrich's theory to Gen. 37 (R. Pirson, The Lord of the Dreams: Genesis 37 and its Literary Context [unpublished Proefschrift Katholieke Universiteit Tilburg, 1999], 10-107).

7.   Cf. E. van Wolde, 'A Text-Semantic Study of the Hebrew Bible, Illustrated with Noah and Job', *JBL* 113 (1994), 19-35; *idem*, 'Textsemantics: A Bridge between Linguistics and Literary Theory', in I. Rauch and G.F. Carr (eds.), *Semiotics around the World: Synthesis in Diversity: Proceedings of the Fifth Congress of the International Association for Semiotic Studies, Berkeley 1994* (Berlin: Mouton de Gruyter, 1997), 267-70.

8.   Armstrong, *Conflicting Readings*, 63. Cf. 'Words typically have more than one meaning, as a quick glance at a dictionary will show. Which meaning is in force will vary according to the situation in which the word is applied. In a reciprocally defining manner that recalls the workings of the hermeneutic circle, the meaning of a sentence is built up out of the words that belong to it, but those words acquire their meaning only by virtue of their position and use in that sentence' (Armstrong, *Conflicting Readings*, 72). Cf. T. Longman III: 'Words are the building blocks of texts; texts are the place where words find their meaning' ('Literary Approaches and Interpretation'), 103.

9.   Cf. P. Cotterell and M. Turner, *Linguistics and Biblical Interpretation* (London: SPCK, 1989), 41-42.

10.   K. Vanhoozer, 'Introduction: Hermeneutics, Text, and Biblical Theology' to: 'Guide to Old Testament Theology and Exegesis', in *NIDOTE*, I, 14-50 (36).

3. *Context*

The word 'context' has a broad range of meanings. In order to avoid confusion I must explain what is meant when I use this notion in this study. I primarily understand 'context' in a literary sense: when speaking about the context of Gen. 37–50 I refer to the surrounding texts—in particular all narratives in Genesis dealing with Jacob and his sons.[11] However, in view of a literary and semantic analysis these narratives offer too limited a scope. Therefore I will consider the Torah as the context of my analyses. The Torah, the Pentateuch or the Five Books of Moses, has of old been considered a work on its own. 'Of old' here means at least from the second century BCE, and perhaps even earlier, since the division is known to Sirach, Philo and Josephus, and is also found in the LXX.[12] In addition, not only is the Torah considered to be a literary work in its own right, it is also recognized that it has functioned as one book since it was edited following the period generally referred to as the Babylonian Exile.[13] There are two reasons for taking this textual unit (i.e. the text of the Torah) as the point of reference in this study. One is that the context of a narrative is one of the primary means to discover its function;[14] in other words, a narrative is elucidated by its context. The second reason for taking the Torah as my point of reference is because in another context, for example, the book of Psalms or Jeremiah, the same word may have different meanings.[15] This

11. The relevant surrounding text is often also called co-text; cf. J. Lyons, *Linguistic Semantics: An Introduction* (Cambridge: Cambridge University Press, 1995), 271.

12. T.E. Fretheim, *The Pentateuch* (Interpreting Biblical Texts; Nashville: Abingdon Press, 1996), 19. Maybe the literary form of the Pentateuch is even older. David Clines in his *The Theme of the Pentateuch* (JSOTSup, 10; Sheffield: JSOT Press, 1978) writes that he is 'prepared to go along with the majority of scholarly opinion and locate its definitive edition in the fifth century B.C.' (11). However, Philip Davies opts for a date sometime during the second century BCE (*In Search of 'Ancient Israel'*, 134-54).

13. Cf. 'Die Bücher Esra/Neh setzen "die Tora des Mose" als normative Größe voraus (vgl. Esra 3, 2; Neh 10, 30; 13, 1; Neh 10 kommentiert Texte aus Ex - Dtn, setzt also den Pentateuch voraus)', E. Zenger, 'B. Die Bücher der Tora/des Pentateuch', in E. Zenger *et al.*, *Einleitung in das Alte Testament* (Kohlhammer Studienbücher Theologie 1, 1; Stuttgart: W. Kohlhammer, 1995), 34-75 (39).

14. Cf. V.P. Long, *The Art of Biblical History* (Foundations of Contemporary Interpretation, 5; Grand Rapids, MI: Zondervan, 1994), 66-67.

15. This restriction to the Torah is based upon a diachronic argument: the editing of the Torah sometime between the fifth and second century BC. Perhaps it would be

can be the case in a temporal perspective—through the years a word may have acquired a different meaning—and it is dependent on the particular literary context, in which a word may have a different meaning—for example, the antonymous Greek word-pair καταβαινω in the Gospel according to John functions in a specific way, and has a special meaning,[16] which is different from its meaning and function in the Synoptic Gospels.

A second meaning of 'context' is the historical context in which the texts of Gen. 37–50 and of the entire Torah came into existence.[17] As indicated in the introduction to this study, I will not elaborate upon the problems regarding the origin and dating of Gen. 37–50.[18] And a third meaning of 'context', which one has to bear in mind, is the context in which the reader of today finds him- or herself: a Western context that differs in many ways from the world that is presupposed by the biblical accounts. Moreover, it is a context in which the Bible has had a pre-dominant role over the last 1500 years (although its influence is rapidly declining nowadays). This latter element implies that the reader is aware of the fact that the Torah is part of the Bible, and therefore is conscious of the position that it takes in the Scriptures: in the Hebrew Bible it is situated both in place and from a chronological point of view before the conquest of the promised land. It is impossible to dismiss this knowledge when studying or analyzing one of the texts of the Torah.[19] When the word 'context' is used in this study, it will mostly refer to the meaning mentioned first, namely, the context in a literary sense, the Torah.

---

better to consider all narrative texts of the Hebrew Bible, since it is not until 2 Kings that the *narratives* of the children of Israel (תלדות יעקב) come to an end. Whenever the textual data of the Torah is insufficient or inconclusive I will extend the scope to the books of Joshua to 2 Kings.

16. Cf. G.C. Nicholson, *Death as Departure: The Johannine Descent–Ascent Schema* (SBLDS, 63; Chico, CA: Scholars Press, 1983); W. Weren, 'Mozes, Jezus en het manna. Een intertekstuele studie van Johannes 6', in *idem, Intertextualiteit en Bijbel* (Kampen: Kok, 1993), 93-132 (100-101).

17. The historical context can actually both refer to the time in which the text was written, but also to the time in which, if any, underlying historical events took place; cf. Long, *The Art of Biblical History*, Chapter 2, 'History and Fiction', 58-87; also Cotterell and Turner, *Linguistics and Biblical Interpretation*, 44.

18. Although I will briefly return to this matter in the Epilogue.

19. However, as Cotterell and Turner indicate, one must be aware of the danger of the interpreter reading his own world into the world of the text because of the differences between both worlds (*Linguistics and Biblical Interpretation*, 69-70).

4. *Biblical Hebrew*

The following analyses will demonstrate that the individual words receive a lot of attention. I assume the meaning of a word not only to be restricted to its lexical meaning, but also to be established by its usage in the text: both by its characters[20] and its narrator.[21] This implies that the context in which a word occurs is of primary importance, and that the usage of a word in one context is compared to its usage in another. On the basis of this comparison several inferences may be drawn; these have results for the interpretation of a part of the text. Therefore, several remarks on the Hebrew language system must be made.

The relatively small lexical stock of the Biblical Hebrew language is based on a still smaller number of roots.[22] The meaning that is attributed to these roots in the dictionaries—although they in themselves carry no meaning[23]—is based on the way in which the lexemes, that are based upon these roots, function in their contexts. Ellen van Wolde argues that, because:

1. Biblical Hebrew has a limited lexicon that consists of a restricted number of lexemes and of an even more restricted number of roots;
2. lexemes can often be derived from more than one root, because consonants may have dropped out in inflected forms;
3. lexemes often correspond with miscellaneous and sometimes even contradictory meanings, the Hebrew paradigm is more general and less specified than, for example, the English paradigm. Besides, these data explain why the syntagmatic or contextual relations in the text are necessary to specify the manifold paradigmatic possibilities. The specification in the syntagmatic textual relations is done by way of language-

---

20. Words spoken by a character consequently deserve to be studied thoroughly.

21. Cf. Armstrong, *Conflicting Readings*, 72: 'If words could not mean several things at once, we would need a new term to convey each nuance of thought and feeling, to capture every different experience, and to report on all new objects we encounter. Polysemy allows words to be used in different, unforeseen situations. It also enables us to extend a word's meaning.'

22. According to B.K. Waltke and M. O'Connor there are 1565 verbal roots (*An Introduction to Biblical Hebrew Syntax* [Winona Lake, IN: Eisenbrauns, 1990], 361).

23. 'The ordinary speaker is unconscious of much of the structure of his or her language. In ancient Hebrew this may well have been the case with much of the element we call "root". It was, after all, well on in the Middle Ages before the principles of the Hebrew root were worked out by Jewish grammarians themselves, and this is so especially of the triliteral root' (J. Barr, 'Three Interrelated Factors in the Semantic Study of Ancient Hebrew', *ZAH* 7 [1994], 33-44 [43]). Also cf. *idem*, 'Did Isaiah Know about Hebrew "Root Meanings"?', *ExpTim* 75 (1964), 242.

markers. Which means that similarities are being created between different words, and that use is being made of the fact that words can
represent different meanings at the same time. They become, technically
speaking, 'iconically' motivated.[24]

Meaning, however, is not restricted to the interaction of the Hebrew language system and the realization in the Hebrew texts. It is the reader who
is a determining factor in the process of establishing meaning. The reader
attaches meaning on the basis of markers that she or he is able to discover
in the text. According to van Wolde it 'is the reader's job to discern markers in the text or, rather, to single out elements in the text as markers',[25]
the reader actualizes the possibilities that are dormant in the text.

Another important point to be mentioned here is the rather special place
the biblical texts have acquired through the ages. I do not mean that they
are considered 'holy Scriptures' or 'word of God' or something of this
nature, but the fact that the texts have become part of the cultural history
of our times. There is hardly a reader to be found who is not acquainted
with the contents of quite a few biblical narratives. Everybody who starts
reading a gospel, or perhaps I should say, until now almost everybody who
starts reading a gospel, knows that Jesus will be crucified and rise from the
dead, and a reader of Exodus knows beforehand that the people of Israel
will in the end reach the promised land. Such facts are part of our cultural
heritage, just as everybody knows about the French Revolution or the
Great War. Facts like these mean that biblical narratives cannot be treated
in the same way as novels or short stories. Before starting to read a particular biblical text the reader is already 'heavily burdened' with the knowledge she or he carries with her- or himself.[26] This knowledge, however,
will probably become less and less in the years to come, so that the gap

24. E. van Wolde, *Aan de hand van Ruth* (Kampen: Kok, 1993), 14. Van Wolde also
gives an example of a specific sort of iconicity (paranomasia) from the garden story in
Genesis. The phonetic similarity between the words ערום ('cunning') and ערומים
('naked') suggests a relation concerning content between 'cunning' and 'naked', a relation that subsequently becomes syntagmatically elaborated. Cf. *idem*, 'A Text-Semantic Study', 26-29.

25. Van Wolde, 'A Text-Semantic Study', 30, cf. *idem*, *Aan de hand van Ruth*, 15-
16.

26. Cf. van Wolde, *Aan de hand van Ruth*, 9: 'The last decade people have become
aware of the fact that a reader is not an autonomous individual who produces meaning,
but that he or she is also determined by his social and cultural surroundings, of ideological, economical, racial, sexual, educational and other codes. Both codes and experiences influence the reader, who is determined by both.'

between the biblical texts and literary texts may be bridged more and more.

In the remainder of this chapter I give a step-by-step description of the way in which I will proceed in the semantic analyses of Gen. 37–50; the next section is concerned with lexical meaning (a semantic analysis), section 6 with contextual meaning (a combination of a semantic and literary analysis) and section 7 with connotative meaning as derived from a text's literary context (a literary analysis). In the actual analyses from Chapter 2 onwards, these three steps are more or less integrated and combined into one.

5. *Lexicon and Meaning*

The first step in the semantic analysis of a particular text is of a more general character. It is not restricted to the text itself and its context. It starts on a rather basic level, and is mainly lexicographical. To find out about a particular word's meaning (or meanings) several dictionaries could be consulted.[27] In this lexicographic investigation one is provided with a wide range of information, such as information about a word's etymology and its cognates in other Semitic languages, its development through time or whether it is Classical Hebrew or only found in Late Biblical Hebrew.[28] One also finds information about a word's relationship to other parts of speech or the distribution of a particular word among the several parts of the Bible.

27. Cf. Cotterell and Turner: 'Most words have several senses; and dictionaries compile the various possible senses of each word, by indicating each sense in terms of synonymous words or expressions' (*Linguistics & Biblical Interpretation*, 78). There is always a problem as concerns terminology. Although Cotterell and Turner speak of 'sense' in dictionaries, I use the terminology by J. Lyons in his *Linguistic Semantics*, and will refer to the 'lexical meaning(s)' of a word instead of its 'sense(s)'.

28. It is important to be aware of (1) the fact that most language-users are unaware of the etymology of the words they use; and (2) 'that many words have evolved over time in such a way that their current meaning is only vaguely related to their original meaning' (J.H. Walton, 'Principles for Productive Word Study', *NIDOTE*, I, 161-71 [163]). The first point is stated even stronger by J.H. Hospers: 'etymological, i.e. diachronic, information should always be irrelevant in a synchronic analysis of language, as genetic relationships in the language are not part of the competence of the native speaker' ('Polysemy and Homonymy', *ZAH* 6 [1993] 114-122 [118]). One should also avoid the trap of anachronism: explaining words in terms of meanings which developed later (cf. Cotterell and Turner, *Linguistics and Biblical Interpretation*, 133-34).

A next step regards a word's syntagmatic relationships in the strictest sense: In which way does the word occur? There are variations of meaning depending on the collocations in which a word is used; for example, there is quite a difference between מכר ל (qal, 'sell to') and מכר אל (qal, 'sell into').[29] The presence of a certain preposition or noun rather than another with the verb can add a nuance or a difference to the meaning of the verb. Or, now and then, a word is part of an expression (e.g. טוב ורע, 'good and bad', a merism), by which the words used have another meaning than the sum of its parts.

A further point is concerned with the question of semantic fields: To which semantic field does the word under investigation belong?[30] The meaning of a word in a text is not only determined by its position in that particular text and its syntactic relations within that text, but also by more or less similar words in the language system. According to VanGemeren, the determination of a word is 'contingent on its relationship with other words'.[31] In other words: What is the special meaning of this word compared to other words belonging to the same semantic field? In what way

29. Information of this particular kind is given structurally in *DCH*.

30. Cf. Lyons, *Linguistic Semantics*, 75: 'But how does one define or identify what a word stands for? Is it possible to say what one word stands for without employing other semantically related words in doing so and without saying in what respect these semantically related words are similar to one another in meaning and in what respects they differ?' And in the same vein, but with regard to future Hebrew lexica, cf. J. Barr, 'Semitic Philology and the Interpretation of the Old Testament', in G.W. Anderson (ed.), *Tradition and Interpretation: Essays by Members of the Society for Old Testament Study* (Oxford: Clarendon Press, 1979), 31-64 (54): 'Since meanings are not really stated by glosses in another language such as English, and actually reside in the differences from other words in Hebrew, and since much emphasis has recently been laid on word-pairs and vocabulary groupings, ways for displaying the relationships of groups of words will have to take a larger place, in comparison with the traditional word entry'. Both *DCH* and *NIDOTE* register a word's semantic fields.

31. And he continues: 'This relation may be *synonymous* (with an absolute, near, or partial overlap), *homonymous* (lexemes that have the same spelling and lexical form, but are unrelated in sense), *polysymous* (lexemes that have multiple related senses), *antonymous* (difference in spelling and form and opposition in meaning), or *hyponymous* (a lexeme that has a different meaning, but shares in some aspects the boundary limits of another lexeme...)', (W.A. VanGemeren, 'Introduction' in *NIDOTE*, I, 5-13 [8]). As Lyons remarks: 'The sense of an expression may be defined as the set, or network, of sense-relations that hold between it and other expressions of the same language' (*Linguistic Semantics*, 80). Cf. Cotterell and Turner, *Linguistics and Biblical Interpretation*, 154-55.

does the word נער ('youth', 'assistant', 'helper') differ from words like
ילד ('boy') and בחור ('young man') and from עבד ('servant')? Or what
exactly is the difference between a כתנת ('robe') and clothes like בגד
('garment') and שמלה ('mantle')—if the difference can be clarified. In this
stage the *Theologisches Wörterbuch zum Alten Testament* (*ThWAT*) and
the *New International Dictionary of Old Testament Theology and Exegesis*
(*NIDOTE*) are often very enlightening. Important in this respect is Walton's
remark that a 'word should be understood in recognition of other related
words that were not selected by the author'.[32] For example, for 'tell' one
might both encounter the verb נגד (hiphil) and the verb ספר (piel).

6. *Context and Encyclopaedia*

The next steps are determined by the context in which a particular word is
found.[33] Nevertheless they are still of a general character. In this stage it is
also important to notice the difference between denotation and reference:

> The crucial difference between reference and denotation is that the deno-
> tation of an expression is invariant and utterance-independent: it is part of
> the meaning which the expression has in the language-system, independ-
> ently of its use on particular occasions of utterance. Reference, in contrast,
> is variable and utterance-dependent.[34]

A lexeme like עץ ('tree') in a dictionary denotes a class of entities in the
external world. It is not until it is used in a text or utterance that it has a
referent (from this specific class).

The denotation of a word reflects the cultural knowledge of the world in
which it occurs; it belongs to the encyclopaedia of a certain language community: what does the world look like.[35] Trying to find the denotation of a
word requires knowledge of this encyclopaedia,[36] which differs from one
language community to another (e.g. lexically the word 'mountain' is a

---

32. Walton, 'Principles for Productive Word Study', 164; and also: 'Whenever
words with overlapping meaning exist, we have a right to ask: Why did the author
choose this one instead of another?' (162).

33. Cf. Lyons, *Linguistic Semantics*, 294: 'One cannot generally determine the
reference of an expression, then, without regard to its context of utterance'.

34. Lyons, *Linguistic Semantics*, 79; see also Cotterell and Turner, *Linguistics and
Biblical Interpretation*, 139-40.

35. Cotterell and Turner refer to this as 'supposition pool' (*Linguistics and Biblical
Interpretation*, 94-102).

36. Cf. J.I. Saeed, *Semantics* (Oxford: Basil Blackwell, 1997), 6-8.

very high area of land with steep sides; however, the word 'mountain' in
England or Ireland denotes something rather different than the word 'mountain' in Tibet or India does). This encyclopaedic knowledge needs to be
elucidated by careful research: historical, archeological and sociological.[37]
It is one thing to know that the word מֶלֶךְ means 'king' (the lexical meaning), but another to know what a king looked like in the ancient Near East
(or rather, in one particular time and place), or what were his functions.
The denotations of words in texts are bound up with a particular time, with
a specific society; the 'reality' they represent is historically and geographi-
cally determined.[38] Obtaining such encyclopaedic knowledge of a Hebrew
language community must be done by examining the context of the text in
which words occur, both literal—there is a kind of circularity here—and
historical.

7. *Connotations and Alluvial Meaning*[39]

In this stage of a word's investigation the aim is to study the meanings
which are added to the word by the actual context (immediate or larger) in
which it functions. Is it possible that something unique is added to the
general meaning of the word? In other words: Does a word get a particular
connotation[40] or is a specific meaning attached to it?[41] 'Here we move
away from objectivity to subjectivity, away from cold grammar to flesh-
and-blood utterances. Words are not, in fact, the neutral entities we might
intuitively assume them to be.'[42] What I refer to here partly agrees with
Cotterell's and Turner's 'specialized sense',

37. Cotterell and Turner, *Linguistics and Biblical Interpretation*, 102.

38. See S. Sykes, 'Time and Space in Haggai–Zechariah 1–8: A Bakhtinian Analysis of a Prophetic Chronicle', *JSOT* 76 (1997), 97-124 (99-101).

39. I think that Cotterell's and Turner's 'discourse concepts' (*Linguistics and Biblical Interpretation*, 151-52) are much alike to what I call the connotations that can be
attributed to words in texts.

40. In H. von Gorp, *Lexicon voor literaire termen* (Groningen: Wolters-Noordhof,
1993), 84, connotation is defined as the entirety of associations that can be evoked by a
word, but which do not belong to the denotation of this word. The connotation of a
word is often strictly personal. However, connotations may become part of the encyclopaedia and/or the dictionary.

41. Cf. J.F.A. Sawyer, 'Root-Meanings in Hebrew', *JSS* 12 (1967), 37-50, esp. section 4, 'Overtones', 46-50.

42. Cotterell and Turner, *Linguistics and Biblical Interpretation*, 46. The above
quotation refers to connotation in general, not to a connotation evoked in a text.

which could either be an idiolect sense, or a sense specific to a particular group, arising out of its distinctive interests. Paul's teaching on baptism, righteousness, charismata, etc., will gradually build up in his churches generally accepted senses of the respective words which are neither lexical senses (for they are not yet sufficiently widely established to be labelled such), nor are they purely Paul's personal usages, or special discourse senses, because they have become part of the general linguistic usage of the Pauline congregations.[43]

Their focus, I think, is too much on the individual author or the receiving community in the past, whereas the actual reader or interpreter remains out of the picture. And it is here, I think, that their view can be expanded. By way of analogy I quote Armstrong on metaphor:

If a metaphor results from an interaction, the meaning of the figure is not a concealed substance but a process and an event. Metaphorical meaning is not something 'there', independently awaiting discovery, but is cocreated by the reader and depends on him or her to make it exist by resolving the incongruity of the figure.[44]

Armstrong's point with regard to metaphor also holds true for the meaning of words in a text: attaching meaning to a word is a process in which the reader has an important role to play. She or he expands a word's lexical meaning by relating it to its context and usage within this context; this is what I would like to call alluvial meaning. Here a semantic and a literary analysis indeed almost merge, but although connotative or alluvial meaning is not an 'objective entity' as is lexical meaning, it can nevertheless be explained and substantiated.

I am aware of the fact that a clear-cut procedure is hardly possible. Nevertheless, the kind of approach I have in mind may run like this. To begin with, one has to look for the presence of any 'regularities' or 'nuances' when the same word is encountered in several texts (e.g. the Torah), in other words one has to ask: Is there a typical usage? These nuances may give the word a special connotation in certain contexts. And if there are any nuances to be discerned, one must ask whether these are applicable to the text under consideration: Do the contents allow for the 'newly uncovered' alluvial meaning?

Interpreting a text like Gen. 37–50 requires several skills of a scholarly reader. She or he not only has to have a certain amount of knowledge of

43. Cotterell and Turner, *Linguistics and Biblical Interpretation*, 166.
44. Armstrong, *Conflicting Readings*, 73.

the world ('encyclopaedic knowledge'), but also has to analyze the text (in a syntactic and semantic way), and finally has to combine the results that the analyses have yielded—here the actual literary analysis starts. It is through the idiosyncratic selection of the elements and the analysis of the results with the goal of achieving a coherent interpretation, that various readers may reach different conclusions.

Based on the method described above, although not describing the entire procedure in detail, Gen. 37–50 will be examined in the remainder of this book. The leading questions in this examination are already posed in the Introduction. The most important of those is: Why does Joseph disappear from the biblical history of Israel?

Chapter 2

ALL IN THE FAMILY

From Gen. 29 onwards the protagonists of Gen. 37–50 gradually enter the story. In this chapter I both consider the episodes in which they make their first appearances and the opening account of the larger tale about the brothers (37.2-4).

1. *Jacob's Offspring*

In Gen. 29.31–30.24 and 35.16-18—before the actual *toledot* of Jacob begin (in 37.2)—the births of Jacob's offspring are related. Both his wives Leah and Rachel and their maids Bilhah and Zilpah conceive by him. Together they deliver 13 children:

Leah:	1. Reuben (29.32)	9. Issachar (30.17)
	2. Simeon (29.33)	10. Zebulun (30.19)
	3. Levi (29.34)	11. Dinah (30.21)[1]
	4. Judah (29.35)	
Bilhah:	5. Dan (30.5)	
	6. Naphtali (30.7)	
Zilpah:	7. Gad (30.10)	
	8. Asher (30.12)	
Rachel:	12. Joseph (30.23)	
	13. Benjamin (35.18)[2]	

1. It is rather curious to find that Dinah is often neglected and left out of overviews of Jacob's children; see, for instance, T.J. Prewitt, *The Elusive Covenant: A Structural-Semiotic Reading of Genesis* (Advances in Semiotics; Bloomington: Indiana University Press, 1990), 45 and 47; and S.D. Kunin, *The Logic of Incest: A Structuralist Analysis of Hebrew Mythology* (JSOTSup, 185; Sheffield: Sheffield Academic Press, 1995), 142.

2. It is remarkable that several conceptions are not mentioned: these are Gad's, Asher's (the sons of Leah), Dinah's (Leah's daughter) and Benjamin's (Rachel's second son). Whenever in the above list a child is on its way the Hebrew says: ‏ותלד ותהר‎...,

In this order of births the story is told, although this need not be the
chronological order—consider for instance, the death and burial of Isaac
(35.27-29), which is told before Gen. 37, but which must definitely have
happened at a later date than the events told there.[3] In Gen. 29.31 the tale
of the births has its beginning: 'And YHWH saw that Leah was hated, he
opened her womb'. Such statement about YHWH's involvement in the
conception and birth of the children is repeated twice—in 30.17 ('and
YHWH heeded Leah and she conceived and bore...'), and in 30.22 ('Then
God remembered Rachel, and God heeded her and opened her womb')—
which means that both Leah's and Rachel's children 'are products of
divine fruitfulness'.[4]

The chapters following Gen. 29 and 30 present some information about
the list of 13. Below I will have a closer look at some of Jacob's descendants, because not all 13 appear on stage, even though their births are mentioned explicitly. It will become clear that apart from Leah's and Jacob's
daughter, Dinah, four sons are singled out, and that not all of their (i.e. the
sons') actions are what one would consider favourable.

Reuben

The first of Jacob's sons to be encountered is Reuben. In 30.14-15 he goes
into the fields and happens to find דודאים (often translated as 'mandrakes')
and takes those to his mother, who in turn passes them on to Rachel and
receives Jacob's nightly services in the bargain, but not after Leah and

---

'she conceived...and she bore'. Moreover, only Dinah's birth is *not* told by way of a
wayyiqtol (30.21 reads: ואחר ילדה בת, 'afterwards she has also born a daughter'). It is
also striking that every newborn's name is explained *except* Dinah's.

3.   When Esau and Jacob were born Isaac was 60 years of age (25.26), he dies at
the age of 180 (35.28). Consequently, at that time Jacob is 120 years old. When Jacob
passes away he is 147 years old—at that moment he had lived in Egypt for 17 years
(47.28). The timespan between Joseph's sale and Jacob's coming to Egypt is 22 years
(for details: see next chapter). Therefore, at the beginning of Gen. 37 Jacob is 108
years old, which implies that the death and burial of Isaac *chronologically* took place
after the events of Gen. 37, even though its account precedes Gen. 37. Also cf. Redford, *A Study of the Biblical Story of Joseph*, 23 n. 2, and M. Sternberg, 'Time and
Space in Biblical (Hi)story Telling: The Grand Chronology', in R.M. Schwarz (ed.),
The Book and the Text: The Bible and Literary Theory (Oxford: Basil Blackwell,
1990), 81-145 (117).

4.   Kunin, *The Logic of Incest*, 122. Kunin draws attention to the fact that God's
role is also emphasized in the naming of the children (122-23). However, this does not
happen all the time, in the naming of Levi, Gad, Asher, Issachar, Dinah and Benjamin
God is not present in the explanation of the names.

Rachel have had an argument (30.15). Because of its resemblance with
דוד ('beloved one') these דודאים may have acquired the connotation of
Liebesäpfel as Westermann names them.[5] Indeed, the fruit makes Leah
fruitful again, or rather, her giving away the fruit opens the way to a new
pregnancy.[6] With the דודאים she has hired (שׂכר) Jacob to sleep with her,
and so she becomes pregnant (30.16). It is therefore not surprising that she
names her newborn son יששׂכר (Issachar). In other words, by way of the
finding of the דודאים Reuben provides both his mother and father with
another son.

In a second appearance, Reuben may have tried to do likewise, although
the son would biologically have been his. In 35.22 the reader is told that in
the time when Jacob was dwelling in the land of Migdal Eder, Reuben
went to lie with Bilhah, his father's concubine. When his father hears about
this, he does not take any actions against his son (at least not until 49.3-4;
if those verses refer to 35.22). No offspring come of this affair. In short,
Reuben seems to have a special talent for disturbing family matters. In
30.14-16 it is because of his finding the דודאים that Rachel and Leah have
their first and only (reported) quarrel, and in 35.22 Reuben insults his
father by sleeping with Bilhah. In the next chapters I will return several
times to Reuben and consider his role in Gen. 37–50.

Joseph
The second son to be explicitly mentioned is Joseph, whose birth previously concluded the register of births in Gen. 30.[7] It is not until the birth of
Joseph that Jacob takes leave of his family-in-law in Paddan-aram and
departs for the land of Canaan.[8] When in Gen. 33 Jacob is going to meet
his brother, Esau, he divides his children among Rachel, Leah and the two
maids: the maids and their sons are put in the front, followed by Leah and
her children, and, last, Rachel and Joseph (33.2). After the brothers' reunion
the maids and their sons step forward and bow down before Esau, as do

5. C. Westermann, *Genesis 12–36* (BKAT, 1.2; Neukirchen–Vluyn: Neukirchener
Verlag, 1981), 580.

6. Cf. B. Jacob, *Das erste Buch der Tora: Genesis* (repr., New York: Ktav, 1968
[1934]), 597.

7. Cf. S. Lehming, 'Zur Erzählung von der Geburt der Jakobsöhne', *VT* 13 (1963),
74-81(79).

8. Cf. the rather special construction of 30.25: ויהי כאשׁר ילדה רחל את־יוסף
ויאמר יעקב אל־לבן ('and it was when Rachel had delivered Joseph that Jacob said to
Laban...').

Leah and her children. Finally, also 'Joseph and Rachel' draw near and bow down (33.7). The order is a reversal of 33.2. It is rather remarkable that Joseph is mentioned before his mother, whereas in the other cases the mothers are mentioned first. By way of the order in which Rachel and Joseph are being depicted in Gen. 33 Joseph already seems to have acquired a special position within Jacob's family.

Dinah

Dinah is the next of Jacob's offspring to play a small yet significant role. A short tale is devoted to Leah's daughter in Gen. 34. On only one other occasion does the reader meet her: in Gen. 46.15.[9] In the tale of Gen. 34, Dinah goes out to see the daughters of the land of Canaan, where Jacob and his family have settled in the vicinity of Shechem (34.1; cf. 33.18). As well as being the name of the geographical location, Shechem is also given as the name of Hamor's son. Of this Shechem the narrator tells that 'he saw her, he took her, he lay with and he raped her' (33.2)—as most translations state. Although I will not pursue the question of rape too far, I must say that I subscribe to Lyn Bechtel's view that the translation 'rape' may evoke something other than Hebrew ענה indicates—she translates the verb as 'humiliate'.[10] The verbal form ויענה is derived from the verb ענה II ('rape, humiliate').[11] The suggestion of 'rape' is often made on the basis of לקח ('take') preceding ענה. However, to 'take' a wife is a common expression in the Bible, and there is no violence expressed (cf. 34.9, 16; 38.2). Comparing Gen. 34 to texts in which 'rape' is the central theme (Deut. 22.25-27; 2 Sam. 13.11-14) Bechtel concludes: 'Without a similar association of force in verse 2, there is no indication of rape in Shechem's "taking" (*lqh*) of Dinah'. And she continues: 'Then, the text goes on to emphasize Shechem's bonding (*dbq*) with her, his love (*'hb*) for her and his speaking to her heart'.[12]

---

9.   Although she is not present in the list of Gen. 35.23-26, Dinah is mentioned in the list of Jacob's children who enter into Egypt (46.8-27).

10.   L.M. Bechtel, 'What if Dinah is not Raped (Genesis 34)?', *JSOT* 62 (1994), 19-36 (24).

11.   The verb form in Gen. 34.2 is a piel; the verbs ענה I ('answer, reply') and ענה III ('be occupied, worried') are not attested in the piel conjugation. ענה II has 'a range of meanings that covers both the positive and negative aspects of several Eng. words, namely, humble, oppress, and afflict' (*NIDOTE*, III, 450), and is mostly found in the piel (two-thirds of approximately 80 occurrences).

12.   Bechtel, 'What if Dinah is not Raped?', 28.

Bechtel's point that Dinah is not raped is even stronger. When looking at Deut. 22.23-24 and 22.28-29 one can ascertain that in the first of both texts both the (young) woman and the man approve of their act: the man lies with the woman, who does not cry for help. The order of the verbs involved is שׁכב ('to lie down') followed by ענה ('humiliate'). 'Note that in this case the word *'nh* follows *škb*, which seems to be the case when rape is not involved.'[13] This same order is found in Deut. 22.27-29, although the lying down is preceded by the male taking (תפשׂ) the maiden. If they are caught the man is forced to marry the girl.[14] The same seems to be the case in Gen. 34, although Shechem is not forced to marry Dinah, and the verb for 'take' is not תפשׂ, but לקח. Also, in the narrator's phrasing, Dinah does not cry for help (like the woman in the law from Deuteronomy). Moreover, in Gen. 34.2 the order of the verbs for 'lying' and 'humiliating' is the same as in both texts from Deuteronomy: Shechem is lying with Dinah and humiliates her. The verb ענה appears to denote a rift in the family relationships. As for the Deuteronomy text in which one encounters a rape, there are the verbs חזק ('overpower') and שׁכב ('to lie down')—the verb ענה, however, is nowhere to be found. In 2 Sam. 13, where there is a rape the reversed order is used: Amnon humiliates/rapes Tamar and lies with her, moreover, before this he also overpowers (חזק) her.[15]

If one has a closer look at the instances in Genesis where the verb ענה is used, it becomes clear that on that basis too there is no indication to ascribe the notion of 'rape' to the verb's occurrence in 34.2. One can hardly assume that Sarai raped Hagar in 16.6 (ותענה), or that the messenger of YHWH wanted Hagar to be raped by her mistress (16.9, והתעני); likewise Abram's seed will be oppressed or humiliated for 400 years in a foreign land (15.13, וענו) and Laban urges Jacob not to humiliate Leah and Rachel and take (לקח!) other women (31.50, אם־תענה).

Apart from the fact that Dinah is not being raped, another element concerning Dinah is of importance, as Bechtel indicates. In her article she

---

13. Bechtel, 'What if Dinah is not Raped?', 25.

14. 'There is voluntary sexual intercourse between two unbonded people' (Bechtel, 'What if Dinah is not Raped?', 25).

15. Cf. Bechtel, 'What if Dinah is not Raped?', 26. One could consequently ask whether the notion of 'rape' is intrinsic to the verb ענה at all, or whether that notion is brought about by the context in which it appears. In Gen. 34.2 the humiliation is the result of Shechem's and Dinah's sleeping together, whereas in 2 Sam. 13 Tamar is humiliated by being forced to have sex.

draws attention to Dinah's 'going out' (ותצא, 34.1).[16] In 34.6 Hamor goes forth as well—'on a diplomatic mission to talk to Jacob'. In Gen. 34 the verb יצא ('going forth') might indicate the crossing of a boundary: 'When Dinah goes forth to see, to get acquainted with, the daughters of the land, she exits and crosses her group/tribal boundary... Dinah is both a figure who "goes forth" and crosses her group boundaries and a marginal figure who engages in sexual activity outside the group'.[17] In this perspective she prefigures the roles of Judah and Joseph who will both marry a woman outside their group (Gen. 38 and 41).[18]

After Shechem has expressed his love for Dinah, Hamor his father goes to Jacob to ask whether Dinah can be his son's wife and whether they can arrange the marriage: 'And Hamor communed with them, saying, "The soul of my son Shechem longs for your daughter; I pray you give her him in marriage. Make marriages with us; give your daughters to us, and take our daughters for yourselves and live in our land..." ' (34.8-10).

Simeon and Levi

However, and here the next sons of Jacob enter the scene, Simeon and Levi are firmly opposed to this marriage, as appears from the final verses of Gen. 34, where they not only kill Hamor and his son, but also the entire city in which Hamor's people live. Jacob strongly disapproves of his sons' behaviour: 'You have brought trouble on me by making me odious to the inhabitants of the land, the Canaanites and the Perizzites; my numbers are few, and if they gather themselves against me and attack me, I shall be destroyed, both I and my household' (34.30). Simeon and Levi respond: 'Should our sister be treated like a whore?' (34.31).[19]

---

16. ותצא may have a sexual connotation, cf. Leah's going out (ותצא) in 30.16, of which Issachar's birth is the result.

17. Bechtel, 'What if Dinah is not Raped?', 32.

18. However, are not all Jacob's sons doomed to marry 'outside' their clan? After all, there are no female 'Israelites' whatsoever. On this matter see also Y.-W. Fung, *Victim and Victimizer: Joseph's Interpretation of his Destiny* (JSOTSup, 308; Sheffield: Sheffield Academic Press, 2000), 52-55.

19. The Hebrew word that is used is a participle of the verb זנה (qal), which according to *HALAT* (I, 264) is to mean 'buhlen, sich m.e. anderen Mann anlassen'; *DCH* (III, 121) comments: 'be or act as a prostitute' or 'fornicate'; and BDB (275) state: 'commit fornication' and 'be a harlot'. One could ask, however, who did treat or is treating Dinah like a whore? Moreover, what does זנה ('whore') in this context actually mean? An answer to these questions will not be pursued here, they may be the subject of another study.

This reaction ought to be distinguished from the sons' collective opinion that was expressed before in v. 7: 'When they heard of it [i.e. of the fact that Shechem had slept with Dinah], the men were indignant and very angry, because he had committed an outrage in Israel by lying with Jacob's daughter, for such a thing ought not to be done'—also compare the way the narrator informs the reader of Jacob's perception of what had happened: 'Now Jacob heard that Shechem had defiled (טמא, piel) his daughter Dinah' (v. 5). Fortunately, there is a way to undo this outrage, as the sons make clear in vv. 14-17, (even though they speak with deceit, במרמה, as the narrator states, in v. 13):

> We cannot do this thing, to give our sister to one who is uncircumcised, for that would be a disgrace to us. Only on this condition will we consent to you: that you will become as we are and every male among you be circumcised. Then we will give our daughters to you, and we will take your daughters for ourselves, and we will live among you and become one people. But if you will not listen to us and be circumcised, then we will take our daughter [*sic*] and be gone.

So, despite their initial disagreement on the marriage between their sister and Shechem, at the end of the day—after their condition is granted—the brothers have to agree, since Hamor and Shechem accept the proposal (v. 18). The brothers, however, were speaking with deceit (v. 13),[20]—they were having a hidden agenda. In Bechtel's view the 'requirement of circumcision is only a clever pretext to render the Shechemites defenceless, so they can take revenge for the shame of the pollution of their group. They are "saving face".'[21] According to the narrator, Jacob's sons (therefore including his much beloved Joseph) had the vile intention to get rid of Hamor and his people. All brothers turn out to be frauds. Two of them, Simeon and Levi, act as angels of death and slay Hamor's clan. The brothers, and especially Simeon and Levi, present themselves as rather untrustworthy and violent. They are men who do not keep their word, and who act against their father's wishes and risk the welfare of the family by their rash actions (34.30).

20. ' "Deceit" frames the whole of the brothers' speech, so that the reader is unable confidently to posit sincerity in any of it, whether in the specific proposal or in its ostensible socioreligious motivation', write D.N. Fewell and D.M. Gunn ('Tipping the Balance: Sternberg's Reader and the Rape of Dinah', *JBL* 110 [1991], 193-211 [202]).
21. Bechtel, 'What if Dinah is not Raped?', 33.

Benjamin

The last of Jacob's sons to be mentioned here is Benjamin. His birth, which is recounted in Gen. 35.16-19, causes his mother's death: 'when they were still some distance from Ephrath, Rachel was in childbirth, and she had hard labour…and her soul was departing… So Rachel died, and she was buried on the way to Ephrath'. Benjamin is singled out from among his brothers and sister in three respects. Whereas the births of the others are all told in Gen. 29 and 30, Benjamin's is not told until ch. 35.[22] This might suggest that there is quite a lapse of time between the births of the 12 and Benjamin, but this is not necessarily so.[23] A second respect in which there is a difference between Benjamin and the other of Jacob's children is that Benjamin is the only one who is born in the land promised to Abraham.[24] His sister and brothers were all born in Paddan-aram, during Jacob's service to Laban.

The third element which shows that Benjamin is treated differently from his brethren is that the others are all named by their mothers, and in all cases (Dinah excepted) an explanation for their names is given—for example, in 30.24 Rachel names her son Joseph (יוֹסֵף) saying: 'May YHWH add (יֹסֵף) to me another son!' This actually happens in 35.17.[25] Before she breathes her last Rachel names her newborn Benoni, 'but his father named him Benjamin' (35.18). So this is the exception that breaks the rule now that Jacob names one of his children.

Besides, no explanation for the name (or names) is given. 'Oni' (in Benoni, בֶּן־אוֹנִי) may have anything to do with the noun אוֹן ('generative power', 'sexual virility', 'physical strength'—this word is used in 49.3 with regard to Reuben[26]), but generally it is said to be derived from אָנָה ('lament'): 'The nom. *'ônî* is found as part of the name Rachel gives her son as she dies in childbirth (Gen. 35.18). This name contrasts neatly with

---

22. For a historical explanation of the rather isolated account of Benjamin's birth compared to the birth of the other children of Israel, cf. James Muilenberg's interesting 'The Birth of Benjamin', *JBL* 75 (1956), 195-201.

23. Cf. Gen. 46, where Benjamin is the father of ten sons.

24. As is correctly noted by Prewitt, *The Elusive Covenant*, 44.

25. Joseph's name might also be linked to 30.23, where Rachel says: 'God has taken away (אָסַף) my disgrace'.

26. The construction בֶּן־אוֹנִי resembles Jacob's רֵאשִׁית אוֹנִי ('first of my strength') in 49.3; in both occurrences אוֹנִי has the same vocalization. Three more times in Genesis does one come across the word אוֹן: 41.45, 50 and 46.20: Joseph is told to be married to Asenath, daughter of Potiphera, a priest of On (written as אֹן or אוֹן, by which is meant the city of Heliopolis).

bin-yamīn (son of good fortune).'[27] There is, however, no reason to exclude the meaning 'son of my strength', or 'son of my vigour'. Consequently Benoni could both mean 'son of my sorrow' and 'son of my 'vigour'. If one chooses the first option ('sorrow'), the naming probably refers to Rachel's suffering while giving birth to her son; but if one opts for the second meaning ('vigour'), Rachel could be hinting at her own fruitfulness by bearing a second son, hereby playing along with the midwife's words in 33.17: 'Do not be afraid, for now you will have another son'.[28]

Jacob, however, does not grant his wife's last wish to name her son 'Benoni'. Instead he names his last child 'Benjamin', which literally translated means 'son of the south' or 'son of the right (hand)', which 'auch "Glückskind" bedeuten kann' ('could mean "child of fortune" as well').[29] The reason why Jacob did call his son 'Benjamin' is not entirely clear (it is hardly conceivable that he was happy about Rachel's passing). However, Speiser's explanation that Benjamin is the 'one on whom the father expects to count heavily for support and comfort; or alternatively, one who promises good fortune, a propitious turn of events'[30] is reasonable, although not satisfactory. Later on in Gen. 43 (and in 42.38 as well) when Jacob is about to send his sons to Egypt for a second time, the name chosen for Benjamin by his mother (i.e. 'Benoni', in the sense of 'son of my sorrow') appears to be more appropriate, because sending Benjamin to Egypt does cause Jacob great sorrow indeed (43.14; see also Judah's speech, 44.30-34). Something similar could be said about the brothers' second stay in Egypt. Benjamin, because of Joseph's false accusation of having stolen the cup, causes his brothers a lot of distress (44.12-13). So, on closer inspection, 'Benjamin' never seems to live up to this name, except perhaps in 45.22 where Benjamin receives 300 shekels of silver and five sets of clothes, whereas his brothers only get one set of clothes and receive no money whatsoever.[31]

27. *NIDOTE*, I, 452, cf. *DCH*, I, 333 and *HALAT*, I, 22.

28. According to E.A. Speiser the orthography supports the meaning 'son of my vigor', but 'the context, however, favors (at least symbolically) "misfortune, suffering" (from a different root), and this interpretation is preferred by tradition (cf. Hos ix 4); it has furthermore good extra-biblical parallels' (*Genesis* [AB, 1; New York: Doubleday, 1964], 274). Contrary to Speiser I think the context supports both meanings of אוני.

29. Westermann, *Genesis 12–36*, 676.

30. Speiser, *Genesis*, 274.

31. For some other possibilities on the meanings of both names 'Benoni' and

Just before the section on the *toledot* of Esau (Gen. 36) and the passing of Isaac (35.27-29) the narrator presents a list of Jacob's male descendants:

> And the sons of Jacob were twelve. The sons of Leah: Reuben (Jacob's firstborn), Simeon, Levi, Judah, Issachar, and Zebulun. The sons of Rachel: Joseph and Benjamin. The sons of Bilhah, Rachel's maid: Dan and Naphtali. The sons of Zilpah, Leah's maid: Gad and Asher. These were the sons of Jacob who were born to him in Paddan-aram (35.22-26).

As observed, the narrator's final statement is not entirely correct, since Benjamin was born in Canaan.

As seen above, three of Jacob's sons (Reuben, Simeon and Levi—who are, incidentally, his three eldest sons) did act without taking the family relations into account: Reuben slept with his father's concubine Bilhah (Rachel's maid) immediately after Rachel's death, [32] and Simeon and Levi did not only jeopardize the family's sojourning in Canaan, but they also deprived their sister of a husband (cf. Deut. 22.28-29).

Another thing to be noted is Jacob's—to say the least—rather awkward behaviour. He denies Rachel the privilege of giving a name to her second-born son, and instead chooses one himself which seems hardly appropriate. In the matter of the דודאים he willingly follows Leah into her bed, whereas when he hears that Reuben has stepped into *his* bed with *his* concubine, Jacob does not do anything, and after the massacre committed by Simeon and Levi he hardly rebukes them.

2. *Father and Sons*

In the beginning of Gen. 37 Joseph is being introduced. His introduction is brought about by a rather peculiar construction היה רעה את־אחיו בצאן (37.2). It may be translated: 'he used to tend the sheep with (את) his brothers', or: 'he used to tend (את) his brothers with the sheep'.

However, the option to interpret את here as a *nota accusativi* involves several problems—it results in a rather awkward translation. This seems to have been recognized by the translators of the LXX; they understood את as a preposition: 'with his brothers' (that is, if they were in the possession of the same Hebrew text as the one we have today). That being decided, the

'Benjamin', cf. V.P. Hamilton, *The Book of Genesis: Chapters 18–50* (NICOT; Grand Rapids, MI: Eerdmans, 1995), 384-85.

32. Some commentators interpret this act as a challenge to Jacob's authority (e.g. N.M. Sarna, *The JPS Torah Commentary: Genesis—בראשית* [Philadelphia: The Jewish Publication Society of America, 5749/1989], 245).

object (the flock) is consequently introduced by the preposition בְּ (which remains untranslated). LXX regards אֵת as the preposition μετά and the flock as the object of the verb: Ἰωσὴφ δέκα ἑπτὰ ἐτῶν ἦν ποιμαίνων μετὰ τῶν ἀδελφῶν αὐτοῦ τὰ πρόβατα ('At 17 years of age, Joseph tended the flock/sheep together with his brothers').

A striking phenomenon when considering the series of prose texts in which רעה occurs, is that the verb only occurs twice in combination with both אֵת and בְּ. Even more striking is that both places are to be found in Gen. 37, viz. in verses 2 and 12 (וילכו אחיו לרעות את־צאן אביהם בשכם), 'His brothers went to tend their father's flock at Shechem'). In v. 12 there is no other way for אֵת to function other than as *nota accusativi*, just as בְּ cannot be interpreted in a way other than as a preposition: 'His brothers went to tend (אֵת) the sheep at (בְּ) Shechem'. With regard to these characteristics—both combinations occur only in Gen. 37 and the function of אֵת and בְּ in 37.12—and because of the grammatical structure, it is on the margins of possibility that v. 2 can be read conformable to v. 12: Joseph used to tend his brothers with the sheep.[33] However, if tending the sheep only means to provide the sheep with sufficient food, than Joseph seems to take care of the nourishment of the brothers in verse 2.[34] He used to bring food to his brothers, who were to be found among the flocks. The distribution of food to people as a meaning of רעה may be the reason for the use of this verb in places like 2 Sam. 5.2 and 7.7—although in these places רעה is usually read as being led by a leader.[35] Joseph's commuting

33. Some commentators notice a case of anticipatory paronomasia in 37.2, like D.L. Christensen ('Anticipatory Paronomasia in Jonah 3:7-8 and Genesis 37:2', *RB* 90 [1983], 261-63) or Hamilton (*The Book of Genesis: 18–50*), 406: 'The syntax of the Hebrew allows for the translation "Joseph was shepherding his brothers", if *'ēt* is understood as the sign of the accusative rather than as the preposition "with". So understood, this verse would provide an excellent introduction to the Joseph story in the form of anticipatory paranomasia. What Joseph is doing during his teen life is exactly what he will be doing in his adult life—caring and providing for those who are dependent on him.'

34. This translation of רעה is found in the Dutch Statenvertaling and the KJV of Gen. 48.15: 'the God which fed me all my life long …' In the LXX it is no exception for רעה to be translated by 'feeding'; 22 times the verb in use is βόσκειν (cf. *ThWAT*, VII, 568). However, it does not occur in 37.2, where the verb ποιμαίνειν is used. In 37.12, 16, on the other hand, the LXX translates רעה by βόσκειν, whereas in 37.13 ποιμαίνειν is used again.

35. Also compare a text like Ezek. 34, a chapter which is strongly determined by shepherds and sheep in a metaphorical way, but in which nevertheless 'eat' and 'food' are explicitly present.

between his father and his brothers in v. 2 becomes more understandable if he provides for his brothers' food too.

In the light of what is written above, it is not unlikely that v. 2 on first reading reads, 'he was shepherding the flock with his brothers', whereas on second (or further) reading—when readers know about Joseph's food policy and the salvation of his relatives—the feasibility of reading 'he was shepherding his brothers with the flock' urges itself upon those readers.

Slander and Gossip

The final part of 37.2 presents three problems. First: What is one to understand when reading רעה דבתם ('their bad report')? And second, Who are supposed to be the ם–('their') or םה–(of 'their father')? To begin with the latter, the most obvious choice seems to be 'the group of four': Dan, Naphtali, Gad, and Asher—the brothers who were mentioned last. However, this conclusion is not obligatory. It is by no means impossible that 'their' in the final clause of v. 2 extends to the previous clause, so to the brothers in the beginning of the verse. The text as it is cannot provide the reader with a definite conclusion. The narrator may be making the most of the ambiguity of the Hebrew language. A more or less similar remark can be made on דבתם רעה.[36]

> *Dibbatam*—their slander—is remarkably ambiguous. Considering the Narrative's otherwise so masterly stylistic competence, such ambiguities are deliberate and call for all the possible interpretations: 'Their slander' can mean the slander *by* or *about* them. Moreover, 'them' can refer to all ten brothers, to the sons of Leah and to the concubines's sons. Consequently, the verse seems to say that Joseph reported the defamations of the two 'parties' about each other and by all Ten about himself.[37]

---

36. The noun דבה does not occur very often in the Hebrew Bible. Except for 37.2 it it used in Num. 13.32; 14.36-37; Ezek. 36.3; Jer. 20.10; Ps. 31.14; Prov. 10.18; 25.10. According to *HALAT*, I, 200, the meaning is 'Gerede, Nachrede'. Possible translations according to *DCH*, II, 383 are: 'evil report, gossip, defamation'. Wilhelm Gesenius' *Hebräisches und aramäisches Handwörterbuch über das Alte Testament* (18. Auflage, 2. Lieferung ד-י) translates 37.2 like: 'Joseph brachte ihre üble Nachrede vor ihren Vater (d.h. er denunzierte sie)' (236). The combination רעה and דבה is also found in Num. 14.37, where it sounds rather negative: 'these men responsible for spreading the bad report about the land were struck down and died of a plague before the Lord' (NIV).

37. E.I. Lowenthal, *The Joseph Narrative in Genesis* (New York: Ktav, 1973), 16. Also compare J.P. Fokkelman, who indicates that רעה is being used predicatively, not attributively (as is the case in many translations:'he brought the evil reports...'); in the

Because the narrator refrains from every kind of judgment, there are quite a few ambiguities that come to light. Therefore one could follow the above quoted suggestion by Lowenthal and not make a decision concerning: (1) which of the brothers are referred to, and (2) what 'spoke ill about them' or 'their slander' might exactly mean. In this perspective, רעה דבתם can be understood in different ways (*beside* one another): (1) Joseph takes the slander which is uttered by others to his father;[38] (2) Joseph takes the slander which is brought about by the brothers to their father; (3) Joseph takes the slander which he himself trumpets[39] to his father.[40] It is questionable whether Joseph's brothers are aware of his behaviour towards them. The narrator reports of Joseph's messages to his father in a neutral way

latter case the definite article should have been placed before רעה. 'That the talk about the brothers is bad is not an objective fact. Instead, the text says: "Joseph brought the rumours about them to their father as bad", which is unpretty English for: he brought this gossip to his father [and presented it] as bad. This means that the text leaves open the possibility, if it does not say so unequivocally, that Joseph himself is the source of, and is responsible for, the negative import of his message' ('Genesis 37 and 38 at the Interface of Structural Analysis and Hermeneutics', in L.J. de Regt *et al.* (eds.), *Literary Structure and Rhetorical Strategies in the Hebrew Bible* [Assen: Van Gorcum; Winona Lake, IN: Eisenbrauns, 1996], 152-187 [156]). See also P. Joüon and T. Muraoka, *A Grammar of Biblical Hebrew* (Subsidia Biblica 14.1-2; Rome: Pontificio Istituto Biblico, 1993, §126a, 455: '*attulit Ioseph rumorem de eis (ut) malum* (= "spoke ill of them")'.

38. According to B. Jacob the 'häßlichen Reden' were about the sons of Bilhah and Zilpah. When talking about the ones spreading the rumours 'liegt (es) am nächsten, an die andern Brüder, die Söhne der Lea zu denken' (*Das erste Buch der Tora*, 696).

39. Sarna translates 'And Joseph brought bad reports of them to their father' (*Genesis*, 255), which not only implies an active role for Joseph with regard to the transmitting of the reports, but may also imply an active role with regard to the reports' content. The same is applicable to Speiser's 'bad reports about them' (*Genesis*, 287).

40. Cf. B. Jacob: 'Zu übersetzen "üble Nachrede über sie", nähmlich von ihm selbst ausgehende, wäre eine üble Nachrede über Joseph selbst, est ist undenkbar, daß dieser von Grund aus edle Charakter hierzu fähig gewesen wäre' (*Das erste Buch der Tora*, 696). Hamilton (*The Book of Genesis 18–50*, 406) on the other hand writes: 'For some undisclosed reason, Joseph *maligned* his brothers to Jacob'. Yet another interpretation is given by J. Peck ('Note on Genesis 37:2 and Joseph's Character', *ExpTim* 82 [1970–71], 342-43); he does so to bring Joseph's actions more into accordance with the following chapters: 'A slightly different rendering could restore unity to the story, by rendering the words as "Joseph brought their (his brothers') slanders against him to their father"'. This takes the Hebrew *dibbatham* as carrying a subjective rather than an objective genetive' (343). Without any grounds is BDB's suggestion *sub voce* דבה: '*evil report*, specif. a (true) report of evil doing' (179).

and does not inform the reader about the brothers' reaction to Joseph's commuting between them and their father.[41]

This latter remark reveals the third problem in this verse: Does Joseph bring those reports only once, or does he make a habit of it? Taking account of text-linguistic studies of Biblical Hebrew, like those made by Talstra and Niccacci,[42] it is probable that 'and he brought' (ויבא, so a *wayyiqtol*) continues the durative value of the participle (היה רעה, 'was shepherding') in the preceding line.[43] In this latter case, Joseph's taking reports about his brothers to his father was not a single event.

This first line of the story of Jacob's *toledot* shows Joseph to be in the position of an assistant (נער),[44] together with the four sons of his father's

41. Although G.W. Coats appears to discern some hatred of the brothers in verse 2, as can be derived from his statement that 'The reason for the brothers' hatred is different in vs. 2 from the ones noted in the following verses' (*From Canaan to Egypt: Structural and Theological Context for the Joseph Story* [CBQMS, 4; Washington, DC: Catholic Biblical Association, 1976], 12).

42. E. Talstra, 'Clause Types and Textual Structure: An Experiment in Narrative Syntax', in *idem* (ed.), *Narrative and Comment: Contributions to Discourse Grammar and Hebrew Bible Presented to Wolfgang Schneider* (Amsterdam: Societas Hebraica Amstelodamensis, 1995), 166-80; *idem*, 'A Hierarchy of Clauses in Biblical Hebrew Narrative', in E. van Wolde (ed.), *Narrative Syntax & the Hebrew Bible: Papers of the Tilburg Conference 1996* (Biblical Interpretation Series, 29; Leiden: E.J. Brill, 1997), 85-118; A. Niccacci, *The Syntax of the Verb in Classical Hebrew Prose* (JSOTSup, 86; Sheffield: JSOT Press, 1990); *idem*, 'On The Hebrew Verbal System', in R.D. Bergen (ed.), *Biblical Hebrew and Discourse Linguistics* (Dallas, TX: Summer Institute of Linguistics, 1995), 117-37.

43. This is not to say that *wayyiqtol* has a durative aspect; ויבא is a verbal form indicating continuation. Cf. Y. Endo, *The Verbal System in Classical Hebrew in the Joseph Story: An Approach from Discourse Analysis* (Studia Semitica Neerlandica, 32; Assen: Van Gorcum, 1996), 269. See also this example from 1 Kgs. 21.25-26: יהוה מאד ללכת אחרי הגללים בכל רק לא־היה כאחאב אשר התמכר לעשות הרע בעיני עשׂו האמרי אשר הורישׁ יהוה מפני בני ישׂראל: אשר־הסתה אתו איזבל אשתו אשר (But there was none like unto Ahab, which did sell himself to work wickedness in the sight of the LORD, whom Jezebel his wife stirred up. *And he did* ויתעב very abominably in following idols, according to all things as did the Amorites, whom the LORD cast out before the children of Israel [KJV]). The depiction of Ahab in v. 25 is a retrospective judgment, that is substantiated in the next verse. The *wayyiqtol* from v. 26 cannot but be interpreted as a continuation of the static (durative/iterative) description of v. 25. The *wayyiqtol* is being used to emphasize the wicked actions of Ahab, which in the narrator's eyes were not of a single kind!

44. The word נער here rather refers to Joseph's apprenticeship than to his age, for

concubines. This job as an assistant allows him to commute between his father and his brothers who are pasturing the sheep. On these errands he transmits negative reports about his brothers to his father—it is not clear what exactly Joseph's role in the reporting of the gossip was.

In vv. 3 and 4 the narrator describes part of the relationships between Jacob and his sons. According to v. 3, Jacob 'loved Joseph more than all his sons',[45] 'because he was a son of his old age (בֶן־זְקֻנִים)'. This is the reason why Jacob makes his son a special robe, a כתנת פסים.

Quite a few commentators and translators have racked their brains on the question of what a כתנת פסים might be. The word כתנת is found 29 times in the entire Hebrew Bible (the root is known from Mesopotamia to Greece; the consonants might indicate a connection with 'cotton'[46]). It is both translated as 'coat' and 'robe'. According to *ThWAT* the word כתנת designates two possible garments; on the one hand, it indicates the 'archa-ische' ('archaic') *ketonet passim*, and on the other the 'einfache' ('simple') *ketonet*, 'ein Leibgewand oder Hemd' ('IV, 398'). The editors of *HALAT* have made a tripartite division with reference to the people wearing a garment like this. It is worn by laymen, by women,[47] and by priests.[48] With regard to the combination כתנת פסים, one often points to the circum-stance that it could indicate a garment 'das nicht zur Arbeit taugt und

that has been mentioned before. For more arguments to opt for 'assistant', see R. Pirson, 'What is Joseph Supposed to Be? On the Interpretation of נער in Genesis 37:2', in A. Brenner and J.W. van Henten (eds.), *Recycling Biblical Figures: Papers Read at a NOSTER Colloquium in Amsterdam 12–13 May 1997* (Studies in Theology and Relig-ion; Leiden: Deo, 1999), 81-92.

45. The narrator does not say whether or not Joseph's feelings for Israel were mutual.

46. *ThWAT* IV, 397-401. Cf. ABD, II, 233 s.v. 'dress and ornamentation': 'The k^etonet was probably the forerunner of the Greek *chitōn* and Roman tunic, and was worn next to the skin…or over the *'ezor*; it often had sleeves'.

47. E.g. Westermann: the robe 'ist nach 2S 13, 18 die Tracht einer Prinzessin. Dieses Kleid ist dann nicht nur ein schönes Geschenk des Vaters für seinen von ihm geliebten Sohn, sondern es hebt Joseph über seine Brüder hinaus; aus der Vorliebe wird das Vorziehen. Die Vorliebe wird öffentlich, und damit wird der Vader mitschuldig an dem Streit, der daraus entsteht… Nicht erst in den Träumen, auch schon bei dem Geschenk des Kleides geht es um die Stellung Josephs zu seinen Brüdern' (*Genesis 37–50* [BKAT, 1.3; Neukirchen–Vluyn: Neukirchener Verlag, 1982], 27).

48. *HALAT*, II, 480-81: 'Laientracht' (Gen. 3.21; 37.3, 23, 31, 33; 2 Sam. 15.32; Isa. 22.21 and Job 30.18), 'Frauentracht' (2 Sam. 13.18-19; Songs 5.3) and 'Priestertracht' (Exod. 28.4, 39-40; 29.5, 8; 39.27; 40.14; Lev. 8.7, 13; 10.5; 16.4; Ezra 2.69; Neh. 7.69, 71; Sir. 45.8).

deshalb nicht für einfache Menschen geschaffen ist. Königstöchter trugen solche Gewänder—Tamar zum Beispiel, Absoloms Schwester' ('that is not suitable for labour, and is therefore not made for ordinary people. The daughters of kings wore such garments—Tamar, for example, Absolom's sister').[49] The odd thing in derivations like these is that despite the fact that כתנת פסים is found only in Gen. 37 and in 2 Sam. 13, the main indication of its meaning is looked for at a royal court, and consequently כתנת פסים is supposed to refer to a royal garment. Whether a כתנת פסים is or is not a royal garment, from 2 Sam. 13.18—'She [Tamar] was wearing a כתנת פסים, for this is how the virgin daughters of the king were clothed, with מעילים'—it becomes clear that a כתנת פסים looks like a מעיל, which is a sleeveless coat (ärmelloses, mantelartiges Obergewand, HALAT, II, 579) —so that a כתנת פסים may be a sort of sleeveless coat as well.

The LXX and the Vulgate have introduced the well-known translation (in 37.3): 'coat of many colours'; LXX: χιτῶνα ποικίλον, and Vulgate: *tunicam polymitam*. Beside this translation one also encounters the meaning: 'long robe with sleeves', in which translators base their case on the post-biblical word פס, which is connected to פסים, and which means the flat of the hand or foot. The robe is supposed to reach down to the ankles and wrists (which of course contradicts the above mentioned possible 'synonymity' with מעיל).[50] According to Speiser, both translations are 'sheer guesses from the context; nor is there anything remarkable about either colors or sleeves'.[51] He offers a solution by referring to Mesopotamian cuneiform inscriptions on which the words *kitû pišannu* appear.

> The article so described was a ceremonial robe which could be draped about statues of goddesses, and had various gold ornaments sewed onto it...the Heb. phrase, i.e. *passīm*, would be an adaptation of Akk. *pišannu*, a technical term denoting appliqué ornaments on costly vests and bodices.[52]

---

49. Dietrich, *Die Josephserzählung*, 72; also Westermann, *Genesis 37–50*, 27; G. von Rad, *Genesis: A Commentary* (OTL; London: SCM Press, 3rd edn, 1970), 346.

50. *HALAT*, III, 892. Hamilton gives a second possible explanation for the 'long robe with sleeves': 'Another attempt has been made to connect Heb. *passîm* with *'epes*, "end, extremity", and with *'opsāyim*, "ankles" (cf. Ezek. 47.3). Thus, a *kᵉtōnet passîm* is a garment extending to the extremities of one's body (hands and feet). Support for the equation of *pas* and *'epes* may be found in the place name Ephes-dammim (1 Sam. 17.1), which is called Pas-dammim in 1 Chr. 11.13)' (*The Book of Genesis: 18–50*, 407-408, cf. 408-409).

51. Speiser, *Genesis*, 289.

52. Speiser, *Genesis*, 290.

My concluding observation with regard to Joseph's robe is brought about by the text of 2 Sam. 13.18, already referred to above, which states that a כתנת פסים was being worn by the daughters of the king before they were married. Thus, here one can notice a similarity between Tamar and Joseph: both Tamar and Joseph are unmarried. Perhaps the robe should be understood in this respect: its wearers are not married.

However this may be, the fact is that Jacob clothes Joseph because of his love for his son. The reason is that Joseph was a 'son of his old age'. The robe is the material representation of Israel's love for Joseph, and it is this quality of the robe that is of importance. It does not really matter what the robe looked like—whether it was multi-coloured or whether it had long sleeves—its function is to depict the love of Israel. The subsequent hate among Joseph's brothers finds its very cause in their father's favouritism of the son of his old age. Israel's behaviour causes the disturbed relationship among the brethren.

So, the reason for Israel's love for Joseph is because Joseph is a בן־זקנים to him. The narrator expresses himself with a verbless clause: כי־בן־זקנים הוא לו, usually translated as: 'because he (was) a son of his old age'. It is a rather curious reason, especially since the differences in age between Joseph and his brothers in Gen. 30 appear not to be great.[53] Moreover, Benjamin is even younger than Joseph. This implies that Israel has several sons to whom the designation בן־זקנים is applicable.[54] Israel loving Joseph because he is a son who was born to him when he was old is not entirely impossible, but it is a rather unconvincing and awkward reason.[55]

---

53. Perhaps Joseph is even older than Zebulun and of the same age as Issachar (Lowenthal, *The Joseph Narrative*, 161).

54. According to Lowenthal the difference in ages between Judah and Joseph may be no more than three years; see *The Joseph Narrative*, 161-63.

55. Another interpretation is presented in Targum Onqelos, where זקנים is not understood as to refer to 'old age', but to 'the elders' who are supposed to sit in the gate, judge and be wise (although such a meaning for זקנים is not present in Genesis); in this targum the clause ארי בר חכים הוא ליה is translated: 'for he was a wise son to him' (A. Sperber [ed.], *The Bible in Aramaic*. I. *The Pentateuch According to Targum Onkelos* [Leiden: E.J. Brill, 1959], 61). Lowenthal interprets בן־זקנים as 'a born leader': '*Ben* is not only "the son of" but also introduces a word of quality, characteristic etc. Also *zaqen* is not only "an old man", but can connote "sage, elder, authority"' (*The Joseph Narrative*, 167). This interpretation appears to be opted for by Josephus as well (*Ant.* 2.9).

In v. 4 the narrator reports on the feelings of the brothers towards Joseph, feelings that have arisen because their father provides Joseph with a special position within their family. Whereas the unusual relationship between Joseph and his father may have been invisible for the brothers in v. 2, now in v. 4 it is told that they are aware of the fact that their father loved him more than he loved them.[56] Therefore, the verse continues, they hated him and were unable to communicate with him in a normal course.

Peace and Wellbeing

What exactly does the latter part of v. 4—ולא יכלו דברו לשלם—mean? As a rule it is translated as 'and they could not speak friendly/peaceably with him' or 'they could not address him civilly'.[57] Can the brothers really not speak to their younger brother in a peaceful manner, or are they really unable to address him civilly?

The word דברו is, as Sarna indicates, unique.[58] Besides 'talking to him' it is possible as well to understand דברו in the meaning of 'his speech' (Sarna). This is why the final clause of a reading followed by v. 4 has a certain equivocation. One could read the verse as 'His brothers could not speak לשלם with him', but also as 'His brothers could not abide his speech לשלם'. Both possibilities indicate a disturbance in the communication among the brothers. However, the narrator's description shows that the brothers are the ones to blame. No blame falls to Joseph. Just as the expression דבתם רעה in the final clause of v. 2 could have different interpretations, it appears that the same holds true for דברו לשלם in v. 4.

The word that concludes v. 4 is לשלם; this notation is only encountered twice in the Hebrew Bible: here in Gen. 37.4, and in Jer. 15.5.[59] The plene spelling לשלום is found more often. One might distinguish two ways in

---

56. See also H.C. White, *Narration and Discourse in the Book of Genesis* (Cambridge: Cambridge University Press, 1991), 241.

57. Instead of דברו the LXX has read דבר לו: καὶ οὐκ ἐδύναντο λαλεῖν αὐτῷ οὐδὲν εἰρηνικόν ('and they could not speak to him peaceably'). Cf. Hamilton's view that 'Targ. Onkelos renders "could not" by "did not wish to" (*wl' bn*) to indicate that the brothers were able to speak to Joseph but chose not to' (*The Book of Genesis: 18–50*, 404).

58. Sarna (*Genesis*, 256): 'Hebrew *dabbero* is unique. Usually the suffix attached to this verb carries a possessive sense, meaning "his speech". The passage would then be translated, "They could not abide his friendly speech". In other words, they rebuffed every attempt by Joseph to be friendly.'

59. NRSV translates: 'Who will have pity on you, O Jerusalem, or who will bemoan you? Who will turn aside to ask about your welfare?'

which לְשָׁלֹם is being used. First, nine cases show a combination with a verb of movement: 'go in peace' or 'get up in peace'.[60] Second, in the remaining cases it is combined with a *verbum dicendi*: 'they asked about the well-being of...'[61] In Gen. 37.4, לְשָׁלֹם is combined with a *verbum dicendi* as well. This might be a clue not to emphasize the notion 'peaceably' or 'friendly (amiably)', which the brothers could not summon towards Joseph (in this case one applies דַּבְּרוֹ to the brothers). I am aware of the fact that although this is not an ideal way of communication, it nevertheless presents a more favourable casting of the brothers. The impossibility of enquiring after someone's wellbeing is more kind than 'they could not speak peaceably to him', which implies the brothers' permanent negative attitude toward Joseph and their constantly treating him rudely.[62] Israel's favouritism of Joseph awakens the brothers' negative feelings toward Joseph. The result of all this is the violation and disruption of the peace (שָׁלֹם), the unity and plenitude of Jacob's *toledot*. This disruption of the family ties manifests itself further when Joseph tells his dreams to his brothers and his father.

Hatred and Envy

In Gen. 37 it is to be noticed that the narrator ascribes emotions only to Israel and to the brothers as a collective—(there are no statements of individual feelings, Reuben's exclamation in v. 29 excepted)—and these emotions are always described in relation to Joseph. As far as Joseph is concerned, however, emotions are entirely absent.

The brother's hatred of Joseph is mentioned three times (vv. 4, 5 and 8). This strongly contrasts with Israel's love in vv. 3 and 4 (שָׂנֵא vs. אָהֵב),

---

60. Gen. 44.17; Exod. 4.18; Judg. 18.6; 1 Sam. 1.17; 20.13, 42; 25.35; 1 Kgs. 20.18; 2 Kgs. 5.19. It is possible for Deut. 20.10 to be counted among these places (if קְרָאת is not read as a verbal form of קָרָא I, but of קָרָא II).

61. Gen. 43.27; Exod. 18.7; Judg. 18.15; 1 Sam. 10.4; 17.18, 22; 25.5; 30.21; 2 Sam. 8.10; 11.7; 2 Kgs. 10.13. In this respect one could note places like Gen. 29.6 and 43.27 (הֲשָׁלֹם as a question: 'everything well?') and Gen. 29.6; 37.14; 41.16; 43.23, 28. In these cases it is always the wellbeing of someone or something that is focussed upon.

62. The brothers' unwillingness to communicate to Joseph can also be seen in the preceding clause, where the verb שָׂנֵא is used. According to *NIDOTE*, III, 1257 the verb 'may express the most intense hatred of the enemies of God (Ps 139.21-22), or that of a violent enemy (25.19), but it may simply express that which is to be avoided, such as serving as a guarantor for a debt (Prov. 11.15)...' This latter meaning could apply to Gen. 37. It is probably no coincidence that the brothers leave Joseph in v. 12.

which appears to be the first cause of their hatred. A little further, however, the increase of the brothers' hatred against their brother is caused by
Joseph's dreams (אֹתוֹ שְׂנֹא עוֹד וַיּוֹסִפוּ; vv. 5 and 8). The verb שָׂנֵא indicates
an emotional condition of aversion and dislike.[63] It implies a growing apart
of the one who hates and the one who is hated. So, Hebrew שָׂנֵא implies
something different from English 'hate'. An illustration of this is to be
found in the case of Leah being hated by Jacob (29.31): because God saw
that Leah was being hated, he opened her womb. The fact that he hated
Leah did not prevent Jacob from sleeping with her and having children
with her.[64] He treats Leah rather unfairly in comparison to Rachel, and this
is what שָׂנֵא expresses.[65]

In his discussion of Gen. 37 Branson regrettably concludes that 'the
term signifies hostility or enmity based on jealousy'.[66] In his conclusion he
states that 'The basic meaning of the Hebrew root שָׂנֵא is "hatred, enmity,
hostility"; however, it has a wide range of connotations expressing both
negative emotions and disruptions of relationships'.[67] The aversion sensed
by someone towards another leads to a total lack of contact (cf. Gen. 37.4).
It is a pity that Branson does not think the meaning he finds in the case of
Leah to be present in the case of Joseph's brothers. Just as Leah sensed a
lack of love on her husband's part, so the brothers experience their father's

63. The verb 'is often used…and in an antithetical function with אָהֵב' (R.D. Branson, *A Study of the Hebrew Term* שָׂנֵא [Boston: Boston University Graduate School,
1976], vi).

64. Cf. Branson: 'The opposite of שָׂנֵא is אָהֵב. Leah wanted her husband to love her
(v. 32), to be joined to her (v. 34). Speiser suggests that שָׂנֵא indicates rejection, not
being loved, and notes the similar use of the term in Deut. 21.15. It seems best to accent
this suggestion understanding the term to signify in this context a lack of emotional
commitment on the part of Jacob to Leah' (*A Study of the Hebrew Term* שָׂנֵא, 45).

65. 'Das Verb *śāne'* "hassen bezeichnet einen emotionalen Zustand der Aversion,
der Abneigung, der durch die at.liche Anthropologie im Herzen" (*leḇ*, Lev 19, 17) oder
in der *næpæš* (2 Sam 5, 8; Ps 11, 5) lokalisiert wird. Es legt nicht not wendigerweise
boshafte Absichten hinsichtlich des Haßerfülltseins nahe, dennoch impliziert es eine
Distanzierung vom Gehaßten, seine Entfernung aus der Umgebung des Hassenden in
sich' (*ThWAT*, VII, 829).

66. Branson, *A Study of the Hebrew Term* שָׂנֵא, 46.

67. Branson, *A Study of the Hebrew Term* שָׂנֵא, 135. In his conclusion he also
writes: 'The emotional content of the root שָׂנֵא swings from aversion of an object or the
disliking of an action to the loathing of some person, even the hating of one which
leads to murder. Within the family context it represents a range of emotions from a
lack of proper affection (Gen. 29.31, 33) to violent rejection (2 Sam. 13.15) or hatred
(2 Sam. 13.22)' (136).

lack of love for them (verse 3). This has repercussions for their relationship with Joseph, and in the way they will react to his dreams.

The second verb used by the narrator to inform the reader of the brothers' state of mind is קָנָא ('envy', v. 11), combined with the preposition בְּ.[68] The source of envy is the fear of losing someone or something,[69] or to be in want of something.[70] The brothers' envy is not Joseph's dreaming but rather their feeling of losing the relationship with their father. The brothers also want the thing Joseph possesses: the love of the father.[71] This is indicated already in vv. 3 and 4 when the narrator twice uses the verb אָהַב, which 'erscheint zugleich als Oppositum als auch als Voraussetzung (les extrêmes se touchent) von *qn*' ('appears both as contrary to a prerequisite [les extremes se touchent] to *qn*') (*ThWAT*, VII, 53.). This is the reason why the envy is mentioned after the dreams as a summarizing statement, and also why it is combined with the statement that 'his father kept the matter in mind'. The brothers' envy of Joseph finds its roots in their father's relationship with them.[72]

---

68. According to *HALAT*, III, 1037, the meaning of קָנָא *cum* בְּ is 'neidisch sein auf'. Examples given are 37.11 and Prov. 24.1. Another possible meaning is 'sich erhitzen, sich ereifern über/gegen'; Gen. 37.11 is given in this category as well; together with 30.1; Pss. 37.1; 73.3; Prov. 3.31; 23.17; 24.19. It is rather remarkable that the occurrence in Gen. 30.1 is not mentioned together with the examples falling under 'neidisch sein'.

69. 'Im zwischenmenschlichen Bereich drückt *qn*' vor allem eine heftige Gemütsbewegung aus, die durch die Angst vor dem Verlust eines Gegenstands oder einer Person ausgelöst wird' (*ThWAT*, VII, 53). B. Jacob ascribes a slightly different meaning to the verb: 'קֵנְאָה ist nicht dasselbe wie שִׂנְאָה, und קַנֵּא בְּ ...heißt: seine Gelassenheit gegenüber jemandes unverdientem Glücksstand verlieren und diesem Gefühl in Reden Luft machen, während der Haß auch schweigen kann' (*Das erste Buch der Tora*, 700).

70. According to T. Muraoka the meaning of קָנָא plus בְּ is 'to envy (somebody's success)' ('On Verb Complementation in Biblical Hebrew', *Vetus Testamentum* 29 [1979], 424-35 [429]).

71. 'Etwa die Hälfte aller Belege handelt von der Eifersucht Gottes' (*ThWAT*, VII, 58); cf. Exod. 20.5; 34.14; Deut. 4.24; 5.9; 6.15. Maybe is it not improbable to think that the 'Eifersucht Gottes' (like the 'Eifersucht der Rachel' in relation to Jacob) is caused by the fear to lose Israel to 'the other gods'. In view of God's words about a punishment into the third and fourth generations, the brothers' reaction against Joseph (the departure to Shechem) is rather mild. Not until his arrival in their camp do they take radical measures.

72. The fear of losing someone or something is confirmed by the occurrence of קָנָא

Thus, as for the brothers, it is obvious that they do not know how to deal with the special position Joseph has in their father's eyes. Their initial reaction is hatred. This hatred pervades their contacts with their younger brother in v. 4. The hatred also has a strong influence on the brothers' response to Joseph's dreams. If they hear him talk about their sheaves bowing down before his, they cannot but interpret the dream in terms of dominance and suppression: 'do you want to be king over us and indeed rule over us?' (v. 8). It is not possible for them to consider the dreams from a detached perspective. A dream in which a נער, an assistant, is bowed down before seems to imply no less than a reversal of the present situation: the least expresses his wish to be first, the servant of all to be lord (בעל). It is questionable, however, whether the brothers' interpretation of Joseph's dream is correct.

in Gen. 30.1. As in 37.11, it is combined with the preposition ב. According to the narrator, Rachel envies her sister because she could not have children, whereas Leah had already given birth to four sons. The barrenness is the source of her envy—not Leah, or the circumstances that Leah does already have children. Rachel fears to lose her husband: she wants to die if she is not going to conceive any children (30.1).

Chapter 3

A TALE OF TWO DREAMS

In this chapter Joseph's dreams and their meaning will be my point of interest. To have a good understanding of his dreams, however, the other dream-pairs in Gen. 37–50 have to be considered as well.

When dealing with Joseph's dreams there are two problems that need to be solved. The first is the brothers' interpretation of Joseph's first dream: 'Do you want to be king over us, and indeed rule over us?' (v. 8). Is this really what the first dream is about? Trying to be king and trying to be a ruler? The second problem surfaces after reading Jacob's answer to Joseph's dream: 'Shall we, I, your mother and your brothers indeed come and bow down to the ground before you?' (v. 10). Jacob's interpretation of Joseph's dream is an impossible interpretation, as will become clear below. However, before turning to Joseph's dreams and their interpretations by the brothers and the father, the first thing to do is consider the dreams prior to Joseph's, because they differ from Joseph's in a significant way.

1. *The Dreams Prior to Joseph's*

In his description of Joseph's dreams the narrator uses the noun חלום ('dream') and the verb חלם ('dream'). Other dreams described with this noun and verb are to be found in Gen. 20.3-7 (God talking to Abimelech); 28.12-15 (God talking to Jacob at Bethel); 31.10-13 (Jacob telling a dream in which God has spoken to him) and 31.24 (God talking to Laban). Apart from these dream-reports there are several occasions when people have had a vision in the night during which God talks to them: 15.12-16; 26.2-5, 24; 46.2-4. The overall connection between these places is the fact that God makes his appearance in the dreams and is talking to the one dreaming. These elements are lacking in Joseph's dreams, but also in the dreams following Joseph's, like those of the cupbearer, the baker and Pharaoh.

Another point, which is observed by Turner,[1] is the non-symbolic nature of the dreams prior to Gen. 37, which means that they do not need any interpretation, as is needed by the symbolic dreams of Gen. 37–41. This makes the dreams prior to and following Gen. 37 not strictly comparable.

2. *The Dreams of Joseph*

It is helpful to consider Joseph's dreams together, before looking at each dream separately. The dreams present some similarities, as well as some differences.

The First Dream (37.5-8)

5a	Joseph dreamed a dream	ויחלם יוסף חלום	5a
b	and told it to his brothers	ויגד לאחיו	b
c	and they hated him even more	ויוספו עוד שׂנא אתו	c
6a	He said to them	ויאמר אליהם	6a
b	Please, listen to this dream	שמעו־נא החלום הזה	b
c	which I have dreamed,	אשר חלמתי	c
7a	and look;	והנה	7a
b	we were binding sheaves in the field	אנחנו מאלמים אלמים בתוך השׂדה	b
c	and look,	והנה	c
d	my sheave had arisen	קמה אלמתי	d
e	and kept standing upright	וגם־נצבה	e
f	And see,	והנה	f
g	your sheaves gathered round	תסבינה אלמתיכם	g
h	and bowed down to my sheaf	ותשתחוין לאלמתי	h
8a	And his brothers said:	ויאמרו לו אחיו	8a
b	Do you intend to be king over us	המלך תמלך עלינו	b
c	and indeed rule over us?	אם־משׁול תמשׁל בנו	c
d	And they hated him even more because of his dreams and because of his words	ויוספו עוד שׂנא אתו על־חלמתיו ועל־דבריו	d

---

1. L.A. Turner, *Announcements of Plot in Genesis* (JSOTSup, 96; Sheffield: JSOT Press, 1990), 145.

The Second Dream (37.9-11)

9a	And he dreamed yet another dream,	ויחלם עוד חלום אחר	9a
b	and told it to his brother	ויספר אתו לאחיו	b
c	and he said		c
d	Look,	ויאמר	d
e	I dreamed another dream,	הנה	e
f	And look:	חלמתי חלום עוד	f
g	The sun, the moon and eleven stars were bowing down before me.	והנה השמש והירח ואחד	g
10a	And he told it to his father and his brothers	עשר כוכבים משתחוים לי	10a
b	And his father rebuked him	ויספר אל־אביו ואל־אחיו	b
c	and said to him:	ויגער־בו אביו	c
d	What dream is this	ויאמר לו	d
e	that you dreamed?	מה החלום הזה	e
f	Must I and your mother and your brothers come to bow down before you on the ground?	אשר חלמת הבוא נבוא אני ואמך ואחיך להשתחות לך ארצה	f
11a	And his brothers envied him,	ויקנאו־בו אחיו	11a
b	whereas his father kept the matter in mind	ואביו שמר את־הדבר	b

These texts do not only show Joseph's dreams to have a parallel pattern, but also show some differences between them. Most striking is the difference in length between both dreams. Nothing but the participial clause from the first dream (v. 7b) is to be found in the second (v. 9g);[2] this second dream lacks further participial clauses and the *yiqtol* and *wayyiqtol* clauses.[3] This makes the second dream less dynamic.

A second observation is concerned with the characters portrayed in the dreams. The first dream presents Joseph and his brothers binding sheaves; next, the dream focusses on the sheaves themselves—*your* sheaves and *my* sheaf. This first dream maintains a relationship between the images in the dream and the characters of the story (Joseph and the brothers—my sheaf

---

2. One could argue that v. 9g should be placed next to v. 7h (instead of next to v. 7b), because both verses have a verb form of the verb חוה ('bow down') in common; however, from a syntactic point of view both verses share the participle.

3. *Wayyiqtol* following *yiqtol* here is not 'correct' Classical Hebrew, since *wayyiqtol* can only follow a form of *qatal* (cf. e.g. GKC §111a, 326: 'As a rule the narrative is introduced by a perfect and then continued by means of imperfects with *wāw consecutive*'; also cf. GKC §49a, 132).

and your sheaves). The second dream presents something completely different: 'the sun, the moon and eleven stars were bowing down before *me*'.[4] The only character appearing both in the dream and in the story is Joseph himself. The dream makes no connection between the heavenly bodies and the characters. The linkage of the dream to the world of the characters is made only by Israel, who connects the celestial bodies to his family.[5]

A third distinction is the way in which the narrator introduces Joseph's dreams. When presenting the first dream he says: 'Joseph dreamed a dream, and he told (נגד, hiphil) it to his brothers' (v. 5a). This is being followed by a comment about the brothers, and not until then is Joseph allowed to tell his dream. The second dream is introduced in another way: 'He dreamed yet another dream and told (ספר, piel) it to his brothers and said' (v. 9a). When Joseph has told his dream, the narrator repeats a part of the verse just quoted: 'And he told (ספר, piel) it to his father and to his brothers' (v. 10a). In this verse Israel appears to be an auditor as well.

Having a closer look at the different verbs used by the narrator to introduce Joseph's dreams might shed some more light on both dreams. Both verbs share the meaning 'tell, make known, declare', but they function in a different way. This is demonstrated upon examination of the places in which both verbs occur in Genesis. Whenever the verb נגד is found, its meaning is plain: 'to tell', which has to be understood as the passing on of (necessary) information (cf. a little further, in v. 16, where Joseph asks the unidentified man: 'Please tell me [הגידה־נא לי] where are they [my brothers] tending their flocks?').[6]

---

4. Wildavsky's remark may seem a bit too strong: 'The most damaging is that this is an idolatrous dream in which Joseph takes the place of the Almighty, thereby worshipping himself. Self-worship is a characteristic of the Pharaoh, who is called the very incarnation of the sun god Ra' (A. Wildavsky, *Assimilation versus Separation. Joseph the Administrator and the Politics of Religion in Biblical Israel* [New Brunswick, NJ: Transaction Publishers 1993], 78).

5. A.L. Oppenheim does not share this opinion: '...the sheaves and the stars "symbolize" the brothers, while the luminaries refer in the same way to his parents. Their reactions show this' (*The Interpretation of Dreams in the Ancient Near East: With a Translation of an Assyrian Dream-Book* [Transactions of the American Philosophical Society, 46; Philadelphia: The American Philosophical Society, 1956], 206).

6. Cf. *NIDOTE*, III, 16; נגד (hiphil) occurs 14 times in Gen. 37–50: 37.5, 16; 41.24, 25; 42.29; 43.6, 7; 44.24; 45.13, 26; 46.31; 47.1; 48.2; 49.1.

Something different is the case when one considers the root ספר, whose qal, niphal, and piel conjugations are to be found in Genesis. To start with the latter, this conjugation is found eight times—six of which in combination with a dream (37.9, 10; 40.8, 9; 41.8, 12); the two remaining occurrences are 24.66 and 29.13. All attestations of ספר (piel) have the meaning 'tell'. The qal and niphal conjugations of ספר occur five times (qal: 15.5; 32.13; 41.49, and niphal: 16.10); the meaning being 'count'. When looking at these places, it is obvious that 16.10 and 32.13 are about the seed (of Abraham and Jacob respectively) that cannot be counted; 15.5 belongs to this category as well: 'Count the stars (הכוכבים), if you can count them… This is how your seed will be' (the 'stars', כוכבים, are to be found in 37.9 as well). And Gen. 41.49 is about counting too: the Egyptians stopped counting the grain because of its abundance. As noted above, there are six cases in which ספר (piel) is combined with a dream, and in four of them the notion of 'counting' appears to be present (40.8, 9; 41.8, 12). In these dreams, numbers play an important role. The cupbearer and the baker behold a vine with three branches and three baskets, whereas in Pharaoh's dreams there appear seven lean or seven fat cows and ears. So, in the piel conjugation of ספר—besides its meaning 'tell'—it also seems to have a connotation of 'counting'. This might account for the presence of ספר in Joseph's second dream, in which numbers undeniably play a prominent role: 'The sun, the moon and eleven stars were bowing down before me' (v. 9g). The importance of the figures and the choice for the verb ספר are evident in comparison with the first dream, in which there is no indication of numbers and the verb ספר is consequently absent. Contrary to the second dream, the first is not clear about the number of brothers (sheaves) involved.[7] This matter will return at the end of the chapter.

Both dreams are followed by the reaction of the characters to whom Joseph tells his dreams. The brothers give their response in v. 8, and Israel rebukes his son in v. 10. Both reactions convey the impudence of the dreams as it is perceived by the father and the brothers. This dreaming is outrageous! Both rhetorical questions show a similar structure. The brothers pose two questions by means of an infinitive absolute followed by *yiqtol*, and Israel makes use of a similar construction after his exclamation 'What dream is

---

7.   Although M. Sternberg supposes there were 11. When writing on the brothers' voyage to Egypt, he states: 'Eleven bowing sheaves foreshadowed, but only ten appear before him' (*The Poetics of Biblical Narrative: Ideological Literature and the Drama of Reading* [Bloomington: Indiana University Press, 1985], 292).

this, that you have dreamed?' The brothers' question is succeeded by the
narrator's statement that 'they hated him even more'. This has a parallel
after the second dream when the narrator says that Israel rebuked his son,[8]
although one could argue that 'they hated him even more because of his
dreams and because of his words (דבריו)' has its counterpart in v. 11: 'His
brothers envied him, whereas his father kept the matter (הדבר) in mind
(שמר)'.[9] By means of these statements the narrator makes a (successful)
try to undermine the comments by the brothers and Israel, in which they
express the outrageousness of the dreams, by ascribing negative feelings to
them: hate (שנא) and envy (קנא).[10] The narrator explicitly relates this to
the dreams by way of the terms 'his words' and 'the matter', both of which
are expressed by the same Hebrew word, דבר. The tale of Joseph's dreams
is concluded by the note that 'his father' kept the matter in mind.[11]

Despite the above-mentioned differences between both dreams, in the bigger part of the studies on Joseph, one comes across the opinion that
Joseph's dreams do not only have the same meaning, but also that they are
obvious and clear. Westermann, for example, says: 'einer Deutung oder
gar eines Deutefachmannes bedarf der Traum nicht; was er bedeuten soll,
ist sofort jedem der Beteiligten klar' ('an explanation or even a professional
explainer is not necessary for the dream; what it means is immediately
clear to anyone hearing it').[12] And Aaron Wildavsky mentions 'dreams so
self-evident in their desire for domination that [they] require no further
interpretation'.[13] Humphreys is of the same opinion; according to him
Joseph's dreams are 'the simplest and need no interpretation'.[14] However,
the interpreters often do not say what the meaning of the dreams might be.
Yet, they see the dreams come true when the brothers arrive in Egypt, and
bow down before Joseph (42.6; 43.26). This asks for a closer examination

8.   Cf. B. Becking, ' "They hated him even more": Literary Technique in Genesis
37.1-11', *BN* 60 (1991), 40-47 (43).

9.   The verb שמר (qal) has as its primary meaning 'bewachen, behüten, beobachten,
erfüllen, halten, Wache halten, ausspähen' (*ThWAT*, VIII, 286).

10.   'The various usages [of קנא] share the notion of an intense, energetic state of
mind, urging towards action' (*NIDOTE*, III, 938).

11.   This element will be considered in the final chapter of this book.

12.   Westermann, *Genesis 37–50*, 28.

13.   Wildavsky, *Assimilation versus Separation*, 70.

14.   W.L. Humphreys, *Joseph and his Family: A Literary Study* (Studies on the
Personalities of the Old Testament; Columbia: University of South Carolina Press,
1988), 111.

of both dreams to see whether they are self-evident and whether they do
have a similar meaning.

3. *The First Dream: We Were Binding Sheaves in the Field*

'Listen to this dream which I have dreamed' (v. 6) are the first words
spoken by Joseph. If somebody's first words are directive or illustrative,
one has to admit that the brothers' designation of Joseph in v. 19 as 'lord
of the dreams' is appropriate. Another important point is Joseph urging the
brothers to listen to his dream: שמעו־נא ('please listen!'). The particle נא
indicates an urgent request.[15] Here in 37.6 it expresses Joseph's wish to be
listened to. In exactly the same way he will address 'the man' (האיש) in
v. 16, who finds him wandering in the fields around Shechem: 'please tell
me (הגידה־נא לי) where to find my brothers'.

The picture Joseph saw in his dream was: 'We were binding sheaves in
the field, and my sheaf had arisen and kept standing upright, and your
sheaves gathered round and bowed down to my sheaf!' (v. 7). The first
clause is a participial clause and gives a description of the situation.
Suddenly a change has come about, indicated by והנה: Joseph's sheaf has
arisen and keeps standing upright; they continue the image from v. 7b. The
following clauses (after yet another והנה) describe the subsequent actions
on a narrative level: your sheaves gathered round (*yiqtol*) and bowed down
(*wayyiqtol*) to my sheaf!

From the brothers' reaction it is obvious that hackles are raised by Joseph
describing their sheaves gathering around his, and bowing down to his. The
change from 'we' (we were binding sheaves) to the sheaves themselves
(your sheaves, my sheaf) will presumably not have caused any problems,
the same can probably be said about Joseph's sheaf standing up: this does
not say anything about the other sheaves. But their bowing down before
Joseph's sheaf goes beyond the pale. The brothers identify bowing down
with being in a position of subordination: 'Do you want to be king over us,
and indeed rule over us?' (v. 8bc), is the brothers' ironic question. They
extrapolate the narrative thread of the dream to their own present and
future.[16] However, it is questionable whether the brothers' interpretation of

15. Joüon and Muraoka, *A Grammar of Biblical Hebrew*, §114b, 374; cf. §105c,
350: 'It is mostly used for the purpose of adding a usually weak entreating nuance,
which is roughly equivalent to a stressed and lengthened *Please* in English'.

16. On Joseph's motivation to tell his dreams von Rad says: 'A vision was for the

the dream is correct. Looking at the places in Genesis in which the verb חוה ('bow down') is found may prove fruitful.[17]

In the Hebrew Bible the form *hištaḥ^awāh* is encountered 170 times. *ThWAT* presents these meanings: 'sich (huldigend, höflich) verneigen ['to bow down (in honour, courteously)'], sich (anbetend) nieder werfen ['to prostrate oneself (in worship)'], niederfallen ['to fall down (προσκυνεῖν)], sich (ehrfurchtsvoll, anbetend) tief beugen, und zwar vor Menschen zur Begrüßung, Huldigung oder Unterwerfung ['fall down' (προσκυνεῖν), 'in cases of hail, honour, or submission'].[18] *ThWAT* also mentions *hištaḥ^awāh* to be used for 'Huldigung vor dem König' ('honouring the king'); the places involved indicate that it is about 'einen Unterwerfungs- oder Auslieferungsgestus' ('a gesture of submission or surrender').[19] Most places, however, refer to the cult.[20] In sum, the basic meaning of חוה is 'bow down'.

If one restricts oneself to Genesis (23 occurrences) it seems highly unlikely that חוה has a connotation of 'submission to someone'.[21] The majority of occurrences in Genesis show that this is not the case.[22] There

ancients so important and obligatory that a demand to keep it tactfully to oneself would not have occurred to them' (*Genesis*, 346-47). However, he does not give any evidence to support this claim.

17. I refer to the root חוה, even though it is not entirely certain to which root 'to bow down' belongs: שחה or חוה; this however has no consequences for the root's meaning. 'Bis vor nicht allzu langer Zeit wurde die Bildung *hištaḥ^awāh* als hitpalel von שחה (*šāḥāh*) erklärt...und in Beziehung zu *šwḥ* und *šḥḥ* gesehen... Ein *hitpalel* von *šāḥāh* müßte aber eigentlicht *hištaḥāh* lauten, so daß die Erklärung des eingedrungenen *w* schon immer Schwierigkeiten bereitete' (*ThWAT*, II, 785). Since the discovery of the Ugaritic verb *ḥwj* the editors of *ThWAT* designate the Hebrew verb to the root חוה (*ThWAT*, II, 785); *NIDOTE* (II, 42) also prefers חוה to be the root. See also Joüon and Muraoka, *A Grammar of Biblical Hebrew*, §79t, 211. Another opinion has J. Emerton, 'The Etymology of *HIŠTA⁴WĀH*', in H.A. Brongers *et al.* (eds.), *Instruction and Interpretation. Studies in Hebrew Language, Palestinian Archeology and Biblical Exegesis; Papers Read at the Joint British–Dutch Old Testament Conference held at Louvain, 1976* (OTS, 20; Leiden: E.J. Brill, 1977), 41-55.

18. *ThWAT*, II, 786. 'Man verneigte sich vor einem Menschen, um ihn ehrfurchtsvoll zu begrüßen oder seine höhere Stellung anzuerkennen' (788).

19. *ThWAT*, II, 788. The occurrences mentioned are to be found in the books of Samuel, Kings and Chronicles, in several Psalms and in Esther.

20. *ThWAT*, II, 789-94.

21. These are: 18.2; 19.1; 22.5; 23.7, 12; 24.26, 48, 52; 27.29; 33.3, 6, 7; 37.7, 9, 10; 42.6; 43.26, 28; 47.31; 48.12; 49.8.

22. In Gen. 22.5; 24.26, 48, 52, חוה has a cultic meaning. Setting aside Gen. 37 one

might be two exceptions, and these are in Gen. 27 and 49. In 27.29 Isaac blesses Jacob: 'Let peoples serve you, and nations bow down to you. Be lord over your brothers, and may your mother's sons bow down to you!' And perhaps also Jacob blessing Judah in 49.8: 'Judah, your brothers shall praise you; your hand shall be on the neck of your enemies; your father's sons shall bow down before you'. One should however be aware of the fact that the meaning of חוה, which occurs twice in 27.29, is strongly determined by the verb עבד ('serve'), which precedes the first of both occurrences, and which forms a parallel construction with חוה. Another important element in this verse is the presence of the noun גביר ('lord, master'). The point now, is that a connotation of subservience is not part of the verb חוה, but that this is a notion that is added by the explicit mentioning of the words עבד and גביר. Concerning 49.8, it should be observed that the entire context is determined by Judah's future kingship.

With regard to Gen. 27.29 it seems that for Jacob it would not have been awkward to establish a link between חוה and submission—a thing he actually does *not* do in his rebuke of Joseph after the second dream. The fact is that a notion of subservience is in no way present in Joseph's dreams. In the larger part of the occurrences of חוה in Genesis, it has a connotation of respect, and sometimes fear. This is undoubtedly applicable to 42.6 and 43.26, 28, in which Joseph's brothers prostrate themselves before the Egyptian governor (cf. 50.18)—although fear may have played a part as well. One shows respect for another country's sovereign; submission is out of the question. The reader must keep her- or himself from the wrong conclusion drawn by the brothers.

It is especially true, in view of Gen. 33, in which Jacob and his family prostrate themselves before Esau (חוה occurs four times) and Esau and Jacob are reconciled, that the reader ought to know that bowing down and subservience are not necessarily the same. Jacob calling Esau 'my lord' and calling himself 'your servant' do not restrict his freedom and are by no means expressions of subservience, let alone that Esau is going to rule over Jacob. To summarize: in Genesis there is no reason to establish a link between חוה ('bow down', meaning 'be subjected'), מלך ('be king') and משל ('rule'), as did the brothers.[23] In 45.8, after he has revealed himself,

bows down for others as a mark of respect, as is customary according to *ThWAT* (see above).

23. My analysis of bowing down to refer to respect (or even gratitude) rather than to subordinance is supported by B. Jacob: 'Daß die Garben der Brüder die seinige umringten und sich vor ihr verneigten, hatte für ihn nicht besagen wollen, daß er sie

Joseph implies that his brothers' interpretation of his first dream was not correct anyhow—even if they would keep to their interpretation of subservience. If Joseph's dream had referred to Joseph's future position of domination, it would have been the Egyptian people over whom he was to be lord: 'God has made me a ruler (מושל) over Egypt'[24]—not over his brothers.[25]

Nevertheless, the brothers' reaction to Joseph's dream illustrates their disapproval of the dream. Their younger brother—their נער ('assistant', 37.2)—expresses a reversal of positions in his dream, and this is something they cannot stomach. All of this might be the reason why this first dream is bracketed by the narrator's comment 'they hated him even more' (vv. 5 and 8).

4. *The Second Dream: The Sun, the Moon and 11 Stars*

Joseph's second dream is being introduced by the narrator when he says that Joseph had another dream (v. 9): ויחלם עוד חלום אחר ('and he dreamed yet another dream'). The word עוד seems a little superfluous, or pleonastic. By dreaming another dream, it is clear that Joseph dreamed once more. Therefore it is possible that the word אחר does not simply mean 'another, following', but rather indicates that Joseph dreamed a dream which is completely distinct from the first (see below).

As for Joseph's first dream, it has become evident that there are some serious doubts regarding the correctness of the brothers' interpretation. The same goes for the interpretation of Joseph's second dream. For a start, there is the observation that Israel's reading of the dream deviates from the brothers'. They interpret it in terms of kingship and domination. This element is lacking in Israel's exegesis. His rhetorical question, however, rather exhibits his astonishment about the dream. But, being the receiver of a dream twice himself (28.12-15; 31.11-13—the latter only according to himself, the narrator does not mention it), he should be able to assess a dream at its true value.

einst beherrschen oder gar tyrannisieren werde (es geschieht ja auch später durchaus nicht), sondern daß er wie ein idealer Herrscher für sie sorgen, sie schützen und am Leben erhalten werde, sie es ihm danken werden' (*Das erste Buch der Tora*, 766).

24. Before making this claim in 45.8 Joseph has sent away his Egyptian servants: 'He certainly does not want the Egyptians to overhear his proud claim of ruling over them' (Fung, *Victim and Victimizer*, 86).

25. The brothers repeat this when they return home (45.26).

In his reading Jacob emphasizes the fact that Joseph's family *has to come* (infinitive absolute construction: הבוא נבוא)[26] and bow themselves down to the ground before Joseph. This act of coming is lacking in the dream: the dream described a situation, a situation that may have lasted a while—judging by the participle.

A problem in Israel's interpretation is that both Joseph's mother and 11 brothers are supposed to be present in the dream.[27] In Gen. 35.19 Rachel died while giving birth to Benjamin.[28] Therefore it is physically impossible that both she and *11* brothers come and bow down before Joseph.[29] If one, nevertheless, wants to stick to 11 brothers, one has to assume that Benjamin is one of the brothers who are going to bow down before Joseph (and is among the brothers who envy Joseph, v. 11). In the case of the stars representing the brothers, the moon might depict Leah, Bilhah or Zilpah. One should keep in mind, however, that such explanations for 'the moon' are contradictory to Israel's words '*your* mother'.[30] To this, one might also add the already mentioned difference with regard to the characters acting in both dreams. In the first dream both Joseph and the brothers were present, whereas the only character in the second dream is Joseph. This is another indication that both dreams have different readings.

26. Cf. also Coats, *From Canaan to Egypt*, 14. In 46.8 all the family do actually come (בוא) to Joseph.

27. Gibson observes that 'It is not so commonly pointed out, however, that the second dream is *not* fulfilled in the epic' (J.C.L. Gibson, *Genesis*, II [The Daily Study Bible; Edinburgh: The Saint Andrew Press; Philadelphia: Westminster Press, 1982], 230). The interpretation as given by Israel is nowhere realized: 'In the received story, Joseph's father does not bow down to him, and Joseph's mother is long since dead, and has no place in the story whatever' (T.L. Thompson, *The Origin Tradition of Ancient Israel*. I. *The Literary Formation of Genesis and Exodus 1–23* [JSOTSup 55; Sheffield: JSOT Press, 1987], 118).

28. One cannot assume that Rachel's death will—chronologically—occur later than the events told in Gen. 37, because in 43.29, Joseph knows that Benjamin is his brother, the son of his mother. Also, Benjamin has ten sons when Jacob and his family enter into Egypt in Gen. 46.

29. Cf. Turner (*Announcements of Plot*, 153): 'taken as a whole, it is an *impossible* dream', and B. Jacob (*Das erste Buch der Tora*, 700): 'Wie gewöhnlich ist dem Traum, der ja selbst schon Unmögliches vorstellt, wäre es auch nur, daß Sonne, Mond und Sterne nie zusammen auftreten, insofern Falsches beigemischt, daß die Mutter Josephs nicht mehr lebt, und es ist unnötig, darunter die Pflegemutter Bilha zu verstehen'.

30. Unless one, as does Lowenthal, regards Israel's reading as ridiculing the dream: 'He ridicules it by pointing out that "the moon" can only refer to Joseph's mother who is already dead' (*The Joseph Narrative*, 20).

In relation to Jacob's interpretation of Joseph's second dream, there is
also the fact that in Genesis he never bows down before Joseph. It rather is
the other way around. In 48.12 Joseph bows down before his father.[31] Here
is, once again, an element that forces a question on Israel's reading of
Joseph's second dream. If Jacob's reading is not correct, what does the
second dream mean? In Gen. 37–50 there are four more dreams—these
might shed some light on Joseph's.

5. *Four More Dreams*

The combination חלם חלום ('dream a dream') occurs in connection to just
four characters in the book of Genesis: in Joseph's dream-pair (37.5, 6, 9,
10), in the cupbearer's and the baker's dreams (Gen. 40.5, 8; 41.11) and in
Pharaoh's dream-pair (41.15). Therefore the three dream-pairs seem to be
tightly connected.

The second dream-pair is encountered in Gen. 40. In prison, one morning Joseph detects the cupbearer and the baker who are highly upset. They
have both had a dream. Both dreams are presented below.

Genesis 40.9-11

(9a So the chief cupbearer told Joseph his dream	ויספר שר־המשקים את־חלמו ליוסף	9a)
b and said to him.)	(ויאמר לו	b
c In my dream,	בחלומי	c
d I saw a vine in front of me	והנה־גפן לפני	d
10a and on the vine there were three branches	ובגפן שלשה שריגם	10a
b as soon as it had budded	והיא כפרחת	b
c it blossomed	עלתה נצה	c
d and its clusters ripened into grapes.	הבשילו אשכלתיה ענבים	d
11a Pharaoh's cup was in my hand	וכוס פרעה בידי	11a
b and I took the grapes	ואקח את־הענבים	b
c and I squeezed them into Pharaoh's cup	ואשחט אתם אל־כוס פרעה	c
d and put the cup in Pharaoh's hand.	ואתן את־הכוס על־כף פרעה	d

31. See D.J.A. Clines, 'What Happens in Genesis', in *idem, What Does Eve Do to
Help? and Other Readerly Questions to the Old Testament* (JSOTSup, 94; Sheffield:
JSOT Press, 1990), 62-63.

Genesis 40.16-17

(16a	The chief baker saw that...	...וירא שׂר־האפים 16a)
b	and he said to Joseph.)	ויאמר אל־יוסף) b
c	Me too, in my dream,	אף־אני בחלומי c
d	I saw that there were three baskets of bread upon my head,	והנה שׁלשׁה סלי חרי d על־ראשׁי
17a	in the top basket were all kinds of baked goods for Pharaoh,	ובסל העליון מכל 17a
b	but the birds were eating them out of the basket on my head.	מאכל פרעה מעשׂה אפה b והעוף אכל אתם מן־הסל מעל ראשׁי

According to Joseph this is how the cupbearer's dream is to be understood: three branches are three days. Within three days Pharaoh will restore the cupbearer to his former occupation. Syntactically the dream looks like this: the beginning is constructed by means of three verbless clauses (vv. 9d, 10ab), followed by two *qatal* clauses (v. 10cd), to which another verbless clause is attached (v. 11a). The dream is concluded by three *wayyiqtol* clauses. The dream shows a steady progression from a situation to actions.

The texts above show the baker's dream to differ from the cupbearer's. Following the introductory remark ('It was in my dream. I saw...') there are verbless clauses ('Three baskets of bread were on my head')—there is no development in the dream, there are no dynamic elements. The baker's dream presents nothing but an image.[32] Both the cupbearer and baker find themselves in their dreams (like Joseph in his dreams). Joseph's interpretation of the baker's dream hardly causes any surprises: three baskets are three days. After three days Pharaoh will hang the baker, so the birds can eat him. Syntactically, there is no sequence in the baker's dream, no succession, no progress. Syntax and semantics go hand in hand: there is no change for the better for the baker.

As a conclusion to this minor excursion on the dreams of Gen. 40, it must be observed that both the verb 'tell' (ספר, v. 9) and the number three are present in the dreams.

---

32. See also W. Richter, 'Traum und Traumdeutung im AT. Ihre Form und Verwendung', *BZ* 7 (1963), 202-220 (204-205). Richter however is not correct when he states that the cupbearer's dreams consist of '*einem* Bild' as well.

The final dream-pair are those of Pharaoh in Gen. 41. They are being told twice: by the narrator (41.1-7) and by Pharaoh himself (41.17-24).[33] Pharaoh's account of his dreams is presented below.

As can be seen in Pharaoh's dreams, he describes the initial situation in his dream by means of participial clauses and the particle הנה: 'in my dream there I was standing on the banks of the Nile, and what I saw…'— Pharaoh is present in his dreams—like the baker, the cupbearer, and Joseph in their dreams. This situation is succeeded by several actions, as is indicated by *wayyiqtol* clauses. These *wayyiqtol* clauses give Pharaoh's dreams a development from a pleasant and rural scene to a dead-end alley.

Genesis 41.17-24

17a	Then Pharaoh said to Joseph	וידבר פרעה אל־יוסף	17a
b	In my dream	בחלמי	b
c	there I was,	הנני	c
d	standing on the banks of the Nile;	עמד על־שפת היאר	d
18a	and what I saw	והנה	18a
b	seven cows, fat and sleek, came up out of the Nile	מן־היאר עלת שבע פרות בריאות בשר ויפת תאר	b
c	and fed in the reed grass.	ותרעינה באחו	c
19a	And what I saw,	והנה	19a
b	seven other cows came up after them,	שבע־פרות אחרות עלות אחריהן	b
c	poor, very ugly, and thin.	דלות ורעות תאר מאד ורקות בשר	c
d	Never had I seen such ugly ones in all the land of Egypt.	לא־ראיתי כהנה בכל־ארץ מצרים לרע	d
20a	The thin and ugly cows ate up the first seven fat cows,	ותאכלנה הפרות הרקות והרעות את שבע הפרות הראשנות הבריאת	20a

33. The narrator both presents more and less action in Pharaoh's first dream. The narrator has the lean cows stand beside the fat cows, whereas Pharaoh remarks that he had never seen such ugly cows in the land of Egypt (cf. vv. 3 and 19). Pharaoh also adds that it was not visible that the lean cows had eaten the fat cows (v. 21). On differences between the narrator's and Pharaoh's accounts of Pharaoh's dreams, see e.g. J. Licht, *Storytelling in the Bible* (Jerusalem: Magnes Press/Hebrew University, 1978), 176; Jacob, *Das erste Buch der Tora*, 746; Redford, *A Study of the Biblical Story of Joseph*, 79-80.

21a	and when they had come into them	ותבאנה אל־קרבנה 21a
b	no one would have known	ולא נודע b
c	that they had come into them,	כי־באו אל־קרבנה c
d	for they were still as ugly as before.	ומראיהן רע כאשר בתחלה d
e	Then I awoke.	ואיקץ e
22a	And I saw in my dream,	וארא בחלמי 22a
b	I saw,	והנה b
c	seven ears of grain growing on one stalk,	שבע שבלים עלת בקנה אחד c
d	full and good,	מלאת וטבות d
23a	I saw,	והנה 23a
b	seven ears, withered, thin, and blighted by the east wind,	שבע שבלים צנמות דקות שדפות קדים b
c	sprouting after them;	צמחות אחריהם c
24a	and the thin ears swallowed up the seven good ears.	ותבלען השבלים הדקת את שבע השבלים הטבות 24a
b	But when I told it to the magicians,	ואמר אל־החרטמים b
c	there was no one who explained it to me.	ואין מגיד לי c

Both in Pharaoh's dreams and in his representation in 41.17-24 one can detect quite a few words relating to food (e.g. אכל, 'eat', and בלע, 'devour'); however, the numbers are even more prominent. According to Joseph these numbers have to be understood as indicating time. Seven fat cows and seven fat ears on the one hand, and seven lean cows and lean ears on the other represent seven years of abundance and seven years of shortage. As were the baker and the cupbearer, Pharaoh is terribly upset by his dreams.

6. *Numbers in Dreams*

As said before, I have some reservations about Israel's interpretation of Joseph's second dream. Because of the resemblances between the dreams of the Egyptians and Joseph's second dream, another interpretation of the latter is possible, an interpretation in which numbers play a prominent role.

In the dreams of Pharaoh, the cupbearer and the baker, the numbers three and seven indicate units of time: days and years. In general it is perhaps necessary to consult a professional dream-interpreter to know whether such a numerical unit is supposed to refer to days or to years.[34] In the case of the cupbearer's and the baker's dreams the unit of time being 'days'

---

34. Richter, 'Traum und Traumdeutung', 206.

was rather evident, because Pharaoh's birthday was to fall within those three days (40.20).[35] The references to years in Pharaoh's dreams, however, was not self-evident.

Another explicit mention of numbers is to be found in Joseph's second dream: 11 stars. In one and the same breath the sun and the moon are mentioned. These celestial bodies are both one of a kind. In other words, it is possible that numbers do play an important part in this second dream. If the symbolic images like the sun, the moon and the stars do not refer to Israel, Rachel and the brothers, what then is their function? What do they refer to? What role do the sun, moon and stars play in Genesis? The sun (שֶׁמֶשׁ) indicates dawn or sunset.[36] Whenever the sun is shining it appears to function as a marker of passed time. This confirms the function given by God to the lights in Gen. 1, as can be read in vv. 14-17:

> And God said, 'Let there be lights in the dome of the sky to separate the day from the night; and let them be for signs and for seasons and for days and years, and let them be lights in the dome of the sky to give light upon the earth'. And it was so. God made the two great lights—the greater light to rule the day and the lesser light to rule the night—and the stars. God set them in the dome of the sky to give light upon the earth, to rule over the day and over the night, and to separate the light from the darkness. And God saw that it was good. (NRSV)

God makes the sun, the moon and the stars to illuminate the earth, but they have another function as well: to separate the day from the night, and to serve as signs for seasons and days and years. So, besides being a source of light, the celestial bodies function to indicate the passing of time.

Above I compared Joseph's dreams and drew attention to the different verbs the narrator used to express the way in which Joseph told his dreams (נגד vs. סָפַר). There I also showed that the verb סָפַר (piel) might have a connotation of counting. This verb is found twice in relation with the second dream and its presence might be a clue for the interpretation of the second dream.

---

35. I do not agree with Jeffers who calls Joseph's dream a 'simple message dream' and the cupbearer's and the baker's dreams (and Pharaoh's) 'symbolic dreams'. According to Jeffers a simple message dream is 'self-explanatory, i.e., it does not need the help of a professional interpreter to understand it', whereas a symbolic dream 'can be solved by professional interpreters only'. A. Jeffers, 'Divination by Dreams in Ugaritic Literature and in the Old Testament', *IBS* 12 (1990), 167-83 (168-69; cf. 170-72).

36. The sun is met in Gen. 15.12, 17; 19.23; 28.11; 32.32; 37.9. The moon (יָרֵחַ) only occurs in 37.9.

Thus, there are several resemblances between Joseph's second dream and the dreams of the Egyptians—the dreams which Joseph at least partly explained by way of terms that indicate the passing of time. These resemblances are (1) the numbers in the dreams, (2) the presence of the verb סְפר, and (3) the dreamer is the only human character present in the dream.

Therefore Joseph's second dream might also be related to the passing of time. Perhaps it can be understood in such a way that it refers to a period of time. The sun, the moon and the stars (1 + 1 + 11) indicate 13 years. This is the exact number of years that Joseph spends in Egypt before he is promoted ruler of Egypt (see 41.46, which says that Joseph was 30 years old when he entered the service of Pharaoh, king of Egypt).[37]

Yet also in a different way the numbers may indicate years. In Gen. 1 the sun and the moon are treated apart from the stars; together they make a pair/couple. Multiplying this pair by 11 (the stars) adds up to a number of 22. And this again is the number of years passing before Joseph and his brothers meet again *as brothers*, and when Joseph is reunited with his father (43.26).[38] It is in the second of seven lean years that Joseph and his brothers are reunited (45.6; 47.18), the twenty-second after his sale to Egypt (13 years in Egypt + 7 fat +2 lean years).[39] The celestial bodies represent

37. The suggestion of Joseph's second dream to refer to 13 years is also made by B. Green, *'What Profit for Us?' Remembering in the Story of Joseph* (Lanham, MD: New York: London: University Press of America, 1996), 123. However, she does not give any reasons why this could be the case.

38. Ackerman too, thinks the first dream to be fulfilled in 43.26: 'With this statement, the narrator stresses that the first dream has been completely fulfilled' ('Joseph, Judah, and Jacob', in K.R.R. Gros Louis with J.S. Ackerman [eds.], *Literary Interpretations of Biblical Narratives*, II [Nashville: Abingdon Press, 1982], 85-113 (92). Another opinion is held by E.-J. Bae, according to whom the first dream is fulfilled in 45.5-8, whereas the second dream finds its fulfillment in 50.19-21 (*A Multiple Approach to the Joseph Story: With a Detailed Reading of Genesis 46,31-47,31; 50,1-11.14* [Rome: Pontificia Universitas Gregoriana, 1995], esp. 90 and 97).

39. This conjuring with figures is not uncommon in the Bible. The ages of the patriarchs are highly interesting with regard to numbers: Abraham's age is 175 years (7×5^2); Isaac's 180 years (5×6^2) and Jacob's 147 years (3×7^2). Joseph's age (110) is the sum of the squares of his forefathers ($5^2 + 6^2 + 7^2$); see L. Ruppert, *Die Josephserzählung der Genesis: Ein Beitrag zur Theologie der Pentateuchquellen* (SANT, 11; Munich: Kösel, 1965), 178-179; S. Gervirtz, 'The Life Spans of Joseph and Enoch and the Parallelism šib'ātayim–šib'îm wěšib'āh', *JBL* 96 (1977), 570-71. J.G. Williams adds that Joseph (whose age is 110 years = $1 \times 5^2 + 6^2 + 7^2$) also fits the pattern 7–5–3–1, that seems to be at work at the patriarchs' ages ('Number Symbolism and Joseph as Symbol of Completion', *JBL* 98 [1979], 86-87). Lowenthal mentions the fact that the

the passing of time before Joseph; that is why he is the only person present in the dream.

'Bowing down' in Joseph's dreams, then, appears to have two distinct functions. The first function, literally 'to bow down', is done by the sheaves of Joseph's brothers. Later, the brothers themselves will indeed bow down before him because he is a ruler of Egypt, not over *them*.[40] So the brothers' bowing down in 43.26 has no connection whatsoever with their own interpretation of Joseph's dream: being subservient to Joseph. When they do bow down it is out of respect for the unknown Egyptian ruler. The second function—the sun, moon and stars bowing down in the second dream—is to establish a connection between both dreams. In the second dream Joseph is the only human present. The celestial bodies' bowing down before him refers to a certain period of time. And this happens to be exactly that particular period of time that will go by before the first dream comes true. In the second dream the sun, moon and stars indicate the passing of time, whereas 'bow down' (חוה), establishes the connection with the first dream. So, when the 22 years have passed by, the first dream comes true: after 22 years all brothers bow down before Joseph (43.26).

In retrospect, the six dreams of Gen. 37–50 show the following pattern. Pharaoh's dreams are one;[41] both the cupbearer's and the baker's dreams refer to the same time span, but are at the same time each other's reversal: one dream points to life, the other to death—finally, Joseph's dreams are

---

sum of the multiplications of Abraham's, Isaac's, and Jacob's ages is 17 (the sum of respectively $7 \times 5 \times 5$, $5 \times 6 \times 6$ and $3 \times 7 \times 7$ is 17 each time), like Joseph's age in 37.2 and exactly the number of years that Jacob spent in Egypt (Lowenthal, *The Joseph Narrative*, 193). More numbers are presented by I. Caine, 'Numbers in the Joseph Narrative', in R.A. Brauner (ed.), *Jewish Civilization: Essays and Studies* (Philadelphia: Reconstructionalist Rabbinical College, 1979), 3-17.

40. Occasions on which the brothers themselves bow down are: 42.6; 43.26, 28; 44.14; 50.18. In 42.6 there are only ten brothers in the company, whereas in 43.26 they have also brought Benjamin (and Simeon has just been released from prison; 43.23). The verb used in 44.14 and 50.18 is נפל (not חוה). Especially in 44.14, after Benjamin is exposed as the one who has taken the cup of the Egyptian lord, the verb נפל might refer to subjection or surrender; the same might be the case in 50.18. Whenever נפל is encountered all 11 brothers are present.

41. So Joseph explains to Pharaoh in 41.25; a little before Pharaoh seems to be of the same opinion: in 41.15 he says to Joseph: 'I have dreamed a dream (חלום), and there is no-one to interpret it (אתו)' (cf. 41.8: 'Pharaoh told them his dream [חלמו], and there was no-one to interpret them [אותם] to Pharaoh'); see Sternberg, *The Poetics of Biblical Narrative*, 398-400.

completely different with regard to their contents—they are not one.[42] The second dream really is אחר ('different', 37.9) from the first; they are most certainly not אחד ('one', 41.25), like Pharaoh's dreams. In this way the pattern emerges that one person has two different dreams (which appear to be interwoven); this is being followed by two people having both one dream with a common element, until at last one person dreams two dreams that are one.

As we draw to the end of this chapter attention should be drawn to one minor feature of the dreams in Gen. 37–50. As was pointed out a little earlier, 'eat' and 'devour' or more general 'food' has a central position in Pharaoh's dreams: cows are eating cows (41.7, 24), and ears are devouring ears (41.4, 20). Joseph's explanation of the dreams shows that the time-span in both dreams has got everything to do with the production of food and the storage of Egypt's food and 'all the lands' during the years to come. Looking back at the dreams of the cupbearer and the baker, it is not hard to detect the motive of 'food' as well. The cupbearer is dreaming about vines and presenting the cup to Pharaoh, and the baker is seeing birds eating baked food. Looking a little further back one might even find a first indication for the food-motive in Joseph's first dream in the binding of the sheaves in the field.[43] If one does not reject this suggestion, one can discern the two motives, food and time, in Joseph's dreams separately, and see them reappear together in the dreams of chs. 40 and 41. Food, that primary need for human survival, will be provided by Joseph. He begins to do so exactly 13 years after his sale to Egypt.

42. Contra D.A. Seybold, 'Paradox and Symmetry in the Joseph Narrative', in K.R.R. Gros Louis, J.S. Ackerman and T.S. Warshaw (eds.), *Literary Interpretations of Biblical Narratives* (Nashville: Abingdon Press, 1974), 59-73: 'Joseph's two dreams are one' (66).

43. See Hamilton, *The Book of Genesis: 18–50*, 410. Turner (*Announcements of Plot*, 148 n. 1) does not appear to be unsympathetic towards this. E.L. Ehrlich however makes no bones about it: 'In diesem Garbentraum einen Hinweis auf den späteren Kornhandel in Ägypten sehen zu wollen (Gunkel), ist zwar verlockend, geht aber zu weit' (*Der Traum im Alten Testament* [BZAW, 73; Berlin: Alfred Töpelmann, 1953], 59). A. Silva points to the high frequency of words related to food in Gen. 37–50, including the sheaves in this agricultural dream (*La symbolique des rêves et des vêtements dans l'histoire de Joseph et de ses frères* [Héritage et project, 52; Quebec: Fides, 1994], 68).

Chapter 4

AN UNEXPECTED PARTY

The separation between the brothers and Joseph, which on the emotional level was expressed by the verbs שׂנא and קנא, is transferred by the brothers to a physical separation a little beyond (37.12). Their absence may prevent an escalation. It is not clear whether the tensions in the family were latent or manifest. Whether they were or were not, the fact remains that Israel commissioned Joseph to go on a mission of peace to his other sons (probably very much like the ones mentioned in 37.2). Not conscious of or anxious about any danger he sends Joseph on his way,[1] and by so doing unknowingly causes the situation his sons sought to avert: another confrontation with the 'lord of the dreams' (v. 19). For the brothers the dreams appear to be the straw that breaks the camel's back. After Joseph's dreaming the situation is no longer tolerable. So, when the brothers finally spot the haughty dreamer from afar, having no idea about his mission, they plot to kill him (v. 18). The motivation for killing him now is primarily found in the dreams: 'Behold, this[2] lord of the dreams approaching' (37.19). The appearance of the dreamer urges them to a murderous conspiracy: 'And now,[3] come, let us kill him and throw him into one of these pits and say

---

1. Cf. Sarna, *Genesis*, 258: 'Clearly, the brothers had hitherto successfully disguised their true feelings and, indeed, there is no record of their having uttered any threats against Joseph'. Hamilton, *The Book of Genesis: 18–50*, 413, writes something similar: 'One must conclude that Jacob is unaware of the simmering rage of the brothers toward Joseph, that the brothers have not in any way, either through language or conduct, conveyed to their father the rancor they feel toward Joseph'. I wonder whether at *this* spot words like 'rage' and 'rancor' are not too strong to describe the brothers' feelings.

2. 'This' is represented by the uncommon form הלזה, that is also found in 24.65. According to Joüon and Muraoka it is a *reinforced demonstrative* (*A Grammar of Biblical Hebrew*, §36b, 115).

3. I do not agree with Deist, who suggests that by means of the particle ועתה the 'narrator intrudes on his characters' in 37.20. According to him a conclusion that is

that a ferocious animal has eaten him. Then we shall see what comes of his dreams' (v. 20). This final part of the brothers' speech again underlines how much the brothers were troubled by the dreams. They twice refer to the dreams (vv. 19 and 20); like the narrator they do not breath a word about the cause of their hatred in vv. 3-4. As was the case with the brothers' reaction to Joseph's dreams ('and they hated him even more', v. 5), here again the narrator informs the reader of their plans before they can express themselves: 'they plotted to kill him' (v. 18).[4] The narrator does not want any doubts to arise as to how the reader should appreciate the brothers' conversation. So, vv. 3-4 illustrated that the seed of the brothers' hatred is in Israel's preferential treatment of Joseph; now, from the conversation, one can infer that the dreaming causes his death sentence.[5]

An earlier account in Genesis told about a fratricide. Hence it is hardly surprising to come across words like דם ('blood'; vv. 37.22, 26), נכה ('smite'; v. 37.21) and הרג ('kill'; vv. 37.20, 26) that were encountered before in Gen. 4, in which chapter the one who is described as a רעה ('shepherd', 4.2) loses his life. The events in Gen. 37, however, will not lead to another fratricide. The brothers no longer turn out to be the close unit they appeared before. Their plans are hardly articulated when Reuben tries to temper their thirst for blood and to change the course of action. And Judah also adds to the effect with his comments.

introduced by ועתה needs a substantiated motivation, as happens always in Genesis when ועתה is found. The motivation, according to Deist, is not found in the characters' speeches, but in the narrative itself. 'Thus, even though ועתה forms part of the characters' speech, it actually concludes the *narrator's* argument' (F. Deist, 'A Note on the Narrator's Voice in Gen 37, 20-22', *ZAW* 108 [1996], 621). However, everywhere in Genesis where ועתה occurs, it is always in a dialogue between two characters, two occurrences excepted; both belonging to the same category as 37.20. In 3.22 and 11.6 there is a soliloquy by God, whereas in 37.20 there is a collective saying by the brothers. It is not necessary for them to give a motivation, 'the reason' for the ועתה-clause. The reason (obviously) is the situation of seeing Joseph approaching. It is particularly the designation בעל־החלמות ('lord of the dreams') that speaks volumes, and which is sufficient reason to motivate the following actions.

4. 'The narrator summarizes for us the essence of this conversation before relating it in direct discourse... It also dispels any remaining sympathy for the brothers' (H.C. White, 'Reuben and Judah: Duplicates or Complements?', in J.T. Butler, E.W. Conrad and B.C. Ollenburger [eds.], *Understanding the Word: Essays in Honor of Bernard W. Anderson* [JSOTSup, 37; Sheffield: JSOT Press, 1985], 73-97 [90]).

5. Contra *ThWAT*, II, 490: 'Die Bevorzugung Josefs vor seinen älteren Brüdern durch den Vater Israel/Jakob erregt deren Neid und Haß, und sie fassen einen Plan, um ihn zu töten (Gen 37, 20)'.

1. *Reuben and Judah*

Two brothers break loose from the collective by talking to their brethren. Reuben takes the floor in vv. 21-22 (and also in 37.29), and Judah gives his opinion in vv. 26-27.

21c	and he (Reuben) said:	ויאמר	21c
d	Let us not take his life.	לא נכנו נפש	d
22a	Reuben said to them:	ויאמר אלהם ראובן	22a
b	Do not shed blood,	אל־תשפכו־דם	b
c	throw him into this pit	השליכו אתו אל־הבור הזה	c
d	that is in the wilderness	אשר במדבר	d
e	but lay no hand on him	ויד אל־תשלחו־בו	e
f	that he might rescue him out of their hand	למען הציל אתו מידם	f
g	and restore him to his father.	להשיבו אל־אביו	g
26a	Judah said to his brothers:	ויאמר יהודה אל־אחיו	26a
b	What profit is it	מה־בצע	b
c	if we kill our brother	כי נהרג את־אחינו	c
d	and conceal/cover up his blood?	וכסינו את־דמו	d
27a	Come,	לכו	27a
b	let us sell him to the Ishmaelites,	ונמכרנו לישמעאלים	b
c	and not lay our hands on him,	וידנו אל־תהי־בו	c
d	for he is our brother,	כי־אחינו	d
e	our own flesh.	בשרנו הוא	e

Fokkelman states: 'Reuben's proposal is defeated by Judah. Of all the words spoken in Dothan Judah's speech carries the day. His proposal to sell Joseph instead of letting him rot in the pit is approved by his brothers; "they listened" in v.27d means that they complied'.[6] One might wonder whether it is justifiable to use the word 'defeated'. 'Defeat' is not the issue here, for when Judah makes his proposal the conditions happen to have changed. Neither is it certain that Judah's speech will carry the day nor that the brothers will endorse his proposal. In v. 23 the brothers follow Reuben's suggestion not to kill Joseph and throw him into a cistern, while

---

6. Fokkelman, 'Genesis 37 and 38', 161. In a note on the same page Fokkelman writes: 'Complying with Judah implies disregarding Reuben's proposal. Note how Reuben's speech to the father in ch. 42:37 is once more overruled by Judah (speaking to Jacob in the beginning of ch. 43).'

the point at issue is whether they are the ones who sold Joseph (on which see below). Both speeches, however, show some remarkable differences; these prove to be of importance when trying to establish Reuben's and Judah's characters and their subsequent roles in the entire story.

Reuben is the first to address his brothers. The reason for his words is given by the narrator in two verses, in v. 21—וַיַּצִּלֵהוּ מִיָּדָם ('and he delivered him from their hands')[7]—and in v. 22—לְמַעַן הַצִּיל אֹתוֹ מִיָּדָם לַהֲשִׁיבוֹ אֶל־אָבִיו ('to rescue him from their hands, to take him back to his father'). Nothing, however, is said about Reuben's motives. Some commentators refer to Reuben's actions as those appropriate for the eldest son.[8] An interesting observation is the following:

> The scrupulous reader…will observe that verse 21 also bears the seeds of ambiguity. First, it states that 'Reuben heard' (of the brothers' plan), which might imply that he had somehow been absent from the brothers' deliberation. Second, it relates that Reuben 'rescued him [Joseph] from their hand', which could mean that the brothers had already laid hands on Joseph.[9]

At first glance, the latter part of this remark might have some importance regarding a problem that arises when reading Gen. 42.21-22. On second thoughts, however, the clause 'he delivered him from their hands' can only

7. P. Saydon suggests to read v. 21 like this: 'he tried to deliver him from their hands'. The conative (or volitive) character is not represented by means of the verb בקשׁ or a synonomous verb followed by ל, but by *wayyiqtol*. 'In these cases it is the context not the grammatical form, which determines the correct meaning of the verbal form' ('The Conative Imperfect in Hebrew', *VT* 12 [1962], 124-26). It is not necessary to translate the verse in the way Saydon does. The narrator informs the reader that Reuben succeeds in saving Joseph's life, even though he cannot—as can be seen later—pull Joseph out of the pit. A situation like this also occured in vv. 5-8, where the narrator told the reader that Joseph had a dream that he recounted to his brothers, which caused them to hate their brother (v. 5). It is not until this statement that Joseph actually tells them about his dream. The same is the case in vv. 18-20.

8. E.g. Westermann: 'Damit nimmt Ruben die Funktion des ältesten Bruders wahr. Wenn in der Familie der Väterzeit Gruppen oder Teile der Familie vom Vater entfernt waren, hatte der jeweils älteste, wenn es notwendig wurde, die Rolle des Vaters zu übernehmen; für diese begrenzte Zeit hatte er die Verantwortung. Wenn die Gruppe nach Hause kam, hatte er auf die Fragen des Vaters zu antworten' (*Genesis 37–50*, 32-33). See also Hamilton (*The Book of Genesis: 18–50*, 418). He also gives another possible reason: 'We know that Reuben has been out of favor with his father ever since the scandalous affair with Bilhah (35:22). Is Reuben's magnanimity to Joseph an attempt to rebuild some broken communication with his father?' (418).

9. E.L. Greenstein, 'An Equivocal Reading of the Sale of Joseph', in Gros Louis and Ackerman (eds.), *Literary Interpretations of Biblical Narratives*, II, 114-25 (118).

be interpreted in an anticipatory way,[10] because not until v. 23 does Joseph
arrive at his brothers' camp. He cannot have fallen into their hands any
time before. Another reason why it is anticipatory is made clear by v. 22:
'to deliver him from their hands'. Here the narrator gives the motivation
for Reuben's speech, which consists of the same keywords as v. 21: 'he
delivered him from their hands' (ויצלהו מידם)—'to deliver him from their
hands' (למען הציל אתו מידם). Deliverance indeed emerges in v. 24: the
brothers throw Joseph into the pit, they did not take a life (v. 20).

Reuben's suggestion amounts to several changes in comparison with the
original plan, the most striking of which is to make his brothers abandon
their intention to murder Joseph. A further alteration regards the spot where
they intended to leave Joseph behind. The brothers were tending their
flocks near Dothan. From their conversation in v. 20 it appears that there
are several pits in their vicinity ('Let us throw him into one of these cisterns' [v. 20]). Neither the narrator, nor one of the characters mentions
anything about the chance of a dead body to be discovered in a pit that is
to be found in fields used for pasturing. If the brothers agree with Reuben's
suggestion not to kill Joseph and let him pine away in 'one of these
cisterns' (v. 20), they should not leave him behind in one of the intended
pits, that is, near their camp. Therefore Reuben suggests to throw Joseph
into a pit 'that is in the wilderness' (v. 22). This implies that the intended
pit is not near the place where he and his brothers find themselves, for if
it were he would not be able to execute his plans to rescue his younger
brother.

Here it is useful to devote a few lines to two words in the text that can
easily put a reader on the wrong track, namely, 'wilderness' and 'pit'. The
word 'wilderness' (מדבר) encountered in Reuben's speech does not only
denote 'the barren deserts of sand dunes or rock that colour the popular
imagination of a desert, but also steppelands and pasture lands suitable for
grazing livestock'.[11] The pit (cistern) the brothers are talking about (בור)
is not a well (באר); the latter are also found in Genesis (e.g. 21.25; 26.19;
29.2). Cisterns are subterranean reservoirs for the storage of water, 'and
were filled by drainage from roofs, streets, or the surface of a slope, or by
water channelled from some other source. Wells, on the other hand, might

10. Likewise A. Berlin, *Poetics and Interpretation of Biblical Narrative* (Bible and
Literature Series, 9; Sheffield: Almond Press, 1983), 118.
11. J.D. Douglas (ed.), *New Bible Dictionary* (Leicester: Inter-Varsity Press; Wheaton, IL: Tyndale House , 1982), 1251.

be fed directly from underground springs'.[12] Cisterns are 'usually pear-shaped with a small opening at the top which can be sealed to prevent accidents'.[13]

The events related to Joseph's sale are situated in the vicinity of Dothan. Dothan is mentioned only in the Hebrew Bible, it is not known from any other written sources.[14] During the Early Bronze Age (3200–2400 BCE) it was a major city-state. The site appears to have been abandoned during the latter part of the Early Bronze Age and the beginning of the Middle Bronze Age (2400–1800 BCE). From the Middle Bronze Age period (1800–1500 BCE) there is hardly anything known.[15] Dothan was situated at the old caravan-route leading from Damascus down to Egypt;[16] which accounts for the sudden appearance of Midianites and Ishmaelites in vv. 24 and 28. The Midianite traders in Dothan approaching the cistern, then, hardly come as a surprise: they come and look for water.

It is not quite clear whether the brothers rejected Reuben's proposal and indeed swapped it for Judah's, as is presumed by Fokkelman. Their actions in v. 23 imply that they at least partially agreed.

Whichever plan the brothers may have executed, it is clear that there are several differences in the way both Reuben and Judah express their proposals. A comparison of their direct discourses will show this. The first thing to notice is the rather authoritative way in which Reuben expresses himself: he uses imperative forms, which denotes a distance between him and his brothers: 'do not shed blood', 'throw him into this pit', 'lay no hand on him'. Judah's reaction, although in the perception of a reader possibly less noble than Reuben's, presents a better understanding of his

---

12. G.W. Bromiley (ed.), *The International Standard Bible Encyclopedia* (4 vols.; Grand Rapids: Eerdmans, 1979), I, 702, s.v. 'cistern'.

13. *New Bible Dictionary*, 210; cf. the illustration on p. 211. See also the comment regarding a text like Exod. 21.33-34 in *NIDOTE*: 'The Book of the Covenant assumes the owner's responsibility for covering cisterns and prescribes damages in case animals fall and are injured' (*NIDOTE*, I, 620).

14. E. Stern (ed.), *The New Encyclopedia of Archeological Excavations in the Holy Land* (4 vols.; Jerusalem: Israel Exploration Society, 1993), I, 372, s.v. 'Dothan'.

15. Cf. *ABD*, II, 226 s.v. Dothan.

16. Cf. A. Negev (ed.), *Archäologisches Lexicon zur Bibel* (v; Munich: Kunstverlag Edition Praeger, 1972), 132, s.v. 'Dothan'. Also according to J. Negenman (*Geografische gids bij de bijbel* [Boxtel: Katholieke Bijbelstichting, 1981], 103), there were many caravans that used to pass Dothan. The plain of Dothan 'provides easy pass for travellers from Bethshan and Gilead on their way to Egypt' (*New Bible Dictionary*, 289).

brothers' psyche: 'What profit is it if we kill our brother (הרג [by using these words referring to their joint speech in v. 20, while at the same time taking the edge off the words]) and cover up his blood?', which is followed by the suggestion to sell Joseph. A fact not to be forgotten, and which is closely related to this proposal, is that Judah is the only one who *really* turns his back on Joseph's death. In Reuben's proposal—as it is perceived by Judah and the other brothers—Joseph dies: he would not have lasted for a long time in the cistern.

There are two words in Judah's speech that deserve close attention: 'profit' (בצע) and 'cover up' (כסה). The root בצע occurs 39 times in the Old Testament; the primary meaning of the verb is 'abschneiden' ('cut off') and 'zwar vermutlich schon frühzeitig als terminus technicus beim Teppichweben gebraucht' ('probably rather early used as a technical term in carpetwaeving') (*ThWAT*, I, 733). Two derivations come from this meaning: 'den Lebensfaden abschneiden' ('to cut off someone's lifeline') and 'ein Stück abschneiden, d.h. seinen Schnitt, Gewinn machen' (to do well, make a profit') (733). The meaning of the noun is derived from the latter. Originally it was value-indifferent, which is supported by occurrences such as 37.26 that 'nicht im materiellen Sinne von Gewinn sprechen' ('do not mention profit in a material sense') (734). The contention of several commentators who emphasize that Judah was motivated by material gain[17] is not supported by *ThWAT*.

The verb כסה means 'to cover up', 'entweder um das Bedeckte unsichtbar zu machen oder um es zu schützen oder zu erwärmen' ('either to make the covered invisible or to protect or warm it') (*ThWAT*, IV, 273). In Judah's speech it points to the first: 'what profit is it if…and cover up his blood?' In other words if they were to hide his (dead) body in a cistern. Murdering their brother may be a tricky business that is better avoided.

Judah's words are distinct from Reuben's since he talks about 'our brother', 'his blood' (דמו; cf. Reuben's דם), 'our brother' and 'our flesh',

---

17. E.g. 'This cleverly sets in motion the motivation of material gain as a counter point to the motive of jealous vengeance. Through a simple transaction they may exchange Joseph for silver, thereby ridding themselves of Joseph permanently (as in death, they think), while not acquiring blood guilt' (White, 'Reuben and Judah', 92; *idem*, 'The Joseph Story: A Narrative which "Consumes" its Content', *Semeia* 31 [1985], 49-69 [64]). Cf. 'Judah, observing a caravan approaching, appeals to his brothers' self-interest, urging that Joseph be sold as a slave…' (Wildavsky, *Assimilation versus Separation*, 81).

respectively.[18] Apart from referring to the family ties, Judah's speech sounds more friendly and less authoritative. Contrary to Reuben's imperatives ('do not shed', 'throw him', 'lay no hand'), which place him in opposition to his brothers,[19] Judah uses cohortatives ('what profit is it if *we*...', 'come', 'let *us* sell...')—these make him share his brothers' position, which is confirmed by the fourfold occurrence of 'our' (נו–); once in v. 26 and three times in v. 27) in the non-verbal forms. The only time Reuben makes use of a cohortative—in v. 21 ('let us not take his life')—is in a rather absolute formulation: the particle לא expresses a prohibition,[20] which again emphasizes the authoritative nature of his speech. It is even possible that Reuben is talking to himself in v. 21, and only in v. 22 addresses his brothers. Only in v. 22 both the subject 'Reuben' and the addressee 'the brothers' are being mentioned explicitly.

The narrator makes an attempt to give a positive description of Reuben by adding noble-minded motives for his suggestion in v. 22. By so doing the narrator attempts to make the reader see Reuben's words in this perspective of noble-mindedness. Yet, he does not entirely succeed in his attempt. This is indicated by the fact that in v. 22 Reuben also takes a position in opposition to his brothers, which appears from the expression 'to deliver him from *their* hands' (v. 21b). In verse 22, 'to restore him to his father', a similar observation might be made, although it is not conclusive in this clause. The personal pronoun 'his' in 'his father' can both refer to Joseph and to Reuben. If the latter is the case Reuben takes a stance at his father's side, whereas the other brothers are on the opposing side.

As said above, both Reuben and Judah talk about blood: 'blood' and 'his blood'. Reuben says: 'Do not shed blood'. Here the verb used, שׁפך, could allude to Gen. 9;[21] the verb is absent in Judah's words: 'What profit is it if...and cover up his blood?' The verb used by Judah (כסה, 'cover up') might point to the fact that Judah wants to expunge every reference to

18. The same observations ('our brother' and 'our flesh') are made by Lamprecht in his dissertation 'Karakterisering in Gen. 37–50', 94.

19. 'Indeed, there is a shift in Reuben's speech [between vv. 21 and 22]; he now eliminates himself from the verbal forms...giving the others full responsibility for carrying out his suggestion' (Berlin, *Poetics and Interpretation*, 118).

20. Cf. Wenham, *Genesis 16–50* (WBC, 2; Dallas: Word Books, 1994), 354.

21. Reuben's אל־תשׁפכו־דם calls Gen. 9.6 to mind: 'who sheds the blood of a human being, by a human being his blood shall be shed' (שׁפך דם האדם באדם דמו יׁשפך); translation by J. Fokkelman, 'Genesis', in R. Alter and F. Kermode (eds.), *The Literary Guide to the Bible* (London: Collins, 1987), 45.

the killing of a fellow human being, not only by the contents of his words, but also by the words he uses.[22]

From the way the brothers act from v. 23 onwards they appear to agree with Reuben's proposition: they seize Joseph, take off his clothes and make him disappear into the pit. 'Through Reuben's words, Joseph is alive but waiting in the pit with knowledge that would be disastrous to the brothers if related to Jacob',[23] White comments. However, heedful of the history of Esau and Jacob, in which Jacob cheats Esau out of his right of primogeniture and blessing, it is highly questionable whether it would have been so 'disastrous' for the brothers if Jacob had found out that his sons had thrown Joseph into the pit.[24] Compared to the things he did himself, throwing someone into a cistern is hardly more than a prank that has gone slightly out of hand. Leaving Joseph behind alive and well could bring the danger that he might get out—which once again might lead to a confrontation with his brothers. It is a good thing that a caravan happens to come along. This provides Judah with another option he presents to his brothers.

The narrator mentions nothing of their reaction. He only says וישמעו אחיו ('his brothers heard', v. 27), which does not imply their agreement or their thoughts on the matter. In v. 21a the same formulation, 'Reuben heard' (וישמע ראובן) is used. In that case, however, it appears to be the cause of Reuben's action *against* his brothers' intention to kill Joseph. This means that 'and Reuben heard' is supposed to have a meaning opposite to agreement. Although it is possible that the same words are used to express an opposite reaction—nothing can be excluded—there is no proof whatsoever that 'and his brothers heard' in v. 27 points to the brothers' approval of Judah's proposal to sell Joseph.[25]

---

22. In Judah's words there are some references to Gen. 9 to be discerned as well; viz. to v. 4, in which the words בשר ('flesh') and דמו ('his blood') appear (cf. 37.22): 'you shall not eat flesh with its life, that is its blood'. Indeed, the brothers are not guilty of this: in 37.25 they sat down to eat some bread. And besides, Gen. 9.4 is not about the killing of a human being.

23. White, 'Reuben and Judah', 93.

24. Something which Jacob may actually have discovered; see 42.36-38 and 50.16-17.

25. Cf. Gen. 35.22—after Reuben has slept with Bilhah, Rachel's maid, the text reads: וישמע ישראל ('and Israel heard'); I cannot imagine that Jacob would have approved of Reuben's actions.

In this section on the brothers it has become clear that two brothers distinguish themselves from the others, although differently. Despite his noble intentions, Reuben disqualified himself in a way by placing himself in opposition to his brothers. Judah, on the other hand, although his purpose to act is not entirely clear, bore his fraternal relations in mind—both towards Joseph and the others.[26] All 11 of them, however, showed themselves to be unable to cope with their father's attachment to their younger brother. This impelled them to avoid Joseph, and leave the area. But then, Joseph's sudden appearance in the vicinity of Dothan offered them the opportunity to get rid of him once and for all. The initially attractive idea of killing Joseph was soon abandoned, and perhaps replaced by the decision to sell him.

From v. 28 the camera switches position, leaving the brothers behind and focussing on the Midianite traders. Reuben will be in the spotlight once more in the discussion regarding Joseph's sale.

2. *The Sale of Joseph*

The verse in which Joseph is sold, 37.28, presents two problems. In the first place, the verse mentions Midianite merchants, whereas v. 25 and the penultimate clause of v. 28 are about Ishmaelites, and in the second place, the question arises by whom and to whom Joseph is actually sold.[27] On the first problem, White comments that it is 'one of the most certain contradictions in the Pentateuch' which has led to a 'perplexing array of contrary and contradictory viewpoints' in major works.[28] With regard to the second problem B. Jacob writes: 'An dieser Stelle ist ein für das Verständnis der ganzen Josephsgeschichte verhängnisvoller Irrtum begangen worden, indem man...annahm, die Brüder hätten Joseph verkauft' ('In this verse, tradition has made a fatal mistake that has had great consequences for the understanding of the Joseph Story, because it was assumed that the

26. Judah, according to Berlin (*Poetics and Interpretation*, 121), 'is the practical one in the family (this comes out later in the story as well)', yet one can also see that 'Judah can hardly be accused of having a soft spot for Joseph' (121).

27. I do not understand why 'The sudden appearance of the Midianites breaks the flow of the narrative and points to an element of disunity in the section' (Coats, *From Canaan to Egypt*, 17). I do not see any difference between the 'sudden appearance of the Midianites' and the appearance of 'a man' in v. 15, who apparently does not break the 'flow of the narrative'.

28. White, 'Reuben and Judah', 79.

brothers had sold Joseph').[29] Both problems are tightly interwoven, as will
be shown below.

28a	There passed by Midianite merchant-men,	ויעברו אנשים מדינים סחרים	28a
b	they drew	וימשכו	b
c	and lifted up Joseph out of the pit	ויעלו את־יוסף מן־הבור	c
d	and sold Joseph to the Ishmaelites for 20 pieces of silver,	וימכרו את־יוסף לישמעאלים בעשרים כסף	d
e	and made Joseph come to/in Egypt.	ויביאו את־יוסף מצרימה	e

To decide how the matter stands exactly with regard to Joseph's sale, in
addition to v. 28 one must also consider several other places. From v. 27
('his brothers heard'), for example, it is obvious that the subject in the
clause are not *all* brothers: Judah is not included. The question then is
whether it is possible that in v. 28 'the brothers' *do* act as is supposed by a
number of exegetes (see below). One also has to take vv. 29-30 into
account, which indicate—if the brothers did sell Joseph—that Reuben was
not among the brothers who are supposed to have sold Joseph either. Is the
conclusion then that both Reuben and Judah were absent?

What now are the arguments to think the brothers sold Joseph? First,
after the brothers spotted a caravan of Ishmaelites in v. 25, Judah proposed
to sell Joseph to them (vv. 26-27). Second, in Gen. 40.15 Joseph informs
the cupbearer: 'For in fact I was stolen out of the land of the Hebrews'—
out of tactical considerations Joseph would not have told anything about a
sale by his brothers. Third, in Gen. 45.4-5 Joseph makes himself known to
his brothers: 'I am Joseph, your brother, whom you sold to Egypt. Now,
do not be distressed…because you sold me here, because God sent me
before you to preserve life'. Fourth, the fact that there is a change of subject in v. 28 (merchants to brothers) without the explicit mentioning of the
new subject is not unusual in Hebrew according to some commentators, as
can be seen from the following quotation by Longacre.

> On first reading, the phraseology of 37.28a implies to the reader who is a
> speaker of an Indo-European language that a new group of people is being
> introduced, distinct from the Ishmaelites which are referred to in 37.25…
> To begin with…Biblical Hebrew is extremely circumspect in the identifica-
> tion of new participants (especially minor ones) who are brought into a

29. Jacob, *Das erste Buch der Tora*, 706.

narrative. Having specifically studied the device of participant introduction, I find it hard to believe that a new group of people (appearing startlingly and unexpectedly on the scene) would be introduced and named in v 28a ('and there passed by Midianites, merchantmen') and *not* be made subject of the next verb. We should expect, 'and they drew out the Midianites and lifted up Joseph out of the pit', or even, 'and the Midianites sold Joseph to the Ishmaelites'—in that the preceding context has led us to expect that the brothers were to sell him. I assume therefore, that according to normal devices in Hebrew participant reference, the brothers remain the subject of the verbs 'draw out', 'lift', and 'sell' in v 28.[30]

I want to comment on these arguments, and after that add another text (Gen. 42.21-22) which is, I think, of eminent importance to have a good understanding of the passages that are concerned with Joseph's sale. I start by discussing Longacre's quotation.

Hebrew is 'extremely circumspect in the identification of new participants', he states, and that is why 'the Midianite merchants…are simply not introduced and integrated into the story as they should be if they are meant to be new participants moving onto the stage'.[31] That is why there is no change of subject, so that the brothers remain the subject of the *wayyiqtol* clauses in v. 28. As an example against this opinion of Longacre's one could refer to 2 Kgs. 1.1-2:

1a	Then Moab rebelled against Israel after	ויפשע מואב בישראל 1a
	the death of Ahab.	אחרי מות אחאב
2a	And Ahaziah fell down from a lattice…	ויפל אחזיה בעד השבכה... 2a
b	and was sick	ויחל b
c	and sent messengers	וישלח מלאכים c
d	and said to them…	ויאמר אלהם... d

All five verbs in the above example are *wayyiqtol* forms. I think it is obvious that the one fallen ill and sending messengers is Ahaziah, not

---

30. R. Longacre, *Joseph: A Story of Divine Providence* (Winona Lake, IN: Eisenbrauns, 1989), 30-31; also see *idem*, 'Who Sold Joseph into Egypt?', in R.L. Harris *et al.* (eds.), *Interpretation and History: Essays in Honour of Allan A. MacRea* (Singapore: Christian Life Publishers, 1986), 75-92, and Fokkelman: 'After v.28a there is an unmarked shift of subject, something which is not rare at all in Hebrew narration. It is unnatural to assign the second and third narrative forms to other persons than the brothers, one reason being that v.28 clearly is the fulfilment of what Judah had just proposed to his brothers' ('Genesis 37 and 38', 164).

31. Longacre, 'Who sold Joseph into Egypt?', 85. According to Longacre one can only speak of participants when they 'are made focal by multiple representation' (85); cf. Chapter 6 from his *Joseph: A Story of Divine Providence*.

Moab. The second verse of 2 Kings 1 starts a new syntactic unit, as does v. 28 in Gen. 37. I do not deny that Longacre's statement is at least partly correct, but as can be seen from 2 Kgs. 1.1-2 it is by no means the rule. There is no reason to presume why the subject of the first clause of v. 28 would not be the same as the subject in the following clauses. This implies that the brothers are not the subject of the trading party. Moreover, what might be the reason for mentioning the passing by of the Midianite merchants if they were *not* the subject of the subsequent clauses? If the brothers pulled Joseph out of the pit and sold him, v. 28a has no function at all. And besides, as said above, if the brothers were to be the subject of the remainder of 37.28 both Judah and Reuben are not included.

Another element in Longacre's quotation, which also concerns the first argument, is that the preceding context had prepared the reader that Joseph was to be sold by his brothers. It is undeniable that Judah had indeed just proposed to sell Joseph, but one also has to agree that the narrator did not say a word about the brothers' consent. The clause 'his brothers heard' by no means implies that the brothers approved of Judah's proposal. The idea of the brothers *not* having sold Joseph is much more provoking. This is, because at first there appeared to be no reason to accept the brothers' interpretation of Joseph's dream, an interpretation that was strongly influenced by their emotions. Then, their efforts to get away from Joseph and to avoid him are obstructed as Jacob sent Joseph to see how they were faring. And now their plan to sell him is being obstructed.[32] The paradox in all this is that the brothers' attempt to get rid of Joseph to prevent his dreams from coming true is being frustrated by the Midianite merchants— and it is exactly this frustration of the brothers' plan that will eventually result in the dreams coming true.

One more reason why the brothers did not sell Joseph can be inferred from three verses. Verse 25 reads: 'they sat down to eat bread', v. 29: 'Reuben returned to the pit'; and v. 30: 'He [Reuben] returned to his brothers'. Verse 29 implies that—at least—Reuben after the casting of Joseph into the cistern, went somewhere else. From Reuben's proposal to throw Joseph into 'that cistern which is in the wilderness' (אל-הבר הזה אשר במדבר), it is clear that the pit is not near to their encampment. After

---

32. As Poulssen states: '...de broers, meer weerloos dan verlegen, [hebben] de greep op de gebeurtenissen totaal verloren' (N. Poulssen, *Brood en Spelen: Over de werking van het oudtestamentische Jozefverhaal (Genesis 37–50)* [Tilburg: Tilburg University Press, 1992], 12). Cf. I. Willi-Plein, 'Historiographische Aspekte der Josefsgeschichte', *Henoch* 1 (1979), 305-31 (313).

the brothers threw Joseph into the pit, they sat down to eat their bread. This was not in the vicinity of the cistern, because if it was, Reuben could not have returned to the cistern, after which he again returns to his brothers (v. 30). So, his brothers were not staying in the area of the pit either, and therefore cannot have pulled Joseph out of the pit, or have sold him.[33]

3. *Who Sells to Whom?*

There are several more passages that play a part when considering Joseph's sale. Among these are Gen. 40.15 and 45.4-5.

40.15	For I was stolen out of the land of the Hebrews	15 כי־גנב גנבתי מארץ העברים

45.4a	'I am Joseph, your brother,	4a אני יוסף אחיכם
b	whom you sold into Egypt.	b אשר־מכרתם אתי מצרימה
5a	Now, do not be distressed…	5a ועתה אל־תעצבו
c	because you sold me here,	c כי־מכרתם אתי הנה
d	for God sent me before you to preserve life'	d כי למחיה שלחני אלהים לפניכם

In the first of the two passages Joseph not only tells the cupbearer and the baker about his guiltless imprisonment, but also about his involuntary Egyptian journey. He does not mention any sale, instead he states that he has been kidnapped from his country. He does not say by whom.[34]

In the second text, on the other hand, where Joseph is talking to his brothers, he is more explicit: 'I am Joseph, your brother, whom you sold to

33. Cf. W. Rudolph, 'Die Josephsgeschichte', in P. Volz und W. Rudolph, *Der Elohist als Erzähler ein Irrweg der Pentateuchkritik?* (BZAW, 63; Giessen: Alfred Töpelmann, 1933), 143-83 (154).

34. Despite the vagueness in 40.15 a reference to the events of Gen. 37 can nevertheless be discerned. According to Redford, Joseph's designation of his home country as ארץ העברים ('land of the Hebrews') is rather odd: 'The writer of the present verse has merely suffered a *lapsus mentis* and introduced an anachronism into his text' (D.B. Redford, 'The "Land of the Hebrews" in Gen. XL 15', *VT* 15 [1965], 529-32 [530-31]). It may however be possible that the narrator by letting Joseph use the word העברים, refers to 37.28 where the narrator mentions that Midianite merchants came passing by (ויעברו); 'and they passed by' is a *wayyiqtol* of the verb עבר, in which the same root-consonants as in העברים ('the Hebrews') can be detected. The narrator, in Joseph's words, may be alluding to this event: 'I have been kidnapped from the land through which people [merchants] pass [literally: "of the passers-by"]'.

Egypt. Now, do not be distressed...because you sold me here, because
God sent me before you to preserve life'. In these verses Joseph twice uses
the verb מכר ('sell').

Therefore I will consider all texts that are concerned with Joseph's sale.
Three times the verb מכר ('sell') occurs, whereas the purchase is the
central issue once ('buy', קנה). At the same time this investigation will
shed some more light on the Ishmaelite–Midianite issue. These, according
to Gen. 37, are two distinct groups.[35] the Ishmaelites are a caravan (v. 25),
whereas the Midianites are 'men, merchants' (v. 28).[36] On the basis of these
data, Hamilton reaches another conclusion. With regard to Judg. 8.22-24
he concludes that Midianites and Ishmaelites partly concur:

> In other words, the two names were used interchangeably to refer to North
> Arabian caravaneers who branched off through Gilead... The interchange
> of 'Ishmaelites' and 'Midianites' in Gen. 37 suggests that at one time the
> Ishmaelites were the most prominent confederation of nomads in southern
> Palestine, and that their name might be attached to and linked with other
> groups.[37]

A further conclusion by Hamilton is that ' "Ishmaelite" is the more generic
term (Bedouin nomad), while "Midianite" is the more specific and ethnic
term'.[38] I cannot agree with Hamilton. His solution seems good, but on the
basis of Gen. 37 that 'at one time the Ishmaelites were the most prominent
confederation of nomads', his conclusion is too rash. Besides, Hamilton
does not take the *Medanites* of v. 36 into account.[39]

---

35. 'In Judg. 8:24, however, the Midianites are said to be Ishmaelites too, because
they wear gold nose-rings. Thus the two texts [Judg. 8.24 and Gen. 37] clearly contradict each other' (E.A. Knauf, 'Midianites and Ishmaelites', in J.F.A. Sawyer and D.J.A.
Clines [eds.], *Midian, Moab and Edom: The History and Archaeology of Late Bronze
and Iron Age Jordan and North-West Arabia* [JSOTSup, 24; Sheffield: JSOT Press
1983], 147-61 [147]).

36. Greenstein, 'An Equivocal Reading of the Sale of Joseph', 116. M. Anbar, on
the other hand, writes: 'nous nous sommes proposé d'expliquer le changement des
noms dans le récit de la vente de Joseph, par l'emploi de trois noms servant à désigner
le même groupe de nomades, et les changements de noms dans la lettre de Mari, dans
Jg 6-8, 1 Ch 5, Jos 22, Nb 32, Jg 4-5 et les inscriptions assy riennes, par l'emploi de
différents noms de tribus pour désigner l'ensemble du groupe auquel elles appartien-
nent' ('Changement des noms des tribus nomades dans la relation d'un même événement', *Bib* 49 [1968], 221-32 [232]).

37. Hamilton, *The Book of Genesis: 18–50*, 423.

38. Hamilton, *The Book of Genesis: 18–50*, 423.

39. According to the Masorete text one has to read 'Medanites' (מדנים) in v. 36;

Apart from Joseph's words in 45.4-5 there are four texts which explicitly deal with his sale and Egyptian journey: 37.27, 28, 36 and 39.1.

> '…let us sell him to the Ishmaelites (לישׁמעאלים)' (37.27).
> and they sold Joseph to the Ishmaelites (לישׁמעאלים) for 20 shekels of silver and made Joseph come to Egypt (מצרימה) (37.28).
> …the Medanites (והמדנים) sold him to Egypt (אל־מצרים), to Potiphar (לפוטיפר)… (37.36).
> Joseph was taken down to Egypt (מצרימה), and Potiphar…bought him from the hand of the Ishmaelites (הישׁמעאלים), who had taken him there (39.1).

Also, there are two ways to denote '(in)to Egypt'. In 37.25, 28, 39.1 and 45.4 one comes across מצרימה ('into Egypt'), whereas אל־מצרים ('to Egypt') is used in 37.36. In the verses, where it says מצרימה (with *he*-locale), this designation, 'into Egypt', means nothing but the direction in which people are travelling: 37.25 shows the caravan heading for Egypt; 37.28 illustrates that the Ishmaelites take Joseph into Egypt; in 39.1 it is clear that Joseph was taken down into Egypt. In 45.4 Joseph says: 'I am Joseph, your brother, whom you sold into Egypt (מצרימה)'[40]—here the direction is the issue as well.[41] And according to 37.36, 'Medanites sold him (אתו) to Egypt'—here 'to Egypt' is also the direction that Joseph was taken when he was sold into slavery, although this might also imply the arrival in Egypt because the receiving party is mentioned next: 'to Potiphar' (לפוטיפר).

As for the verb מכר ('sell'), it is clear that when somebody (or something) is sold to someone else, the verb is complemented with the preposition ל: v. 27, 'to the Ishmaelites'; v. 28, 'to the Ishmaelites'; v. 36, 'to Potiphar'. In 45.4 the verb is not complemented: Joseph does not mention the receiving party.[42]

LXX, Targum Onkelos and Neophyti read 'Midianites', Targum Pseudo-Jonathan on the other hand reads 'Medanites'. According to *HALAT* one must assume the Medanites to be Midianites (מדינים, *HALAT*, II, 521). Although I do not think it a good idea to insert a yod now and again—whenever it appears to be convenient, and although 'This is a counsel of despair' according to Y.T. Radday ('Humour in Names', in Y.T. Radday and A. Brenner [eds.], *On Humour and the Comic in the Hebrew Bible* [Bible and Literature Series, 23; Sheffield: Almond Press 1990], 59-97 [70]), I think the Medanites in v. 36 to be Midianites (see below). Radday calls attributing the distinction between Medanites and Midianites to different traditions, 'too easy a way out, I think'—to which I wholeheartedly agree.

40. See also 45.5: 'because you sold me here' (כי מכרתם אתי הנה).
41. Cf. in Gen. 12.10, 11, 14; 26.2; 41.57; 46.3, 4, 6, 7, 8, 26, 27; 48.5; 50.14.
42. For an etymological point of view, cf. 'Die Zusammenstellung von *mkr* mit

From these observations, there is no option but to conclude that Joseph
was sold to Ishmaelites (37.28; 39.1), who took him down to Egypt (39.1),
and subsequently sold him to Potiphar (37.36). Above, the question of
who sold Joseph to the Ishmaelites was clarified: the Midianites pulled
Joseph out of the pit and sold him to the Ishmaelites.

Now, two problems remain to be solved. First in 45.4-5 Joseph mentions neither Midianites nor Ishmaelites: he does not refer to the people
who have sold him; he only remarks that—in his perception—his brothers
had sold him to Egypt. This contradicts the narrator's statements considered above. And second, 37.36 poses a problem because the verse says
that 'the Medanites (המדנים) sold him to Egypt, to Potiphar', a completely
unexpected, and seemingly new party—a group never again appears in the
biblical texts.

I will start with the latter. The easiest solution, as seen in most translations, commentaries and exegetical studies, is to insert a yod, and turn the
Medanites (מדנם) into Midianites (מדנים). In that case Gen. 37.36 reads
'The Midianites had sold Joseph to Egypt...', which is supposed to mean
'the actions of the Midianites made Joseph arrive in Egypt (because of the
trading activities of the Ishmaelites)'. This solution not only looks nice,
but is also in accordance with the text: Midianite traders pull Joseph out of
the cistern (v. 28b), sell him to the Ishmaelites (v. 28c-d), who take him to
Egypt (v. 28e). So, in the end, the Midianites *did* cause Joseph to arrive in
Egypt and be sold to Potiphar. In Gen. 39 the story of the sale is continued
by the statement that Potiphar bought Joseph out of the Ishmaelites' hands
—the perspective having changed from the selling to the buying party.
One could, however, wonder with Radday[43] whether this is not too large a
simplification.

A rather ingenious, but unsatisfactory, solution which puts a stop to the
three-party system of Midianites, Ishmaelites, and Medanites is given by

einer Ortsangabe, wohin jemand "übergehen" wird (Gen 45, 4f. Jo 4, 7...), oder mit
'æl und Ortsname (Gen 37, 36) zeigt an, daß dieses Verb ursprünglich nichts mit
Kauf/Verkauf zu tun hatte, obwohl diese Bedeutung nicht selten konnotiert werden
muß... Nur Personen oder Güter, die *b^{e}kæsæp* (Gen 37, 28)...übergeben werden,
werden sicher verkauft. In diesem Zusammenhang erst hat *mkr* die echte Konnotation
des Verkaufens, wobei das Verb als solches aber nach wie vor "übergeben, aushän-
digen" bedeutet' (*ThWAT*, IV, 872). Cf. p. 870: 'Eine Überprüfung der älteren Belege
von *mkr* zeigt jedoch, daß dieses Verb sich nicht spezifisch in das Wortfeld "kaufen/
verkaufen" einordnen läßt'.

43. Radday, 'Humour in Names', 70.

Radday. His suggestion is not to read מדנים as a hypothetical tribe, that is mentioned nowhere else in the Bible, but to understand it as a plural of מדון ('strife, dissension', like Prov. 6.19 and 10.12). Joseph consequently is not sold by Medanites, but by 'dissensions' (among his brothers). Understood like this both the narrator's texts, in which Joseph is not sold by the brothers, and Joseph's own words, in which he states that his brothers did sell him to Egypt, are given their due. While the brothers were arguing about what to do with their brother, Midianites came along, pulled Joseph out of the pit and sold him to Ishmaelites who took him to the south. Thus, the 'strife' among the brothers eventually took him to Egypt.[44]

Although I am not too keen on inserting a yod into מדנים, so that the Medanites turn into Midianites, I think this to be the best solution.[45] Moreover, the word used in 37.36, המדנים, has the definite article. Accordingly, it has to refer to something (i.e. a group of people) that has been mentioned before—and therefore Radday's 'dissensions' cannot hold and besides, it has to be kept in mind that the word המדנים ('dissensions') is the subject of v. 36. It is hardly conceivable that Joseph was actually sold to Potiphar by *dissensions*. In sum, the Midianites sold Joseph to Egypt (via the Ishmaelites) to Potiphar.

The remaining problem to be dealt with is Joseph's remark about his brothers selling him to Egypt. Both Joseph and the reader know that Joseph's brothers did not deliver him in Egypt. This, however, does not exclude the possibility that Joseph thinks his brothers are involved in his Egyptian sojourn. His account of the events in the region of Dothan gives the impression that he (initially) had not the faintest idea of what had really occurred as can be seen in 40.15: 'I have been kidnapped from the land of the Hebrews'.[46] Joseph does not seem to know anything more than that he had been thrown into a cistern by his brothers, after which other

44. Radday, 'Humour in Names', 70.

45. B. Jacob's view of the Midianites/Medanites problem is the same as his view of the two alternative names of Dothan in Gen. 37. Verse 17 has both דתינה ('to Dothan') and בדתן ('in Dothan'): in one form occurs a yod, in the other there is none (cf. *Das erste Buch der Tora*, 709).

46. Hamilton's suggestion that Joseph tells the cupbearer that he was stolen and therefore 'deliberately adjusted the story' because 'To have mentioned that he was sold by his brothers would make the cupbearer suspicious, rather than trusting' is not convincing (Hamilton, *The Book of Genesis: 18–50*, 424).

people pulled him out—although, of course, it is not impossible that he supposed his brothers' involvement.

Between 40.15 and 45.4-5 Joseph hears his brothers talking to one another a few times. One of these conversations is of particular importance. After Joseph has accused the brothers of spying and has put them into prison for three days, they again come before the Egyptian lord. Joseph summons them to bring their youngest brother to Egypt, while one of them is to remain in custody. According to Gen. 42.24 Joseph spoke to his brothers by means of an interpreter, so the brothers could not know that Joseph was able to hear their conversation in 42.21-22.

21a	They said to one another:	ויאמרו איש אל־אחיו	21a
b	Alas, we are paying the penalty for what we did to our brother;	אבל אשמים אנחנו על־אחינו	b
c	we saw his anguish when he pleaded with us,	אשר ראינו צרת נפשו בהתחננו אלינו	c
d	but we would not listen.	ולא שמענו	d
e	That is why this distress has come upon us.	על־כן באה אלינו הצרה הזאת	e
22a	Then Reuben answered them and said:	ויען ראובן אתם לאמר	22a
b	Did I not tell you	אמרתי אליכם לאמר	b
c	not to wrong the boy?	הלוא	c
d	But you would not listen.	אל־תחטאו בילד	d
e	And also his blood,	ולא שמעתם	e
f	behold, it is required.	וגם־דמו הנה נדרש	f

When hearing his brothers talking like this, Joseph put two and two together and concluded that his casting into the pit was not the only ride his brothers had taken him for.[47] Reuben's words may have led him to conclude that the sale was their idea, to which Reuben had opposed himself. This is expressed by the dissension among them: 'Didn't I tell you...but you would not listen' (42.22b-d). Because this is what he guesses, Joseph cannot be more explicit in ch. 45 when he makes himself known to his brothers. Moreover, Joseph as well as the reader, remain in the dark about the moment at which Reuben may have uttered the above words. Were they part of his speech (before, during or after 37.21-22), or did he not say these words until Judah had made his suggestion (while Midianites were

---

47. 'Joseph konnte wirklich glauben, daß die Midjaniter ihn im Auftrage der Brüder aus der Grube gezogen und an die Ismaeliter verkauft haben' (B. Jacob, *Das erste Buch der Tora*, 813).

busy selling Joseph to Ishmaelites). Or it is possible that the words are his restatement of 37.21-22 (one cannot expect Reuben to remember the precise wording after a period of 20 years)? Whoever may have sold Joseph, as Joseph hears it now: in one way or another his brothers, Reuben excepted, appear to be involved in the sale.

As for the narrator's text, it is clear that Joseph has been sold by the Midianites to the Ishmaelites, who again sold him to Potiphar. However, as regards Joseph's words, a reader might draw the conclusion that Joseph suspected the brothers to have sold him—via the two parties—to Egypt.

A striking thing, by the way, is the narrator's (and the brothers') mentioning of Joseph's state of mind in Gen. 42. In Gen. 37 the narrator apparently could not resist emphasizing the brothers' negative feelings towards Joseph, and Jacob's disposition with regard to Joseph (his love in v. 3 and his grief in vv. 34-35). Joseph's state of mind was kept out of consideration. Thus, it is rather remarkable that retrospectively Joseph appeared to be a feeling human being as well. Even more striking is that after hearing his brothers talk about his fear in Dothan (42.21), he lets his tears flow down (42.24).

The texts concerning the sale of Joseph show, be it rather unequivocally, that the brothers did not sell Joseph. Joseph is hauled out of the cistern into which he was thrown by his brothers, by Midianite merchants. These in turn sell him to Ishmaelites[48] who take him to Egypt, where he is bought by Potiphar.

4. *Reuben and his Brothers*

In the first section of the present chapter I examined Reuben's speech in 37.21-22; now I will have a closer look at his words spoken in 42.22. What catches the eye is the apparent lack of change in Reuben during the 21 years that have passed, or, one should rather say, the narrator's way of presenting Reuben shows no significant difference. He again takes a stance in opposition to his brothers': 'I warned you then!'[49] In v. 21 the brothers

---

48. Ishmaelites being involved in the sale once more emphasizes the lack of true family relations in Genesis. According to Gen. 25.12-18 the Ishmaelites are the sons of Joseph's great-grandfather Abraham. The same can be said about Midian and Medan, both mentioned as sons of Abraham in 25.2. Ishmaelites, with Hagar as Ishmael's mother, have a more tight connection with Egypt.

49. Likewise Humphreys, *Joseph and his Family*, 83.

were speaking collectively: 'we did not hear'. Reuben on the other hand
is saying: 'you did not hear' (cf. 37.21, 27). Preceding these words he addresses his brothers and says: 'Did I not tell you?' By stating this he is
pleading to keep himself free of any responsibility regarding Joseph's
adventures. He also makes use of an imperative while addressing his
brothers (v. 22), as he did before in Gen. 37. He does not make a passion-
ate plea for his younger brother either, even though the usage of 'the lad'
(הילד)—which is new compared to Gen. 37.21-22 (where he could not say
any more than calling Joseph 'him' twice: אתו and בו) but is not new in
comparison with 37.30—may have the looks of it. There is, however, a
strong contrast between Judah's 'our brother, our flesh' (37.26-27) and the
brothers' 'our brother' (42.21) on the one hand, and Reuben's designation
of Joseph on the other. The way in which Reuben acts and talks matches
his talking in Gen. 37.22. Even though, with regard to his actual words,
only the word דם ('blood') is used in both places, Reuben's behaviour in
Gen. 37 is more or less repeated in Gen. 42. This attempt to create a distance between himself and his brothers again—after all these years—and
his attempt to plead himself free is no credit to Reuben.[50] No indeed, one
might even blame him for this, especially since it was *his* suggestion to
throw Joseph into the cistern alive.[51]

In 37.29 a new unit of Gen. 37 is opened[52] when Reuben returns to the
cistern on his own and much to his dismay discovers that Joseph has
disappeared: והנה אין־יוסף בבור ('and look, Joseph was not in the pit'). In
this observation 'the pit' (בור) has its seventh (and final) occurrence; at the
same time it is the twelfth mentioning of Joseph's name in Gen. 37. It is
exactly on this occasion that one of Jacob's 12 sons is no longer present.
Struck by grief, Reuben tears his robe (ויקרע את־בגדיו, v. 29), which Jacob
is about to do shortly too[53] (ויקרע יעקב שמלתיו, v. 34) after receiving

---

50. Contra R. Syrén, *The Forsaken Firstborn. A Study of a Recurrent Motif in the
Patriarchal Narratives* (JSOTSup, 133; Sheffield: JSOT Press, 1993), 132.
51. A more or less similar analysis of Reuben's direct speech in Gen. 42 is given
by Ackerman, 'Joseph, Judah, and Reuben', 101.
52. The final clause of v. 28 appears to have taken much more time than is allowed
for by the temporal frame of Gen. 37 (37.36 excepted): 'This is perhaps to indicate that
there is a break between the events of v. 28 and the following verses' (Berlin, *Poetics
and Interpretation*, 120).
53. Together with 44.13 these are the only occurrences of the verb קרע in Genesis.
When used in combination with the tearing of clothes it may indicate terror, dismay,
bewilderment and sorrow 'über ein unheilvolles Ereignis, das den die Handlung

Joseph's *ketonet passim*.[54] After expressing his distress, Reuben returns to his brothers and informs them: הילד איננו ('the boy is not there').[55] From the continuation of his words, which resemble a lament, Reuben's self-directedness can once more be observed. He does join his brothers, but he is not wondering about what they have to do. He only seems to be concerned about himself: ואני אנה־אני־בא ('and I, where am I to go?', v. 30).

If the brothers *did* sell Joseph, they did not inform Reuben about the ins and outs of the matter. This may fit perfectly the idea people have about such 'brother-selling rogues', but the implication is that one has to add two essential things to the text. These are the sale by the brothers (Reuben excepted) and their keeping it concealed from Reuben. However, as shown above, it is highly unlikely for the brothers to have sold Joseph. The verses concerning Reuben are another indication of the brothers' innocence with regard to the sale of Joseph; in his ignorance Reuben acts as a *pars pro toto*.

How or what the brothers were thinking in connection with Joseph's disappearance does not really seem to matter because the narrator keeps silent about it in the text. The brothers, however, may have understood Reuben's words in v. 29 (הילד איננו) in a way in which a similar verse is often understood and translated. The final clause of Gen. 42.13 in the NRSV, for example, is translated: 'and one is no more', which I presume to mean that the person involved is dead. The Hebrew word representing 'no more' is איננו.[56] The very same word is used by Reuben in 37.30. So, his brothers may have understood Reuben to say that Joseph had died in the pit. This subsequently urges them to take Joseph's robe and dip it into the blood of a goat and send it to their father. טרף טרף יוסף ('Joseph has surely been torn to pieces'), is Jacob's exclamation in v. 33, after recognizing his son's garment. This appears to be the only thing a blood-stained robe might

Ausführenden direkt oder indirekt betroffen hat oder zu betreffen droht' (*ThWAT*, VII, 190).

54. Jacob tears his שמלה (often translated as 'mantle') and Reuben his בגד (someone's ordinary clothes). What specific garment is being referred to is hard to detect.

55. This expression in a way resembles Gen. 42.13: ואחד איננו ('and one is no more'). The fact that Joseph 'is not there' does not necessarily imply him to be dead; cf. Gen. 42.36 ('Joseph is not there and Simeon is not there', twice איננו) and also 44.26, 30, 34.

56. Cf. Judg. 4.20 where Sisera tells Yael to say to anyone coming to her tent that no one (אין) is inside.

evoke. Taking some steps and going to look for a possibly wounded son is not something Jacob can think of. His חיה רעה אכלתהו ('some ferocious animal has devoured him'; which beautifully corresponds to the original murder-plan, v. 20) does not leave any shadow of doubt about Jacob's opinion: Joseph is no longer among the living. The robe, stained by the blood of a she-goat,[57] is clear enough for Jacob: it implies a Joseph torn to pieces (v. 33). Jacob subsequently prefers to tear his clothes, put on sack-cloth and mourn for many days. He refuses any consolation from his sons and daughters[58] (v. 35)—his attitude towards them appears not to have changed compared to vv. 3-4; he expresses his attachment to Joseph by lamenting over him: כי־ארד אל־בני אבל שאלה ('I will go down to my son, to Sheol, mourning')[59] (v. 35). The participle is from the verb אבל. The grief this verb expresses is not primarily a state of mind, it rather indicates an 'outward appearence', which is determined by laid down mourning-rituals that are often mentioned—such as in v. 34.[60] The narrator's final remark on Jacob for some time (Jacob does not enter the stage again until 42.1) is in v. 35: ויבך אתו אביו ('and his father wept for him').[61]

57. 'It is ironic that Jacob, who earlier deceived Isaac with 'ōrōṯ hā'izzîm ("skin of the kids") in 27:16, is now deceived by a garment dipped in the blood of a goat (se'îr 'izzîm)' (Hamilton, The Book of Genesis: 18–50, 426).

58. Jacob having more daughters than one (Dinah) can also be seen in Gen. 46.7, 15.

59. The Sheol, suddenly appearing in Jacob's words (and also in 42.38, cf. 44.29, 31), shows that—even though nothing is told about it—behind the textual world, communicated by the narrator, there appears to be another world that gives depth to this textual world. Something similar can be said about the Egyptian words that the reader will come across shortly. There is 'a sense that the author knew more than he was telling, that behind this immediate story there was a coherent, consistent, deeply fascinating world about which he had no time (then) to speak' (T. Shippey, The Road to Middle-earth [London: George Allen & Unwin, 1982], 171).

60. See ThWAT, I, 47. To put on (שים) sackcloth (שק) belongs to the mourning-rituals, as also do 'das Bestreuen des Kopfes mit Staub oder Asche, das Sitzen auf der Erde, das Scheren von Bart und Kopfhaar. אבל ist offenbar terminus technicus für die Gesamtheit dieser Bräuche, die bei einem Todesfall zu beobachten sind' (47).

61. Cf. Gen. 27.38 where Esau wept (ויבך). There are 15 occurrences of the verb בכה in Genesis; 10 of which are in chs. 37–50. Joseph weeps 7 times: 42.24; 43.30; 45.14, 15; 46.29; 50.1, 17. In 37.35 Jacob weeps for the supposed death of Joseph, whereas Joseph in 50.1 weeps for the actual death of his father.

Chapter 5

DESCENTS INTO THE UNKNOWN

In the chapters following the episodes discussed so far, two sons of Jacob's have left their family: when the traders are taking Joseph down to Egypt, Judah takes leave of his brothers and is about to establish a family of his own (Gen. 38).

Once Joseph has arrived in Egypt he is bought by Potiphar and enters into Potiphar's service (Gen. 39). Due to an unjust accusation he is cast into prison, the place where he acquires himself a name for interpreting dreams (Gen. 40). This in turn results in his rise to power because of his ability to give an explanation for Pharaoh's dreams (Gen. 41).

The major part of this chapter will be devoted to Joseph. However, since Judah will enter the spotlight some more times in the remainder of Gen. 37–50, his encounter with Tamar needs to be dealt with briefly as well.[1]

1. *Judah and Tamar*

In Gen. 38 Judah leaves his brothers when Joseph is being taken to Egypt ('at that time') and goes down (ירד) to live with an Adullamite (v. 1) and marries the daughter of a certain Shua (v. 2). He and Bat-Shua will have

---

1.   There is no need to mention several recurring motifs in Gen. 37–50, like the function of garments or the pit (בוֹר) into which Joseph is cast (37.24), which is found again in 40.15 and 41.14, since many of those have been noticed before; among others by U. Cassuto, 'The Story of Judah and Tamar', in *idem*, *Biblical and Oriental Studies*. I. *Bible* (Jerusalem: Magnes Press/Hebrew University, 1973), 29-40, Lowenthal, *The Joseph Narrative*, 49; Seybold, 'Paradox and Symmetry in the Joseph Narrative'; Humphreys, *Joseph and his Family*, 96; V.H. Matthews, 'The Anthropology of Clothing in the Joseph Narrative', *JSOT* 65 (1995), 25-36; Green, *'What Profit for Us?'*. More resemblances between ch. 37 and ch. 38 on the one hand and chs. 39–50 on the other include the traders' merchandise (37.25) and the brothers' presents (43.11), Judah's and Pharaoh's rings (38.18 and 41.42 [although different words are used]), and the marriages of both Judah and Joseph to a non-Israelite woman (38.2; 41.45).

three sons: Er, Onan and Shelah. Judah then takes a wife, Tamar, for his firstborn. This is the overture of the famous tale of Tamar and Judah.

During the last two decades, the story about Tamar and Judah has been the object of a substantial number of studies, in many of which the importance of Tamar (according to Thomas Mann 'she could be called the most amazing figure in this whole story—few will be found to deny it'[2]) and her role toward Judah is emphasized and highlighted.[3]

Tamar's husband, Er (עֵר), is put to death by YHWH, because he was wicked (רַע) in the eyes of God (v. 7). Consequently his brother Onan has to do his duty as a levirate for his brother. However, every time he went into his sister-in-law he spilled his semen on the ground—which is also wicked in the eyes of God. As a result of this, Onan is put to death by God as well. Because Judah assumes his sons' deaths to be caused by Tamar, he is not too enthusiastic about her marrying his youngest son, Shelah (v. 11). He sends her to her father's house to wait until Shelah has come of age. Then Judah's wife dies, and after the period of mourning Judah goes up to Timna to shear his sheep. Tamar realizes that she has not been given Shelah yet, even though he is already an adult. She puts off her widow's dress, changes her clothes and goes up to Timna as well. When Judah sees her he takes her for a prostitute and asks her: 'Come, let me come into you'. After some negotiations the deal is done. Judah promises her a kid from

2.   T. Mann, *Joseph and his Brothers* (London: Minerva, 1997; first published in Great Britain by Secker & Warburg, 1970), Foreword, xii (translation of *Joseph und seine Brüder*, 1933–1943, by H.T. Lane-Porter).

3.   Among the studies in which the constructive role of Tamar is emphasized are S. Niditch, 'The Wronged Woman Righted: An Analysis of Genesis 38', *HTR* 72 (1979), 143-49; R. Alter, *The Art of Biblical Narrative* (New York: Basic Books, 1981); J.W.H. Bos, 'Out of the Shadows Genesis 38; Judges 4:17-22; Ruth 3', *Semeia* 42 (1988), 37-67; N. Morimura, 'Tamar and Judah—A Feminist Reading of Gen 38', in T. Schneider und H. Schlüngel-Straumann (eds.), *Theologie zwischen Zeiten und Kontinenten. Für Elisabeth Gössman* (Freiburg: Herder, 1993), 2-18; D.M. Gunn and D.N. Fewell, *Narrative in the Hebrew Bible* (Oxford: Oxford University Press, 1993), 34-45; A. Wildavsky, 'Survival Must Not be Gained through Sin: The Moral of the Joseph Stories Prefigured through Judah and Tamar', *JSOT* 62 (1994), 37-48; E. van Wolde, 'Texts in Dialogue with Texts: Intertextuality in the Ruth and Tamar Narratives', *BibInt* 5 (1997), 1-28; A.J. Lambe, 'Genesis 38: Structure and Literary Design', in P.R. Davies and D.J.A. Clines (eds.), *The World of Genesis: Persons, Places, Perspectives* (JSOTSup, 257; Sheffield: Sheffield Academic Press, 1998), 102-20. On Gen. 38 in general, see E. Salm, *Juda und Tamar: Eine exegetische Studie zu Gen 38* (Forschung zur Bibel, 76; Würzburg: Echter Verlag, 1996); Fokkelman, 'Genesis 37 and 38'.

his flock if she will sleep with him. As a prepayment he gives her a pledge: his ring, his cord and his staff. Tamar now gets pregnant by her father-in-law and returns home. After a while, Judah is informed of Tamar's condition—which he thinks an outrage. However, as soon as Tamar confronts him with his ring, cord and staff, he swallows his words: 'she is in the right, not I' (צדקה ממני, 38.26).[4] When her time has come, Tamar gives birth to two sons, Perez and Zerah. From the book of Ruth it becomes clear that via Tamar and Perez, Judah and Tamar are the founding parents of the royal line to come (Ruth 4.18-22).

The main result of the research on Gen. 38, a 'spectacular story about a woman's taboo-breaking',[5] is that the story shows how Tamar opens Judah's eyes and teaches him to take responsibility and secure his family's future.[6] Judah approves of the way she has acted, as is shown by his words 'she is in the right, not I'. He declares himself guilty of having looked after private interest at the expense of his daughter-in-law.[7]

2. *Joseph in Egypt*

Gen. 39 picks up where the last verse of Gen. 37 left off: Joseph is taken down (ירד) to Egypt, and bought by Potiphar, a servant of Pharaoh and captain of the guard,[8] out of the hand of the Ishmaelites, who had taken him there (39.1).

Following the opening verse, Gen. 39–41 consists of three episodes. In the first, Joseph's stay in the house of Potiphar is being narrated (39.2–20);

---

4. Translation by Fokkelman, 'Genesis 37 and 38', 172. Fokkelman also makes the interesting observation that Onan's 'criminal act of withholding seed is to a certain degree committed by Onan's father as well' (177).

5. Thus Fokkelman in his eye-opening study 'Genesis 37 and 38', 167.

6. D. Steinmetz, *From Father to Son. Kinship, Conflict and Continuity in Genesis* (Literary Currents in Biblical Interpretation; Louisville: Westminster/John Knox Press, 1991), 45-49; 117-20. Yet, as Barbara Green rightly observes, Judah's first responsibility was to protect his family. That exactly was the reason why he did not send his son Shelah to Tamar to do his levirate duty (*'What Profit for Us?'*, 74); the same idea is expressed by Wildavsky, *Assimilation versus Separation*, 105.

7. Cf. W. Brueggemann, *Genesis* (Interpretation: A Bible Commentary for Teaching and Preaching; Atlanta: John Knox Press, 1982), 310.

8. 'Captain of the guard' (שר הטבחים) is one possible translation; the expression could also be translated 'chief of the butchers, chief of the slaughterers'—this translation is rather ironic when applied in 37.36: whereas the chief of the slaughterers had bought Joseph, a little before Joseph's brothers slaughtered a goat. The observation was made by Steinmetz, *From Father to Son*, 44.

the second episode is about Joseph's time in prison (39.21–40.23); the final episode presents Joseph's glorious exodus from prison (ch. 41). The two sections in which Joseph finds himself in the services of Potiphar and the captain of the guards show a similar structure. Both present several introductory verses (39.2-6 and 39.21-23), after which the tale follows. Both introductions start with the same formula: ויהי יהוה את־יוסף (39.2-21). Also, in both introductory paragraphs Joseph makes a fine impression on his employers; they both leave everything in Joseph's hands.[9] When the narratives proceed, the first clauses are similar as well ויהי אחרי הדברים האלה (39.7 and 40.1). In both episodes Joseph goes from the frying pan into the fire.[10] After his encounter with Potiphar's wife, Joseph ends up in prison, and after giving a correct interpretation of the cupbearer's dream, the latter forgets him. Joseph gains nothing from it.

The third episode is well marked by its introduction. Its first verse both establishes a connection with the previous episodes, and sets it apart from them: 'it happened after two years' (ויהי מקץ שנתים ימים, 41.1). Joseph's subsequent release from prison finds its cause in his ability to interpret other people's dreams—initially the cupbearer's and the baker's (in episode two), and finally the dreams of Pharaoh.

In the following section I will discuss the way Joseph leaves the services of Pharaoh's servants and enters into the service of Pharaoh himself.

3. *The Interpretations of the Dreams*

When discussing the dreams in Gen. 37 (see my Chapter 3) I drew attention to the fact that both dreams were interpreted by Joseph's brothers (the first) and by Jacob (the second). I also showed that the brothers' interpretation as presented by the narrator is probably not correct—because Joseph is never and nowhere going to rule over them—and that Jacob's interpretation is not correct either, since it is impossible that both Joseph's mother

---

9.   Both in v. 3 and v. 23 the narrator uses the hiphil participle of the verb צלח ('make prosperous, make successful'; *NIDOTE*, III, 804).

10.   It is interesting to note that the reasons why both Joseph and the cupbearer and the baker are put in prison are related to חטא (qal, 'sin'; 39.9; 40.1), a verb that is found only seven times in Genesis (five of which are in Gen. 37-50: 39.9; 40.1; 42.22; 43.9; 44.32; the remaining two cases are in Gen. 20, vv. 6 and 9). The verb unites both episodes in which Joseph is a servant (in Gen. 39 to Potiphar and in Gen. 40 to the chief jailor, who may be the very same Potiphar; cf. 37.36; 39.1; 40.3-4; 41.10, 12). Cf. Hamilton, *The Book of Genesis: 18–50*, 475.

and 11 brothers are able to bow down before him. Joseph did not give an interpretation of his dreams. During his stay in the Egyptian prison he appears to have acquired the art of interpreting dreams.

After his initial successful career in Potiphar's house, Joseph ends up in prison because of his refusal to meet the demands of Potiphar's wife. During his time in prison Joseph comes to know two more servants of the Egyptian monarch: the chief of the cupbearers and the chief of the bakers. One night they have both dreamed a dream. On seeing them in the morning Joseph asks why they are troubled. After they have told him about their dreams—which they do not understand (ופתר אין אתו, 'there is no one to explain them', 40.8), Joseph replies: הלוא לאלהים פתרנים ספרו־נא לי ('Do not interpretations belong to God? Please tell them to me', 40.8).[11] 'Following this question, the cupbearer tells his dream and then—quite amazing—Joseph interprets the dream: זה פתרנו ('this is the interpretation'; 40.12, 18). How is one to read Joseph's statements: 'Do not interpretations belong to God?' and 'this is the interpretation'. I will return to this below. Near the end of the episode the cupbearer is restored to his former position, and the baker is executed,[12] 'just as Joseph had interpreted (פתר) to them' (40.22). Whoever interpretations belong to, Joseph's interpretations are obviously correct.

In Gen. 41 another two dreams are dreamed, this time by Pharaoh (vv. 1-7). On his awakening he turns out to be rather disturbed by his dreams, and he sends for all the magicians of Egypt and the wise men. He relates his dreams to them, 'but there was no one interpreting them to Pharaoh' (ואין־פותר אותם לפרעה, 41.8).[13] The impasse is broken by the cupbearer

11. הלוא may also be emphatic: 'Interpretations belong to God, don't they'; cf. Joüon and Muraoka, *A Grammar of Biblical Hebrew* §161c, 610, Waltke and O'Connor, *An Introduction*, 648 n. 48.

12. Although the narrator does not state why the baker is executed and the cupbearer is restored to his former position, one may detect a possible reason. On the occasion of his birthday Pharaoh summons both the baker and the cupbearer. He also throws a banquet for his servants (40.20). The Hebrew for 'banquet' is משתה (literally 'drinking'); the word is derived from the verb שתה ('drink'). Now it may become clear why Pharaoh did not restore the baker, but did restore the cupbearer. When drinking one needs somebody to hold a cup, a baker is not required.

13. Most translations and commentaries translate 'and there was no one who could interpret them to Pharaoh'. However, there is no modality expressed in the verse. It only says that no one is interpreting the dream, it does not say that the magicians and wise men are unable to interpret them. It probably is not unreasonable to assume that they actually were able to interpret the dreams, but were unwilling to be the bearer of

who all of a sudden remembers Joseph interpreting his and the baker's
dreams two years before (41.9-13). Joseph is immediately sent for: he is
taken out of the pit (מן־הבור, 41.14), he has his clothes changed, and is
brought before Pharaoh. The latter tells Joseph about his dream and says
that there is no one who interprets it (ופתר אין אתו, 41.15—the same
words as used in 40.8 by the cupbearer and the baker). He continues to
say: 'I have heard of you: "you hear a dream to interpret it"'. Joseph
replies: 'It is not I, God will give Pharaoh a favourable answer' בלעדי
(אלהים יענה את־שלום פרעה; 41.16). Pharaoh then recounts his dreams
(vv. 17-24) and repeats his statement that there is no one to explain it to
him (ואין מגיד לי, v. 24).[14] Then Joseph again takes the floor: 'Pharaoh's
dream is one and the same, what God is about to do, he has told (הגיד)[15]
Pharaoh' (v. 25). To his subsequent explanation he adds: 'this is the word
I have spoken to Pharaoh, what God is doing he has shown to Pharaoh'
(v. 28). After the explanation of the second part of the dreams he once
more introduces God into his speech: 'And the doubling of Pharaoh's
dream means that the thing is fixed by God, and God will shortly bring it
about' (v. 32).[16]

Joseph then cleverly presents a solution for the problems that Egypt is
going to face during the next decade and a half (41.33-36). In this respect
he surpasses the Egyptian magicians and wise man that Pharaoh had sent
for earlier. Apart from giving an explanation for the dream, he also knows
how to face the problems lying ahead. 'This word was good in the eyes of
Pharaoh and in the eyes of his servants' (v. 37). Joseph's words result in
Pharaoh putting him in charge of all Egypt (vv. 40-45).[17]

bad news. See also Pharaoh's words in 41.15; like the narrator he does not say anything about people being unable to interpret the dreams. The remark that in 'both Genesis and Daniel non-Israelite magicians and astrologers are incapable of giving an interpretation of the dream (Gen 41.8, 15)' in *NIDOTE* (V, 723) consequently is not correct
as far as Genesis is concerned—nothing is said about their incapability.

14. Instead of the verb פתר (41.15) Pharaoh now uses the verb נגד (hiphil; 41.24).

15. Once more the verb נגד (hiphil). It is clear that Joseph picks up the word that
Pharaoh used just before, to make his point.

16. Yui-Wing Fung draws attention to the fact that quite a few commentators
neglect the fact that—in Joseph's view—it is God who brings about the famine. So, in
Joseph's opinion the famine is most certainly no natural disaster. Joseph also refrains
from giving a reason *why* all the earth should meet with a famine (Fung, *Victim and
Victimizer*, 109-19).

17. Which, of course, contradicts Joseph's claim in 45.8: 'God has made me ruler
of all Egypt'. It was Pharaoh who put Joseph in charge over Egypt, not God.

This overview of Joseph's words in connection with the dreams of the Egyptians reveals two things. The first is that in Joseph's opinion the interpretations of the dreams are God's (40.8) and that God makes known the interpretations of the two dreams of Pharaoh which are, in fact, the same (41.28, 32). Then, despite saying that the interpretation of dreams belongs to God, it is Joseph himself who interprets the dreams. Moreover, it is Joseph who makes known to Pharaoh what is going to happen during the years to come—not God. Joseph here ventures out onto thin ice. His remarks are straightforward, but there is quite some ambiguity here about how to read them. Indeed, even though the narrator does not deny Joseph's claims, he does not confirm them either. The second finding, which is closely connected to the first, is that Pharaoh designates Joseph as someone in whom he discerns the spirit of God (41.38)—which is different from 39.3, where it was the narrator according to whom Potiphar saw that YHWH was with Joseph. The subsequent question here is: How did Pharaoh arrive at this conclusion?

The answer to this is to be found in the manner in which Joseph addresses Pharaoh. As appears from the quotations from Gen. 41 given above, Joseph repeatedly refers to God while he is speaking to Pharaoh: 'God has made known to Pharaoh' (v. 25), 'what he is about to do' (v. 25), 'God has shown to Pharaoh' (v. 28), 'what he is about to do' (v. 28). By means of the twofold dream 'God has fixed' (v. 32), and 'God is going to bring about soon' (v. 32). Six times Joseph asserts that God has done something or is about to do it. In the way Joseph presents the interpretation of the dream, he tries to make Pharaoh see things the way he does. To put the matter more bluntly, he imposes his view on Pharaoh. Even stronger, from the way in which Joseph formulates the dream's meaning, it is obvious that he manipulates Pharaoh in such a way that Pharaoh considers both dreams in the way that Joseph wants him to understand them.[18] To do this, Joseph introduces the highest authority to support his interpretation: God has made known; God has shown; God has fixed; and God is going to do and going to bring about.

As soon as one regards Pharaoh's reaction to Joseph's explanation, it becomes clear that Joseph has succeeded in convincing Pharaoh of the correctness of his interpretation of the dream and solution to the crisis. According to the narrator, Pharaoh very much approves of Joseph's words —as do his servants (41.37). Hereafter Pharaoh twice relates Joseph's

18. Wildavsky reaches similar conclusions in the chapter 'The Dreamer Is the Dream', in his *Assimilation versus Separation*, 69-92; see also 107-109.

ability to interpret the dreams to God: 'Can we find a man like this, one in whom is the spirit of God?' (41.38), and 'After God has all this made known to you, there is no one as discerning (נבון) and wise as you' (41.39) —here Pharaoh repeats Joseph's words 'discerning and wise' from 41.33. The occurrence of the word נבון is noteworthy. Apart from the occurrences in vv. 33 and 39 it is only found two more times in the Torah,[19] but here it seems to allude to נבון ('fixed'), which Joseph had used just before in 41.32 to refer to God's decision to bring things about soon. To answer the immediate future which is fixed (נבון) by God, Joseph proposes to look for a man who is discerning (נבון) and wise. This man—at least in the eyes of Pharaoh—is Joseph himself.[20] So, just as the coming years of plenty and the years of famine are—according to Joseph—fixed by God, Joseph has fixed a secure position for himself in the house of Pharaoh.

Interestingly, Pharaoh also seems to refer to Joseph's words from 41.25 where he said 'what God is to bring about, he has told (הגיד) Pharaoh', even though he modifies and enforces the phrase somewhat. In 41.39 Pharaoh says: 'After God has all this made known (הודיע) to you...' By this change it becomes clear that Joseph has wrapped Pharaoh around his finger. At first Joseph explains that God has told Pharaoh what he is about to do—whereas after Joseph's explanation and proposal for a solution Pharaoh more or less reverses Joseph's initial remark, and also enforces Joseph's position by stating that it is not himself to whom God has told what is going to happen, but that it is to Joseph that God has made known 'all this'.

From the dream-episodes as told in Gen. 40 and 41, it becomes clear that during his imprisonment Joseph has both acquired the art of reading dreams and the art of making people see things the way he does. Or to put it more positively, 'Joseph is able to convince people to trust him and depend on him'.[21]

4. *Manasseh and Ephraim*

Joseph's interpretation of Pharaoh's dreams and his solution for the crises during the times of famine, result in his rise to power and glory. He has

19. Deut. 1.13; 4.6; outside the Torah it is found another 17 times, nine of them occurring in Proverbs.

20. Both words are niphal participles of the verbs כון respectively בין.

21. J. Hadda, 'Joseph: Ancestor of Psychoanalysis', *Conservative Judaism* 37 (1984), 17-21 (19).

become Egypt's second in command and is given Asenath, the daughter of the priest of On, as a wife (41.41-45).

Following this account of Joseph's rise in Egypt, the next episode (41.46–42.5) presents a picture of seven years passing swiftly by. During these years Joseph develops a special agricultural policy, by which Egypt ought to be able to face the imminent famine: the people of Egypt have to hand over one fifth of their crop to Pharaoh during the years of plenty. This will be stored for food in the cities, so that the land will not perish when the famine comes over the land (41.34-36). During those seven years of abundance ('it was beyond measure') Joseph gathered all the food and stored it in the cities (vv. 47-49).

In this very same period two major events in Joseph's life come about, which are described like this:

> Before the years of famine came, Joseph had two sons, whom Asenath daughter of Potiphera, priest of On, bore to him. Joseph named the firstborn Manasseh (מְנַשֶּׁה), 'For', he said, 'God has made me forget (נַשַּׁנִי, piel) all my hardship and all my father's house'. The second he named Ephraim (אֶפְרַיִם), 'For God has made me fruitful (פָּרָה, hiphil) in the land of my misfortunes (עָנְיִי)' (41.50-52).

In these verses several important points are made: (1) Joseph and Asenath become the parents of two sons; (2) this happens before the years of famine start, so Joseph is fruitful in the years that the land is fruitful, in the years of plenty; (3) just as Rachel and Leah had previously given their sons names while referring to God, so does Joseph. It is this element of naming, in which Joseph makes two word-plays, that is worth commenting upon.

Unfortunately, there is not much to say about the verb נָשָׁה. Apart from 41.51, it is only found once more in the Torah (Deut. 32.18);[22] its remaining occurrences are in poetic texts, and apart from these sparse occurrences, Gen. 41.51 is the only attestation of the piel conjugation of נָשָׁה ('cause to forget'). There 'the name Manasseh is explained in terms of God's causing trouble to be forgotten'.[23] If, however, one examines the

---

22. According to the concordance of אבן־שושן, 785. According to *ThWAT*, V, 663-64, there are only seven attestations of נָשָׁה in the Hebrew Bible, among which they do not mention Deut. 32.18. BDB, 674, is of the same opinion.

23. *NIDOTE*, III, 185. Of נָשָׁה qal (in Lam. 3.17) *ThWAT* writes: '"Vergessen" wäre fast mit "nicht erfahren" gleichbedeutend' (V, 664). If the piel is a causitive of this, the implication would be that—in Joseph's perception—God has caused him not to be aware of his father's house.

reason why Joseph named his firstborn Manasseh, the observation must be that there are two things mentioned by Joseph that God has made him forget. These are his hardship *and* his father's house—which, of course, he could not have literally forgotten; if he had, he could not have mentioned them. As for the hardship, since it is stated in 41.46 that Joseph is 30 years of age, it is clear that Joseph has spent at least 13 years in Egypt before his first son was born. His presumption that God helped him to leave his situation of servitude—also considering the statements in 39.3 and 21 that YHWH was with Joseph—is in all respects understandable. However, the second part of the naming—'God has made me forget my father's house' —is hard to comprehend. He was, after all, his father's favourite. This remark on forgetting his father's house sheds a not entirely favourable light upon Joseph. All the more so, since Joseph has been the man in charge for at least a year now (and perhaps even more)—and he has not made any attempt yet to contact his family in the land of Canaan. Nor will he for the years to come![24] By giving this explanation with regard to Manasseh's name, Joseph appears to attribute his own neglect of his father's house to God, or perhaps, his willingness to forget his father's house.[25]

The name of Ephraim (אֶפְרָיִם) is related to the root פרה. In 41.52—'God has made me fruitful in the land of my misfortunes [or affliction]'—the phrase 'land of my misfortunes' (אֶרֶץ עָנְיִי) appears to confirm the hard times Joseph has had, and which he referred to when naming Manasseh.

The word עֳנִי 'expresses the condition of pain, suffering, and anguish resulting from affliction' (*NIDOTE*, III, 451). 41.52 is the fourth time the word עֳנִי is encountered in Genesis. It is the second time that it is used by a character to describe her or his difficult sojourn in a foreign land. (In 31.42 it was Jacob who said to Laban that God had seen his affliction and the labour of his hands.) Yet it is also the third time that it is used in the context of a birth. (In 29.32, after she had delivered her firstborn, Leah named her child Reuben and said: 'Because YHWH has looked on my

24. Perhaps Joseph understood his assignment in 37.14 (go and look at the *shalom* of your brothers) as a continuation of his father's rebuke after his second dream. Perhaps that is why, once he has risen to an unprecedented height, he refrains from entering into contact with his father. He keeps distant from both his brothers and his father. It is indeed an intriguing question why Joseph did not contact his father. For several possible reasons, cf. A. Ages, 'Why Didn't Joseph Call Home?', *BR* 9 (1993), 42-46. See also Chapter 7: Many Farewells.

25. See also Fung, *Victim and Victimizer*, 104-109.

affliction; surely now my husband will love me'.) As was the case in 41.52, the birth of the son seems to indicate a new era—the period of affliction comes to an end when the son is born (and Leah does conceive another six children). The very first occurrence of עני in Genesis fits this pattern as well. The messenger of YHWH tells Hagar that she will bear a son, whose name shall be Ishmael 'for YHWH has given heed to your affliction' (16.11).

As was seen above, the word עני is always used by a character—not until Exod. 4.31 is it employed by the narrator (cf. the use of the verb ענה II in piel conjugation, 'oppress', in Exod. 1.11-12). The characters refer to a situation of affliction or oppression in which they find themselves. Apart from indicating a new era for the character him- or herself, the word also appears to carry a geographical connotation (except in Leah's case). Hagar and Ishmael leave (must leave) their oppressive surroundings (Gen. 16; cf. ch. 21), and Jacob departs from the land of his father-in-law, Haran, to Canaan. Joseph, on the other hand, does not leave the country of his misfortunes. On the contrary, after his elevation from prisoner to vizier, and after the period of the famine, he remains in Egypt instead of returning to the land of Canaan.[26]

In the naming of his sons, Joseph expresses the opinion that he has forgotten his labour and his father's house as soon as the land of his affliction has become a land of good fortune. By so saying, however, it is clear that he has not forgotten about his father's house—might he be willing to forget it?—and that he only consideres his sojourn in Egypt prior to his rise as unfortunate. He interprets the change of his fortunes as the work of God: 'God has made me forget' and 'God has made me fruitful'.

It is clear that in Joseph's perception God played a prominent part during his time in Egypt. This is most obvious in the naming of his sons.[27] The prominence of God also confirms the essential role that Joseph ascribes to God, while interpreting the dreams of the Egyptians—which resulted in his rise to Egypt's second in command.

---

26. This geographical notion is also present in the book of Exodus, where Israel's God gives heed to his people who are in misery (4.31) and takes them out of Egypt; cf. Deut. 16.3 and 26.6-8.

27. In 48.9 Joseph says to his father that God has given him his sons.

Chapter 6

ACCUSATIONS AND REVELATIONS

As soon as the years of the famine have started all the world turns to Egypt to buy grain (41.57). When Jacob learns about this he sends his sons there to get some food as well (42.1-3)—Benjamin is not allowed to accompany them, for Jacob feared that harm might come to him (v. 4). And so the brothers arrive in Egypt and go before Joseph (v. 6). Joseph seems to be taken aback by their arrival, otherwise his rather preposterous charge of their being spies (when all the world is coming to Egypt) is hard to explain.[1] In this chapter I will discuss the brothers' visits to Egypt (chs. 42 and 43–45), as well as Jacob's descent to the south (chs. 46–47).

1. 'Your Servants are 12 Brothers, Sons of One Man'

In 42.6 the brothers arrive in Egypt and bow down (וישתחוו) to the ground before the Egyptian vizier.[2] Joseph appears to have recognized his brothers immediately (v. 7). The narrator continues to say that Joseph 'acted as a stranger to them and spoke to them in a harsh way' (v. 7). After a short dialogue between Joseph and his brothers the narrator once again comments that Joseph recognized his brothers, and adds: 'but they did not recognize him' (v. 8). After this second mentioning of Joseph recognizing his brothers, the narrator also says that Joseph remembered his dreams (v. 9). Apparently the brothers' appearance in Egypt brings back memories of Joseph's dreams (of Gen. 37). This remembering evokes Joseph's

---

1. The accusation does not seem 'wise' at all; contra G. von Rad, 'Josephs-geschichte und ältere Chokma', *Gesammelte Studien zum Alten Testament* (TBü: 8; Munich: Chr. Kaiser Verlag, 3rd edn, 1965), 272-80, who discerns in Joseph the ideal young man of wisdom literature, esp. 274-76; also cf. G.W. Coats, 'The Joseph Story and Ancient Wisdom: A Reappraisal', *CBQ* 35 (1973), 285-97, and M.V. Fox, 'Wisdom in the Joseph Story', *VT* 15 (2001), 26-41.

2. This is not, as shown before, 'the outcome envisioned in Joseph's first dream of ascendancy over the rest of his family' (Ackerman, 'Joseph, Judah, and Jacob', 86).

accusation—'You are spies (מרגלים, piel participle)! You have come to see the weakness of the land' (v. 9).[3] This is the first of two false accusations Joseph makes against his brothers (the second is in Gen. 44 where he charges the brothers, or, more precisely, Benjamin, with having stolen his goblet). Joseph accuses his brothers of spying; the verb underlying the participle is רגל, which in the piel conjugation can both mean 'spy' and 'slander'. The connection between both meanings 'is obvious: slander, like spying, is stealthy and hidden'.[4] Considering the accusation in this way, the reader can detect an allusion to Joseph's former occupation, which the narrator reported in Gen. 37.2: 'and he brought their evil reports (רעה דבתם) to his father'. In his youth he himself was the messenger (or provider?) of slander: he used to be a spy himself. Now, Joseph appears to be accusing his brothers of an act he was not unfamiliar with himself. The recollection of his dreams causes images of the past to return to the surface: the dreams evoke his own spying in his teenage years. And this now enters Joseph's mind as an appropriate accusation. So, on seeing his brothers Joseph remembers his dreams (42.9)—it will not be long before it becomes clear that dreams (and 'spying') are not the only things Joseph begins to remember.

According to 42.7 Joseph spoke to his brothers in a harsh way. By talking to them like this he confirms what he had expressed some time before in the naming of Manasseh: 'God has made me forget all my sufferings and *my father's house*' (41.51). During the first conversation (42.7-16) the Egyptian is rather gruff towards the brothers, while during their second meeting (vv. 18-24) something has changed. Hearing his brothers argue about his younger self 20 years before, Joseph has to turn away and weep (42.24). Yet, during their initial encounter, Joseph's 'forgetting of his fathers' house' is beginning to ebb away already. After the brothers' assertion that they are 12 brothers, sons of one man from the land of Canaan, and that their youngest brother is at home, and the other is gone (cf. 42.13), Joseph demands to see their youngest brother. His wish to see the youngest brother is repeated in 42.20: 'You have to bring back your youngest brother to me'.[5] That Joseph is becoming more and more conscious of

---

3.   Joseph's reference to the weakness (literally 'nakedness') of the land, 'may be a subtle play back to ch. 37, when his brothers stripped him of his cloak and placed him, nude or semi-nude, in a cistern' (Hamilton, *The Book of Genesis: 18–50*, 520).

4.   *NIDOTE*, III, 1047.

5.   It is clear that, because he holds one of the brothers in custody, he is not too sensitive about his father's house, and his father's state of mind (cf. 42.36; 43.14).

the past, to be specific, of his father's house, is even more clearly to be seen during the brothers' second stay in Egypt. On their arrival in his house the first thing Joseph asks is 'How is your father doing?' (הֲשָׁלוֹם אֲבִיכֶם; 43.27), and then, after having met Benjamin, he is off to his own quarters to weep once more (43.30).[6]

Now I will turn my attention to the often-heard notion of Joseph's testing his brothers.[7] In 42.15-16 Joseph twice uses the verb בחן ('test'):[8]

> This is how you shall be tested: as Pharaoh lives, you shall not leave this place unless your youngest brother comes here! Let one of you go and bring your brother, while the rest of you remain in prison, in order that your words may be tested, whether there is truth with you; if not, as Pharaoh lives, surely you are spies.

Following the charge is the brothers' imprisonment for three days. Some scholars interpret the brothers' subsequent conversation in vv. 21-22 as a confession of their deed in Gen. 37.[9] However, as shown in a previous Chapter, these verses (vv. 21-22) mainly express Reuben's self-centeredness—they illustrate (as does 42.37) that he is not fit to be the spokesman of the family. And as for the brothers' reference to Gen. 37: what they refer to is dependent on one's reading of Gen. 37. Did or did not the brothers sell Joseph? If they did, they might be referring to their act of casting Joseph into the pit, as well as to the selling of their brother to the Ishmaelites, in 42.21-22. If, on the other hand, they did not sell their brother, they are only referring to their act of casting Joseph into a pit—of which they may have been reminded by their being cast into prison. However, as I showed in Chapter 4, the brothers did not sell Joseph—even though he may be thinking that his brothers were involved in the sale (as he apparently does in 45.4).

6.   He actually weeps seven times: 42.24; 43.30; 45.1, 14; 46.29; 50.1, 17; cf. Lowenthal, *The Joseph Narrative*, 72, 180.

7.   Turner correctly summarizes: 'By far the commonest suggestion for explaining Joseph's actions is some variation of the following. Joseph's intention is to test his brothers to see whether they have reformed, repented and shown loyalty to Benjamin and Jacob, as preconditions for his forgiveness and his reconciliation with them' (*Announcements of Plot*, 156). Cf. also his refutation of such interpretations (156-59).

8.   The verb occurs 32 times in the Old Testament; there are only two occurrences in the Torah; none in the Former Prophets. In the poetical and prophetical books in most of the places it is God (YHWH) who does the testing, cf. *NIDOTE*, I, 637.

9.   Cf. Humphreys, *Joseph and his Family*, 43: 'Guilty of a crime committed many years past, they find themselves falsely accused of another crime'.

To return to the notion of 'testing': Joseph expresses his intention to 'test' his brothers twice (42.15-16): if they are not able to present their younger brother—as Pharaoh lives (חי פרעה)—they are spies. This implies that the testing is linked to the accusation of spying. When the brothers are released from prison Joseph has modified his plan. 'Do this, and you shall live, I fear God' (v. 18): one of them is to remain in prison, the others are free to go, yet they have to bring Benjamin to have their imprisoned brother released (vv. 19-20). The notion of 'testing' has disappeared, never to return. As has the accusation of being spies. What has returned, however, is something of major importance: Joseph's mentioning of 'God'. To enforce his words Joseph initially said 'as Pharaoh lives' (twice, vv. 15 and 16)—this phrase has now changed into 'I fear God' (את־האלהים אני ירא, 42.18):[10] the meeting with his brothers has definitely brought about some kind of change in Joseph.

Before concluding this section on the brothers' first visit, I would like to draw attention to the following. Even though Joseph did not actually make himself known to his brothers during their first encounter he (perhaps unintentionally) may have given them a hint that might have led them to identify him as their brother, but they did not get the hint.[11] Genesis 42.14 is a rather remarkable verse. Most translations run like this: 'Joseph said to them: "It is just as I told you: you are spies"'. This is rather awkward after the brothers' words in the preceding verse: 'Your servants are 12. We are brothers, sons of the same man in the land of Canaan; the youngest is now with our father, and the other one is gone' (v. 13).[12] In translations like the one just offered Joseph's words in v. 14 appear not to have anything whatsoever to do with the things the brothers said in the preceding verse. The following proposal might be a possible solution. The last words in v. 13 are: והאחד איננו (literally, 'and the other is not'). Immediately after these words, Joseph says (ויאמר): הוא אשר דברתי אלכם לאמר מרגלים אתם אלהם יוסף). Why should the personal pronoun הוא be considered to be

---

10. Or 'I fear gods', as Morris correctly observes. He also expresses his discontent with Joseph's behaviour and the usage of the expression 'as Pharaoh lives'; cf. G. Morris, 'Convention and Character in the Joseph Narrative', *Proceedings of the Eastern Great Lakes and Midwest Bible Societies* 14 (1994), 69-85 (80).

11. Perhaps they could not have picked up the hint, because Gen. 42.23 states that 'there was an intermediary (המליץ) between them'. The conversation between the brothers and Joseph seems to have been bilingual.

12. Both translations are taken from Hamilton, *The Book of Genesis: 18–50*, 518.

referring to something indefinite, whereas it might also be understood as to refer to Joseph himself? Then, Joseph speaking in v. 14 utters something of an anacoluthon: he is about to say something, but he swallows his words before he has said them all, and he continues by saying something else. After the brothers' remark 'the other is not', Joseph replies 'It is he, who…', after which he composes himself, and continues 'I have spoken to you, saying: you are spies'. Joseph might have been about to say 'It is he, who has spoken to you: you are spies', herewith revealing his identity, which he sucessfully avoids doing just in time. Joseph appears to be torn between his emotions (willing to make himself known) and his reason (abstaining from making himself known to his family; something he managed to do during the seven years of plenty).

2. *Judah's Plea and the House of Jacob*

In Chapter 4 I showed that Reuben set himself apart from his brothers. This is clearly to be seen in his speeches in 37.21-22, 29, and 42.22. At the end of Gen. 42 (vv. 37-38)[13] and the beginning of 43 (vv. 2-14) there are two more distinct but related incidents. From these, it appears that Reuben is not as diplomatic as Judah. It is clear that Reuben is not fit to persuade Jacob to allow Benjamin to join the brothers on their second journey to Egypt. Because of his experience of losing two grown-up sons, Judah succeeds in persuading his father and consequently receives Jacob's permission to take Benjamin along.[14] On telling their father that they have to take Benjamin to Egypt, Reuben assures his father 'You may put both of my sons to death if I do not bring him back to you. Entrust him to my

13. As in 37.22, Reuben expresses his intention to return (שוב, hiphil) a younger brother to his father. In Gen. 37 he did not succeed, and here in ch. 42 Jacob does not seem to be too confident about Reuben's good intentions. And rightly so. Cf. Alter, *The Art of Biblical Narrative*, 170-71.

14. See Fokkelman, 'Genesis 37 and 38', 181. Reuben's offer of the lives of his two sons makes Ackerman write: 'The brothers have changed. As the story repeats itself, we must notice the great difference between their attitude toward Jacob's suffering over the report of Joseph's loss with the bloody garment and their description of why Simeon was taken and what they must do with Benjamin. They are now sincere, compassionate for their mourning father, desperate to set things straight' ('Joseph, Judah, and Jacob', 92). There is, however, no support for this in the text. The narrator does not say anything about 'sincerity' or 'compassion for their mourning father'. In fact, the only place where the narrator speaks about the brothers' comforting their mourning father is 37.35!

care, and I will bring him back' (42.37)—which illustrates his blindness (or rather, deafness) to the reason why his father is not willing to send Benjamin. This appears from Jacob's words in the previous verse: 'You have deprived me of my children.[15] Joseph is no more and Simeon is no more, and now you want to take Benjamin. Everything is against me!' (42.36). Reuben appears not to be able to think in terms of limiting the possible deaths in the family.[16] If Benjamin were to die, or at least not to return, the family would be diminished by two more deaths—a thing Jacob most desperately wants to avoid. Judah appears to understand his father's dilemma: he can only offer to take responsibility for his younger brother: 'If I do not bring him back to you and set him here before you, I will bear the blame before you all my life' (43.9).[17] Judah's understanding of his father seems to have grown out of his experiences with his own family, of which Gen. 38 related earlier.[18] In the remainder of this section I will focus upon and examine Judah's speech in Gen. 44 and look at what this speech accomplishes—and why.

On their second journey to Egypt the brothers meet the wishes of the Egyptian vizier and bring Benjamin.[19] After an enjoyable stay, during

15. From these words it seems that Jacob is aware of the things that occured years before in Dothan.

16. Contra Boecker who writes that Reuben 'gegenüber Juda der radikalere ist, der sich entschlossener für den Bruder einsetzt, diesmal für Benjamin' (H.-J. Boecker, 'Überlegungen zur Josephsgeschichte', in J. Hausmann and H.-J. Zobel [eds.], *Alttestamentlicher Glaube und Biblische Theologie: Festschrift für Horst Dietrich Preuss* [Stuttgart: W. Kohlhammer, 1992], 35-45 [43]).

17. Cf. Hamilton, *The Book of Genesis: 18–50*, 536-37, 540-42; Ackerman, 'Joseph, Judah, and Jacob', 99-105. Ackerman (104-105) notes that Israel's unwillingness to let Benjamin go parallels Judah's earlier unwillingness to allow his son Shelah to perform the levirate duty. As in Gen. 38, where Tamar made Judah aware of the importance of taking reponsibility for the family, now Judah convinces his father Israel to let him take Benjamin to Egypt for the sake of the family's future.

18. Cf. A.J. Lambe, 'Judah's Development: The Pattern of Departure–Transition–Departure', *JSOT* 83 (1999), 53-68.

19. Turner has the interesting suggestion that Joseph wants the brothers to bring Benjamin, because he thinks that when they bring Benjamin, his father will come as well—in order to fulfill the second dream: 11 brothers are needed to fulfill the second dream; in addition his father has to come and bow down before him (*Announcements of Plot*, 160-62). Despite the attractiveness of this interpretation I do not think that it is correct. During their initial conversation in Gen. 42 the brothers nowhere describe their father's attachment to their younger brother; Turner's argument that Judah in his

which they are reunited with Simeon who had been held in custody since
42.24, the brothers are falsely accused of having stolen Joseph's goblet,
which is—much to their dismay—found in Benjamin's bag. On this discovery they all rend their clothes and return to Joseph to plead their
innocence. The Egyptian dignitary is not impressed; he keeps his distance
and is about to enslave the thief. To avert this evil thing to happen Judah
takes the floor.

16a	Judah said:	ויאמר יהודה 16a
b	'What can we say to my lord?	מה־נאמר לאדני b
c	How can we speak?	מה־נדבר c
d	And how can we justify ourselves?	ומה־נצטדק d
e	The God has found the misdeed of your servants.	האלהים מצא את־עון עבדיך e
f	Look, we are slaves to my lord,	הננו עבדים אדני f
g	both we and the one in whose hand the goblet was found'	גם־אנחנו גם אשר־נמצא הגביע בידו g
17a	And he said:	ויאמר 17a
b	'It is far from me to do like that,	חלילה לי מעשות זאת b
c	the man in whose hand the cup was found	האיש אשר נמצא הגביע בידו c
d	he shall be my slave,	הוא יהיה־לי עבד d
e	you go up in peace to your father'	ואתם עלו לשלום אל־אביכם e

Before turning to Judah's lengthy speech of vv. 18-34, I will first consider
the above verses. 'What can we say to my lord?', 'how can we justify
ourselves?', Judah wonders. What is happening to the brothers is beyond
their comprehension: 'God has found the misdeed of your servants'. Therefore they will all stay to become the Egyptian's slaves, not just the one in
whose possession the goblet was found. In his speech Judah talks about
'justifying ourselves' (צדק, hithpael, v. 16d), and mentions their 'misdeed'
(עון, v. 16e), which God has found. The root צדק only occurs once more
in Genesis, in ch. 38—also in Judah's direct speech: 'she is in the right,
not I' (38.26), he says about his daughter-in-law. On that occasion he
admitted his fault: he had not allowed Tamar to conceive a child by his

speech (44.22) refers to this initial conversation in which the father's attachment was
stated assumes too much. As I will illustrate, Judah in my opinion ascribes words to
Joseph (and to themselves) to make his point and convince the vizier of his position,
not to literally repeat the former conversation. Based on the brothers' words Joseph
could hardly have arrived at the conclusion that Turner believes he came to.

son Shelah. Now, however, despite his words, he is struck dumb. There is no way to account for what has happened to them. So, God must be involved: God has found their עָוֹן, their misdeed. What this 'misdeed' might be, he does not say (the theft of the goblet?, the slaying of Shechem's people?), and Joseph does not ask. The word עָוֹן is probably a generic term for acting against God or against a human being—it does not indicate a specific transgression.[20]

The fact, however, remains that Joseph only strikes at Benjamin. One might ask: Why does he do so?[21] Is it because of Benjamin's part in the Dothan incident? A cup for a pit, instead of an eye for an eye?[22] The narrator does not give any information on the why of Joseph treating Benjamin this way and perhaps the 'why' is not even relevant.[23] Notwithstanding the tears he shed the day before on seeing Benjamin (43.30), Joseph was still able to control himself and device a nefarious plan to frame his younger brother and separate him from the others (or had he schemed this goblet-business long before?). Despite Judah's words in v. 16—the offer to remain as slaves—Joseph does not concede this point: only the man in whose possession the goblet was found is to be his slave; the others are allowed to return to their father. Joseph's mention of their father incites Judah to his impressive speech.[24] A speech that strikes home as far as Joseph is concerned. Judah is willing to sacrifice his freedom in exchange for Benja-

---

20. Cf. *ThWAT*, V, 1164: 'In der Mehrzahl der Fälle [i.e. in the older historical narratives] bezieht er sich auf das Vergehen von Menschen an Menschen, das seine unabwendbaren schlimmen Folgen für den Täter nach sich zieht'. However, according to Green 'Judah's strategy indicates that he may well think Benjamin guilty' (*'What Profit for Us?'*, 151).

21. This action definitely contradicts C.T. Fritsch's 'He is a God-fearing lad who is morally upright and pure' ('"God was with him": A Theological Study of the Joseph Narrative', *Int* 9 [1955], 21-34).

22. According to Exum, the alleged theft of Joseph's cup by Benjamin may be an allusion to Rachel's actual theft of her father's teraphim: the mother actually did steal, whereas the son is accused of stealing, which he did not (J.C. Exum, *Fragmented Women: Feminist (Sub)versions of Biblical Narratives* [JSOTSup, 163; Sheffield: JSOT Press, 1993], 134-35).

23. Nevertheless, in the next chapter I will propose a possible reason.

24. This, as is contended by Westermann (*Genesis 37–50*, 146), Fokkelman ('Genesis 37 and 38', 181) and Hamilton (*The Book of Genesis: 18–50*, 569: 'The lengthiest human speech recorded in Genesis is that of Judah before Joseph'), is not the longest speech in Genesis. The person speaking the most is, of course, Jacob. His farewell speech in Gen. 49 consists of 268 words, Judah's of 223 only.

min's, for—as will be seen right away—Judah's plea is a plea for the father
—it is Jacob's fortune that is at stake.

18c	Excuse me, my lord, let your servant speak a word in my lord's ears,	בי אדני ידבר־נא עבדך דבר באזני אדני	44, 18c
d	and do not be angry with your servant,	ואל־יחר אפך בעבדך	d
e	because you are equal to Pharao.	כי כמוך כפרעה	e
19a	My lord had asked your servants, saying:	אדני שאל את־עבריו לאמר	19a
b	'Do you have a *father* or a brother?'	היש־לכם אב או־אח	b
20a	And we said to my lord:	ונאמר אל־אדני	20a
b	'We have an old *father*	יש־לנו אב זקן	b
c	and a younger late arrival	וילד זקנים קטן	c
d	and his brother is dead.	ואחיו מת	d
e	He alone is left of his mother	ויותר הוא לבדו לאמו	e
f	and his *father* loves him.'	ואביו אהבו	f
21a	You said to your servants:	ותאמר אל־עבדיך	21a
b	'Bring him down to me,	הורדהו אלי	b
c	so that I can set my eyes on him.'	ואשימה עיני עליו	c
22a	And we said to my lord:	ונאמר אל־אדני	22a
b	'The boy cannot leave his *father*;	לא־יוכל הנער לעזב את־אביו	b
c	would he leave his *father*,	ועזב את־אביו	c
d	he would die'.	ומת	d
23a	And you said to your servants:	ותאמר אל־עבדיך	23a
b	'If your younger brother does not come down with you,	אם־לא ירד אחיכם הקטן אתכם	b
c	you shall not again see my face.'	לא תספון לראות פני	c
24a	And as we went up to your servant, my *father*,	ויהי כי עלינו אל־עבדך אבי	24a
b	we told him my lord's words.	ונגד־לו את דברי אדני	b
25a	Our *father* said:	ויאמר אבינו	25a
b	'Return and buy us something to eat,'	שבו שברו־לנו מעט־אכל	b
26a	we said:	ונאמר	26a
b	'We cannot go down:	לא נוכל לרדת	b
c	only if our younger brother is with us	אם־יש אחינו הקטן אתנו	c
d	can we go down,	וירדנו	d
e	because we cannot see the man's face	כי־לא נוכל לראות פני האיש	e
f	if our younger brother is not with us.'	ואחינו הקטן איננו אתנו	f

27a	And your servant, my *father* said to us:	ויאמר עבדך אבי אלינו	27a
b	'You know	אתם ידעתם	b
c	that my wife bore me two sons.	כי שנים ילדה־לי אשתי	c
28a	One has gone away from me,	ויצא האחד מאתי	28a
b	and I said:	ואמר	b
c	"He surely must have been torn."	אך טרף טרף	c
d	I have not seen him since.	ולא ראיתיו עד־הנה	d
29a	You take also this one away from my face,	ולקחתם גם־את־זה מעם פני	29a
b	and evil befall him	וקרהו אסון	b
c	you will bring down my grey head in sorrow to Sheol.'	והורדתם את־שיבתי ברעה שאלה	c
30a	Now, if I would come to your servant, my *father*	ועתה כבאי אל־עבדך אבי	30a
b	and the boy is not with us—his soul is tied up with his soul–	והנער איננו אתנו ונפשו קשורה בנפשו	b
31a	and he were to see	והיה כראותו	31a
b	that the boy is not there,	כי־אין הנער	b
c	he would die,	ומת	c
d	and your servants would bring the grey hair of your servant, our *father*, grieving to Sheol.	והורידו עבדיך את־שיבת עבדך אבינו ביגון שאלה	d
32a	Also, your servant has pledged himself for the boy before my *father*, saying:	כי עבדך ערב את־הנער מעם אבי לאמר	32a
b	'If I will not bring him to you,	אם־לא אביאנו אליך	b
c	I will have sinned before my *father* all days.'	וחטאתי לאבי כל־הימים	c
33a	Now, please let your servant stay instead of the boy, to be a slave for my lord,	ועתה ישב־נא עבדך תחת הנער עבד לאדני	33a
b	and let the boy go up with his brothers.	והנער יעל עם־אחיו	b
34a	For how can I return to my *father*	כי־איך אעלה אל־אבי	34a
b	if the boy is not with me.	והנער איננו אתי	b
c	Otherwise I will see on the evil thing	פן אראה ברע	c
d	that my *father* will meet.	אשר ימצא את־אבי	d

As did the brothers in the previous dialogues between themselves and the Egyptian, Judah expresses himself politely. He addresses Joseph as 'my lord', and names himself and his brothers as 'your servant' and 'your servants' (or 'your slaves', cf. 50.18).[25] He also calls their father 'your servant'. He probably observes the proper forms. In his plea he refers to their former conversation with Joseph, to their conversation with their father on their return from Egypt, and to the dialogue between the brothers and Jacob on the eve of their second departure for Egypt.

In a stimulating and interesting article O'Brien shows that Judah presents the information in his speech in such a way that his speech very much contributes to the characterization of Joseph, and this is, I think, the way Judah's speech is to be understood.[26] Since readers of Genesis have witnessed all the conversations Judah refers to, it is legitimate to say that Judah is manipulating the facts to change Joseph's decision to keep Benjamin in Egypt as a slave.

Taking Joseph's 'you go up in peace to your father' (44.17) as his point of departure,[27] Judah centres the vizier's attention on 'their father' and on the fact that he has pledged himself to their father, as can be read in 43.9: 'I myself will be surety (ערב) for him'.[28] Interestingly, the noun derived from the verb involved, ערבון ('pledge'), is—like צדק (used in 44.16)— found in Gen. 38 (in vv. 17, 18 and 20). So, here the words used by the narrator (which are quite exceptional in the book of Genesis) suggest a connection between both Judah's performances in ch. 38 and chs. 43–44. In the former, Judah not only tried to observe his pledge (he sent his friend looking for the alleged prostitute and to present her the ערבון, 'pledge'), but he also declared Tamar in the right when she presented him his belongings. Here, too, Judah appears to have learned his lesson from his experiences with Tamar well, and accepts his responsibility.

In his monologue Judah retrospectively inserts 'father' into Joseph's words during their first encounter. In the conversation back then (42.13-16, 20), the brothers themselves stated that they were the sons of one man,

25. The brothers would then become slaves, like the Egyptians became slaves during the famine (47.13-26).

26. Cf. M.A. O'Brien, 'The Contribution of Judah's Speech, Genesis 44.18-34, to the Characterization of Joseph', *CBQ* 59 (1997), 429-47; for a detailed analysis of Judah's reports: 434-43.

27. Judah also takes the word כמו ('equal to', 'like') from Joseph, who used it in 44.15: 'don't you know that a man like me (כמני) would be aware of it?' Joseph in his turn may have derived it from Pharaoh's 'there is no one as sensible and wise as you (כמוך)' (41.39). Pharaoh uses it first to describe Joseph, after which Joseph uses it to describe his ability. Then Judah uses it to compare Joseph to Pharaoh.

28. Cf. G.W. Savran, *Telling and Retelling: Quotation in Biblical Narrative* (Indiana Studies in Biblical Literature; Bloomington: Indiana University Press, 1988), 60.

and that they had a brother whom they had not taken with them (42.13); now Judah states that Joseph asked them whether they had a father and a brother.[29] Also Judah mentions—for the first time—that their father is an old man who loves (אֹהֵב)[30] his youngest son (v. 20).[31]

As is clear from Judah's speech the wellbeing of his father is his main concern;[32] by expressing this concern he plays along with Joseph's interest in his father. According to Savran, 'he cannot have missed Joseph's concern for the wellbeing of their father in 43.27'.[33] Therefore, I have italicized the word 'father' in Judah's speech quoted above, in which it has a predominant position. 'Father' (אָב) occurs no less than 14 times.[34]

In the first part of his speech Judah elaborates both on the fact that the Egyptian vizier insisted on having the younger brother brought down to Egypt (vv. 21, 23 and 26), and on his father's attachment to this younger brother (v. 20): if the boy were to leave his father he would die (vv. 22,[35] 29, 31 and 34). After he has emphasized the close relationships between Jacob and the youngest son, and also after having repeated the urgency of the request to bring Benjamin down to Egypt, Judah presents his father speaking a second time (v. 27—Jacob's first reported words are in verse

29. It is the same strategy he applied in 43.7 when he tried to persuade Israel to let Benjamin join them on their trip to Egypt.

30. Cf. 37.3: 'Israel loved Joseph more than all his sons, because he was a son of his old age to him'. The narrator calls Joseph a בֶן־זְקֻנִים ('a son of his old age'). In 44.20 Judah calls Benjamin a יֶלֶד זְקֻנִים, which I have translated as 'a late arrival' (literally, 'a child of old age'). It should, by the way, be noted that only Judah makes mention of Jacob's attachment to Benjamin, the narrator never does, and—considering Jacob's last words to Benjamin (49.27)—there does not seem to be too much love for his youngest son.

31. It is also the first occasion on which Judah explicitly expresses the idea that Joseph is dead: וְאָחִיו מֵת ('and his brother is dead'). (I take 'his' to refer to the 'late arrival'; it could also refer to Jacob: the brother who is dead would in that case be Esau—a detail about which which Joseph could not have known. When Jacob was born Isaac was 60 years old; he died at the age of 180 years [25.26; 35.28] when Jacob was 120, so after Joseph's sale to Egypt.)

32. See also Humphreys, *Joseph and his Family*, 84.

33. G. Savran, 'The Character as Narrator in Biblical Narrative', *Prooftexts* 5 (1985), 1-17 (7).

34. Cf. Lowenthal, *The Joseph Narrative*, 101.

35. Interestingly, 'he would die' could also be taken to refer to the younger brother. The syntax of v. 22b-d does allow for this interpretation: syntactically it makes sense that the subject in all three clauses is the same.

25[36]): 'You know that my wife bore me two sons. One has gone away from me, and I said: "He surely must have been torn to pieces". I have not seen him since.' Judah quoting Jacob's words is the first time Joseph hears anything of what his father seems to know and think about him. This is some kind of news indeed! Not until now does Joseph hear about his father's concern, and becomes aware of his father's pain about the loss of his favourite son: 'My wife bore two sons to me'. It appears from Judah's words that Jacob considers Rachel's sons as special. However, and there is no mistake about this, he presumes the elder of them to be dead (44.28b).[37]

I briefly return to Judah's quotation of Jacob's 'he must surely have been torn apart' (אַךְ טָרֹף טֹרָף; v. 28b). It is obvious that Judah has modified Jacob's words from 37.33, which were there and then preceded by 'an evil beast has eaten him' (חַיָּה רָעָה אֲכָלָהוּ); words that shortly before Jacob uttered them, were suggested by the brothers to lead their father up the garden path (37.20). Judah also leaves out Joseph's name from his quotation of Jacob's words, and he adds the particle אַךְ ('surely'). However, although Judah does not mention the '*evil* (רָעָה) beast' some influence of these words may still be detected. Following 'he must surely have been torn apart', Judah demonstrates his father's affection for the remaining son[38]—'if tragedy befalls him, you will bring down my white head in *sorrow* (בְּרָעָה) to Sheol' (44.29).[39] In this expression one might see a reference to רַע (from Jacob's lament in 37.33). Another adaptation of Jacob's words by Judah can be seen from the phrase 'if tragedy befalls him' (אָסוֹן וּקְרָהוּ). This is an allusion to 42.38. On that occasion Jacob expressed his worries about Benjamin's trip to Egypt: some accident might befall him 'on the way' (וּקְרָאָהוּ אָסוֹן בַּדֶּרֶךְ). In 44.29 Judah omits 'on the way' because Benjamin has arrived in Egypt as sound as a bell. It is in Egypt that tragedy has come upon him: the goblet of the Egyptian has been found (מָצָא) in Benjamin's bag (44.12)—a tragedy that Judah now tries to remove, because how is he to return to his father if the boy is not with

---

36. This is in fact a literal quotation from 43.2.

37. Joseph being dead might have been the brothers' opinion before they came to Egypt a second time too; see 42.36 where Jacob, as mentioned before, appears to know about the Dothan-incident.

38. This, of course, is another allusion to an expression by Jacob, viz. 37.35. In Gen. 37 Jacob sighs 'I go down to my son, mourning (אָבֵל) to Sheol'. In 42.38 he himself alludes to his former words, altering them in such a way as to demonstrate that it is his sons who might bring him down to Sheol.

39. When Judah repeats this in v. 31 he replaces בְּרָעָה by בְּיָגוֹן ('in grief'), which was used by Jacob in 42.38.

him? He would rather not see the *evil* (בֶרַע) thing that his father would meet (מצא; v. 34).[40]

In this clever speech Judah makes two essential points. First, he enlightens Joseph about the latter's ignorance about his father, and also about his fathers' ignorance regarding Joseph's fate. In this respect I very much agree with O'Brien who writes that 'Judah's subsequent reports, predictions, and interpretations unwittingly trap Joseph in a web of uncertainty about the fate of his father'.[41] And, second, Judah stresses Jacob's feelings towards both Joseph and Benjamin: if Benjamin were not to return the father would die. Judah's words strike a chord.[42] It does not take long before Joseph cannot restrain himself, sends away his servants, and finally reveals his identity to his brothers (Gen. 45).[43]

During the conversations with Joseph, Judah and the brothers have had several indications that may have given them cause to discover the Egyptian's true identity. I will mention these indications one-by-one.

40. So, Ackerman's 'The brothers have come in the course of the story to choose unity over separation' ('Joseph, Judah and Jacob', 98) cannot be correct: if Judah (or any other) takes Benjamin's place, there still would be separation: both from the remaining brothers, and from their father.

41. O'Brien, 'The Contribution of Judah's Speech', 447. Cf. Savran: 'The true beauty of Judah's remarks lies in his ability to affirm explicitly his own responsibility, while effectively "blaming" Joseph for his father's anticipated death' ('The Character as Narrator', 8; cf. Savran, *Telling and Retelling*, 61-62, 87).

42. Joseph neither enslaves Benjamin nor Judah. To compensate for this he seems to enslave all Egyptian citizens, the priests excepted (47.18-22); the actions recounted in 47.13-22 might take place in the second year of the famine (47.18)—just as the second meeting with the brothers does. Wildavsky devotes a section to the question 'Did the Egyptians Enslave the Hebrews because Joseph Enslaved the Egyptians?' (*Assimilation versus Separation*, 13-15). Also cf. Caine: 'the action of Joseph is construed as the cause of the enslavement of the Hebrews. Since Joseph had, in effect, sold the Egyptians while protecting his family, it is poetic justice that his family's seed should have been sold, in effect, into slavery. He who had himself been sold, then sold others, had his people sold. On a smaller scale, the person who strove mightily to be remembered (40.14) was forgotten (40.23 and Exod. 1.8)' ('Numbers in the Joseph Narrative', 11). On Joseph enslaving the Egyptians also B. Dov Lerner, 'Joseph the Unrighteous', *Judaism* 38 (1989), 278-81. A more positive reading of Joseph's actions in 47.13-27 is to be read in Bae, *A Multiple Approach to the Joseph Story*, esp. 41-73.

43. Judah's speech 'transforms the harsh ruler Joseph into the emotional brother Joseph' (T.L. Hettema, *Reading for Good. Narrative Theology and Ethics in the Joseph Story from the Perspective of Ricoeur's Hermeneutics* [Kampen: Kok, 1996], 200), I would rather say 'the emotional *son* Joseph'.

First, during their second Egyptian stay there were two occasions on which the brothers—much to their amazement—were treated according to their age (43.33; 44.12). This certainly is peculiar when meeting a stranger. A second important point in this regard is the Egyptian's insistence during their first trip on bringing their younger brother (42.15, 16 and 20). Why would the Egyptian have wanted to see the youngest anyway? Bringing their brother certainly does not refute the accusation of spying. Besides, no one could ever prove that the one the brothers would bring *really* was their brother, unless, of course... Therefore, the request to see the younger brother more or less implied that the Egyptian was indeed able to judge whether the person brought before him was or was not this alleged younger brother.

Furthermore, and Judah and his brothers could hardly have failed to notice this, there is the obvious interest of the Egyptian—and this is notable as well—in their father's wellbeing: it is the first thing he asks when he speaks to them during their second stay (43.27);[44] he does so even before inquiring after Benjamin (v. 29). When he has seen Benjamin, and this is another indication, the Egyptian says 'My son, may God be gracious to you'. This also must strike Judah (and his brothers) as rather odd—not to mention the occasions on which the Egyptian ran from one room to another to shed some tears (42.24; 43.30). A fifth clue refers to Gen. 37, where the brothers saw a caravan passing that was heading towards Egypt (37.25); after seeing the caravan Judah suggested the sale of Joseph—whether or not the brothers sold him, the inevitable conclusion for them to make is that their brother was taken down to Egypt. So, the brothers know where their brother (if he were still alive) ought to be found. Well, if Judah (and the brothers) did have some suspicions about the Egyptian (that he might be Joseph) it is no longer surprising that he very much emphasized the suffering of his father in his speech. He knew that Jacob loved Joseph very much, because he was a בן־זקנים to him, a 'son of his old age' (37.3)—would that not also be the reason why Judah called Benjamin a ילד זקנים, literally, 'a youth of his old age'? Judah's having some possible suspicions might explain why he played upon the Egyptian's state of mind by emphasizing Jacob's feelings for Benjamin *and* Joseph, and by letting the Egyptian know that his father thought Joseph to be dead.

44. Cf. Savran, *Telling and Retelling*, 60.

3. *The Brothers and Joseph*

As has become clear from the above analysis, it is hardly legitimate to say that Joseph is about to reveal himself because he notes that his brothers have changed.[45] A first and rather obvious reason is that it is only Judah who is talking to Joseph: even if Judah had changed, this hardly says anything about the brothers.[46] Just as Reuben's proposal to Jacob (42.37) did not imply that the other brothers were also willing to sacrifice two of their sons, Judah's speech likewise does not imply that the others approve of his speech or that they think the way he does. A second reason is that the manner in which, and the motives why Judah argues with Joseph need not indicate a change on Judah's part; he has simply pledged himself to his father (43.9). As he tried to meet his commitments in Gen. 38 towards the alleged prostitute (vv. 17-18, 20 and 23), Judah now tries to live up to his promise to his father, which is protecting Benjamin. He is an outstanding example of the expression 'an honest man's word is as good as his bond'. Yet, with the passing of the chapters, the narrator does present Judah as having undergone a gradual transformation.[47] From his attempt to get rid of Joseph (ch. 37) via his lesson to take responsibility for his family (ch. 38) he arrives at his speech in ch. 44, in which he cleverly manoeuvres Joseph from the position of a harsh Egyptian ruler to someone who shows compassion for an old man who is about to be bereaved of his second son. And it is not until this change provoked by Judah that Joseph can once more become a brother among his brothers.[48]

45. Like Westermann, *Genesis 37–50*, 150-51, or White, *Narration and Discourse*, 260: 'The basis of the reunion of Joseph must thus be his reconciliation with the brothers. But this can only take place authentically if the brothers themselves also now undergo a transformation, as both Jacob and Joseph have done in the preceding narrative'; White also stresses the importance of change on Joseph's part, e.g., his weeping during the reunion with Benjamin (43.23) 'marks another step in the breakdown of his resistance to reconciliation' (264).

46. Cf. Coats, *From Canaan to Egypt*, 43: 'Judah does not offer himself in the place of Benjamin because of a basic character trait. To the contrary, the reasons for his offer arise from the exigencies of his surrounding circumstances'; see also p. 84: 'He had no real choice. One wonders, had the circumstances been different, whether Judah could have committed himself to that kind of future'. Disagreeing with Coats is White, *Narration and Discourse*, 266-67.

47. Cf. Sternberg, 'Time and Space in Biblical (Hi)story Telling', 131.

48. According to R.L. Cohn the 'development of Genesis characters reaches its climax in Joseph' ('Narrative Structure and Canonical Perspective in Genesis', *JSOT*

The authoritarian Egyptian vizier who for quite some time managed to keep his distance from his addressees, is by Judah's speech turned into a vulnerable human being who is no longer able to restrain himself.[49] During the previous meetings with his brothers Joseph now and then had to turn away and weep. The weeping indicates a gradual change towards his brothers, or perhaps better: towards his father's house.[50] Finally, Judah's account about their father was more than he could bear. Contrary to 43.31, where he 'refrained' (אפק) himself, in 45.1-3

> Joseph could no longer control (אפק) himself before all those who stood by him, and he cried out: 'Send everyone away from me'. So no one stayed with him when Joseph made himself known to his brothers. And he wept so loudly that the Egyptians heard it, and the household of Pharaoh heard it. Joseph said to his brothers, 'I am Joseph. Is my father still alive?' But his brothers could not answer him, so dismayed were they at his presence.

With regard to the latter part of the last verse cited, O'Brien makes the rather interesting and provoking suggestion that 'Joseph's self-disclosure is normally given as the reason for the brothers' silence and dismay, but could it not be their realization of what Joseph has done to their father that reduces them to stunned silence?'[51]

Joseph's words are revealing: 'I am Joseph. Is my father still alive?' These words indicate that Joseph does not think the brothers have changed: they may have fooled him all along. On their arrival in his house,

25 [1983], 3-16 [13]). I consider this only partially correct. Quite the contrary is expressed by Thompson: 'Genesis 37–50 does not seem to concentrate on the personality of Joseph, nor can his personality be said to "develop". In the tradition as a whole he is seen neither as ideal nor as good' ('The Joseph and Moses Narratives', 178). Both Cohn's and Thompson's remarks do hit the mark, yet not completely. Joseph does indeed show some substantial development; however, one might wonder whether the portrayal of one of the characters of Genesis reaches its climax in Judah.

49. According to Fung, Judah's willingness to become Joseph's slave to save his father's life, triggers Joseph's response in 45.4-11 in which he presents his past experiences in terms of 'divine providence': 'Reflecting on Judah's act of sacrifice, he concludes that God providentially has allowed him to be sold (or "sent" in his new understanding) into slavery in order to save many lives' (*Victim and Victimizer*, 75; see his entire second chapter: 'Joseph's Claim of Divine Domination', 56-100). It is only through Judah that Joseph perceives himself to be God's instrument.

50. Contrary to Ackerman: 'The descriptions of Joseph's weeping indicate a gradual change in his attitude toward his brothers as he perceives that they have changed' ('Joseph, Judah, and Jacob', 95). In one respect I agree with Ackerman: Joseph's perception is of primary importance.

51. O'Brien, 'The Contribution of Judah's Speech', 445.

when Joseph asked them 'how is your father?', the brothers answered that their father was doing well (43.27-28). Now he asks them the same question, the possessive pronoun changed from 'your' to 'my'—he does not say 'our'. All he can think of in these circumstances (and which is perfectly understandable) is himself: *I am* Joseph, is *my* father still alive? His words, however, may be an illustration of the doubts he still has toward his brothers.

Turner suggests 'that the characterization of Joseph is a subtle one. He is presented neither as a complete villain nor complete saint, but like most humans has elements of each.'[52] Joseph has indeed retained genuine love for his family, but during his Egyptian years he has suppressed his feelings for his family—as has become manifest in the naming of his firstborn. He is subject to an internal conflict: he is torn between the love for his family and the life he has led so far at the royal court, without his father and his brothers. Now he has a family of his own: a wife, two sons and Pharaoh (to whom he has become a father, 45.8). From the moment his brothers appear before his eyes, his emotions begin to become unwound (as seen by his weeping)—his spirit, however, does not want to give in.[53] Little by little the family ties get the better of him, and when Joseph finally hears about his father's suffering, his feelings gain the upper hand. As stated before, from now on he can no longer refrain from avoiding his family.

After Joseph has made himself known to his brothers, he continues:

> And now do not be distressed, or angry with yourselves, because you sold me here; for God sent me before you to preserve life. For the famine has been in the land these two years; and there are five more years in which there will be neither plowing nor harvest. God sent me before you to preserve for you a remnant on earth, and to keep alive for you many survivors. So it was not you who sent me here, but God; he has made me a father to Pharaoh, and lord of all his house and ruler over all the land of Egypt (45.5-8).

Thus, in his speech he expresses his belief that everything that has happened to him was intended by God. It was God who turned one thing into another. In 50.20 he explicitly repeats this opinion: 'Even though you intended to do harm to me, God intended it for good, in order to preserve a numerous people, as he is doing today'. There appear to be no hard feelings toward his brothers on Joseph's part.[54]

52. Turner, *Announcements of Plot*, 163-64.
53. The incident with the goblet is illustrative: yet another attempt to keep them from leaving.
54. There is, however, no forgiveness as can be seen from 50.17 where the brothers

However, despite Joseph's words to his brothers in Gen. 45, some difficulties still remain. Fung points to the contradictions that will arise if one
takes all of Joseph's claims of God's interference into consideration. For
example, 'If God has made him forget his father's house as he claims, how
could he later lay claim to the opposite idea that God has used him to keep
alive his father's house?'[55] And also, how can Joseph's statement that God
is going to bring about the famine (41.25, 28, 32) coexist with 'God sent
me before you to preserve for you a remnant on earth, and to keep alive
for you many survivors' (45.8). Does God bring about destruction to keep
alive many survivors?[56]

In this context I would also like to draw attention to the circumstance
that it is only Joseph who weeps at the reunion (45.2, 14, 15; cf. also 46.29);
the only one of the brothers who apparently sheds some tears is Benjamin
(45.14). This contrasts with Gen. 33, where Esau and Jacob meet again
after 20 years: 'and Esau ran to meet him, and embraced him, and fell on
his neck and kissed him, and they wept' (33.4). In Gen. 45 Joseph (and
Benjamin) are the only ones who appear to be glad—the brothers were
stunned (45.3; cf. the remark by O'Brien quoted above). The question
remains moot whether one can speak about a reconciliation on the
brothers' part. In 45.15 the narrator states that Joseph kissed his brothers
and wept about them, 'and after that his brothers spoke to him' (ואחרי כן
דברו אחיו אתו). This verse is often seen as a transformation of 37.4: 'and
his brothers could not speak to him peaceably' (ולא יכלו דברו לשלם),
after which everything is going to turn out well. However, one should note
that 37.4 does not say that the brothers are not speaking with Joseph, for
they did after all talk to him in 37.8! Neither does 45.15 state that the brothers spoke to Joseph 'in peace' (לשלם). It is by no means certain that the
brothers did trust Joseph, despite Joseph's reassuring words in 45.5-11.
Their distrust becomes manifest further on in 50.15-17, where his brothers
explicitly express their fear.[57] It is highly unlikely, then, that one can

twice ask to be forgiven. In his reply Joseph does not forgive: 'do not fear, am I in the
place of God?' (50.18). Also he keeps talking about his brother's 'evil' against him in
50.20. Cf. W. Brueggemann, 'Genesis L 15-21: A Theological Exploration', in J.A.
Emerton (ed.), *Congress Volume Salamanca 1983* (VTSup, 36; Leiden: E.J. Brill,
1985), 40-53 (46-47).

55. Fung, *Victim and Victimizer*, 108.
56. Fung, *Victim and Victimizer*, 109.
57. This, actually, is the very first time the brothers' words to Joseph after his reve-
lation are mentioned. Joseph, on the other hand, addresses his brothers several times;
apart from 45.1-13 he does so in 45.24; 46.31-34; 50.19-21, 24-25.

discern a profound change of attitude on the brothers' part from ch. 37 to the reunion in ch. 45. In ch. 37 they were envious of Joseph because they feared the reversal of positions he dreamed about (at least, that is how they interpreted his dream), and in 43.18-23 (cf. 42.35) they were still afraid, and so they remain until the end of Genesis.[58] The only one who actually did change is Judah—and this is particularly illustrated in ch. 38, an episode Joseph knows nothing about.[59]

A further clue for the brothers' distrust of Joseph is found in ch. 46. On the occasion of their entering into Egypt, Joseph orders his brothers to reply to Pharaoh's question 'what is your occupation?' in a certain manner: 'You shall say: "Your servants have been keepers of livestock (מקנה אנשׁי) from our youth even until now, both we and our ancestors"—in order that you may settle in the land of Goshen, because all shepherds (צאן כל־רעה) are abhorrent to the Egyptians' (46.34). And what do the brothers actually reply when they meet Pharaoh? Almost the reverse of what Joseph told them to say.

> Pharaoh said to his brothers: 'What is your occupation?' And they said to Pharaoh: 'Your servants are shepherds (רעה צאן), both we and our ancestors'. And they said to Pharaoh: 'We have come to reside as aliens in the land; for there is no pasture for your servants' flocks (מרעה לצאן) because the famine is severe in the land of Canaan. Now, we ask you, let your servants settle in the land of Goshen' (47.3-4).

So, Joseph asked his brothers to say that they were 'keepers of livestock', a general description of their occupation. Joseph's question implied that they ought not to mention their being shepherds—this piece of information Joseph intended to convey to Pharaoh himself (46.32), probably because of the latter part of 46.34: 'because all shepherds are abhorrent to the Egyptians'.[60] That the brothers' mentioning of their being shepherds was a

---

58. 'With astonishing pointedness the great story ends where it began. So much has happened—and nothing has happened! The sheaves are bowing to Joseph, the stars are saluting him. But he and his brothers still stand apart, mistrust between them; old men, terrified, lying in the dust before the fortunate one, himself no longer young' (M. Samuel, 'Joseph—the Brilliant Failure', *BR* 2 [1986] 38-51 continued on p. 68).

59. I am in agreement with Fokkelman, according to whom Judah—by his growth —'has become the most important brother' ('Genesis 37 and 38', 181).

60. According to Hamilton (*The Book of Genesis: 18–50*, 603) there 'is slim, if any, indication in Egyptian literature that Egyptians held shepherds in contempt, unless one sees here a popular understanding (Manetho, Josephus) of the term *hyksos* (invaders from Asia in the 17th century B.C. who ruled over Egypt for approximately a century, with their capital at Avaris in the Delta), later held in contempt by Egyptians as

problematic statement is perhaps illustrated by the fact that Pharaoh did not respond to them (47.3). This might be the reason why there is a second introduction of the brothers' talking to Pharaoh (v. 4): after a few discomforting moments of silence the brothers speak to Pharaoh once more, after which Pharaoh ignores the brothers and directs his attention to Joseph (v. 5) and tells him that his father and brothers are allowed to settle in Egypt (v. 7).

4. *What About Joseph?*

So far it is clear that in Joseph's opinion God's hand can be discerned in the things that happened to him prior to and following his release from prison. This is obvious in the naming of his sons. In his revelatory speech to his brothers, Joseph appears to have elaborated upon the opinion about God making him forget his father's house and hardship, and making him fruitful. In 45.5-11 he seemed to interpret his trials and tribulations as being transformed by God into something positive, into something good. Apart from this, there is yet another thread present in Gen. 37–50, in which the divine plays a prominent part.

Above, when discussing Joseph's interpretation of the dreams in Gen. 40 and 41, it was clear that Joseph made several claims in which he referred to God: 'do not interpretations of dreams belong to God?' (40.8), he said to the cupbearer. After this disclaimer it was Joseph who presented an interpretation of the dreams. The claim appears to have been accepted by those with whom Joseph was dealing—as was most clearly expressed in Pharaoh's 'Can we find a man like this, one in whom is the spirit of God?' (41.38) and 'after God has made all this known to you, there is no one as discerning and wise as you' (v. 39).[61] Yet, there are some more episodes in which Joseph appears to venture into the realm of the divine.

"shepherd kings"'. Also cf. B. Halpern, 'The Exodus from Egypt: Myth or Reality', in H. Shanks (ed.), *The Rise of Ancient Israel* (Washington, DC: Biblical Archeological Society, 1992), 86-113 (92-99). Unfortunately M. Görg in his monograph *Die Beziehungen zwischen dem alten Israel und Ägypten von den Anfängen bis zum Exil* (Erträge der Forschung, 290; Darmstadt: Wissenschaftliche Buchgesellschaft, 1997), does neither give any information on this question, nor why the Egyptians' abhor to eat with Hebrews (43.32).

61. If one were to read these verses in combination with Joseph's התחת אלהים אני ('Am I in the place of God?', 50.19), one could hardly expect another answer but 'Yes'. Brueggemann ('Genesis L 15-21', 47) also mentions the option to read an affirmative

When the brothers, on returning from their first Egyptian journey, stay at an inn and one of them discovers the money in his sack, they all loose heart and start trembling, saying: 'What is this that God has done to us?' (42.28).[62] On their homecoming the others empty their sacks as well, and they also find the money in their bags, 'and they were afraid (וייראו)' (42.35). Although Joseph has put the money in their bag, the brothers are of the opinion that it was done by God. Their view is confirmed during their second journey. One of the Egyptian servants expresses the same view.[63] After Joseph has invited the brothers to join him in his house, the brothers go there together with Joseph's servant and tell him about the money in their bags. Joseph answers: 'Rest assured, do not be afraid (אל־תיראו); your God and the God of your father must have put treasure in your sacks for you; I received your money' (43.23).

The next episode in which the divine is present is the one in which the brothers are accused of stealing Joseph's goblet. After their arrest, Joseph asks his brothers: 'What is this deed that you have done? Do you not know that a man like me practices divination (נחש)?' (44.15). For this divination Joseph uses his goblet (גביע), as can be seen by his servant's words: 'Is this not the one from which my lord drinks? He practices divination (נחש) in it' (44.5). The verb נחש (piel) means 'seek or give an omen, practice divination' ('Vorzeichen suchen und geben, wahrsagen').[64] This practice of divination was widespread in the ancient Near East.

> Mantic/divination attempted to tell the future or bring to light hidden knowledge through various means, including the interpretation of signs or omens, communication with the dead, or the use of magical powers. The

to Joseph's question: 'all through the narrative the brothers perceive him as acting as though he were God, or as though he thought he was God'.

62. On this passage Wildavsky comments: 'We as readers know that it is Joseph who has done this to them, not the God of their fathers. Joseph is acting like a god. Joseph has now done more than just become an Egyptian. As a high-ranking Egyptian official, he has assumed, on his own, the position of God, which the brothers acknowledge verbally, if unknowingly' (*Assimilation versus Separation*, 116 n. 18).

63. There is no textual support for Hamilton's 'We know from this verse that Joseph has already informed his steward about his brothers and the restored money. Probably it was this same steward to whom Joseph gave the order in the first place to replace the money in the brothers' grain bags' (*The Book of Genesis: 18–50*, 550). Not until 44.1 is the steward involved in putting back the money (and the goblet).

64. *NIDOTE*, III, 84; *ThWAT*, V, 385. It occurs 11 times in the Hebrew Bible (Gen. 30.27; 44.5 (twice), 15 (twice); Lev. 19.26; Deut. 18.10; 1 Kgs. 20.33; 2 Kgs. 17.17; 21.6; 2 Chron. 33.6).

latter shows that divination was not completely distinct from magic; this is shown in the Old Testament in passages where magic is spoken of along with mantic, indicating the interrelatedness of both practices (Exod 7.11; Lev 19.26; Deut 18.10-14; 2 Kgs 21.6).[65]

For his divination Joseph made use of a cup, or goblet:

> The technique of divining by means of a goblet is well known from the ancient world. The practice took various forms, including the employment of water, oil, or wine. The practitioner professed to be able to interpret either the surface patterns formed when a few drops of one liquid were poured onto another or the movement of small objects floating on or sinking in a fluid. The aim of the exercise was to determine the future, locate the source of trouble or apportion blame or credit.[66]

With regard to Joseph's usage of the goblet to practice divination, two more things have to be mentioned here. First, the connection between the goblet and the divine (apart from the verb נחשׁ) also appears from the few occurrences of the word 'goblet' (גביע) in the Hebrew Bible. It is found in Exod. 25.31-34 and 37.17-20, where it is said to become part of the lamp-stand in the Sanctuary. It also occurs in Jer. 35.5, where 'goblets' (to drink wine from) are found in the rooms of the house of YHWH (35.2).

Second, in Joseph's youth, when he and the entire family were about to leave for Bethel (Gen. 35.1-4) all of them were instructed by Jacob to get rid of the foreign gods they were carrying with them; after which Jacob buried them under the oak at Shechem (cf. 37.14, where Joseph is found by 'a man' in Shechem, and possibly also 48.22, where Joseph receives a piece of land as an inheritance from his father). According to Lev. 19.26 and Deut. 18.10 the sons of Israel are not allowed to practice divination (נחשׁ, cf. 2 Kgs. 17.17; 21.6; 2 Chron. 33.6).[67] Joseph's use of the divining

65. *NIDOTE*, III, 945.

66. *NIDOTE*, I, 800, s.v. גביע; cf. Hamilton, *The Book of Genesis: 18–50*, 559.

67. *NIDOTE*, I, 800 naively comments: 'Although augury or interpreting omens was subsequently strictly forbidden as a pagan custom (Lev 19.26; Deut 18.10) no law on divination was as yet promulgated in Joseph's day. Did the narrator of Gen 44 consider the custom harmless and consonant with faith in Yahweh?', not realizing that the narrator in Gen. 37–50 never explicitly approves or disapproves of something. And with regard to the law not yet in existence: what to say about Joseph's 'How then could I do such a wicked thing and sin against God' in Gen. 39.9? There was no law about sleeping with someone else's wife yet either. So what does one have to conclude from the non-existence of a law that Joseph seems to refer to in 39.9? That there was no such law, or that Joseph expressed a public opinion?

cup, then, may be another indication that he has forgotten his father's house during the years spent in Egypt (cf. 41.52).[68]

From this perspective of Joseph and the divine, the brothers' designation of Joseph as בעל החלמות ('lord of the dreams', 37.19) also receives a new meaning: he is not only the one who tells the dreams, but he is also the one who plays the part of God or a god in his own dreams[69]—the one for whom people bow down.[70] And later on, in Gen. 40 and 41, he is once again 'the lord of the dreams' because he is the interpreter of the dreams—and according to Joseph's own words 'interpretations belong לאלהים, to God [or "to gods"]' (40.8).[71]

Quite a few elements in the story of Jacob's sons add up and contribute to a portrayal of Joseph in which the divine not only plays an important role, but in which Joseph—now and then—presents himself as having divine knowledge, or in which he seems to absorb characteristics that are reserved and restricted to God or gods.

68. Hamilton, *The Book of Genesis: 18–50*, 557 n. 10: 'Wanting to dissociate Joseph from any participation in forbidden religious activity, Targ. Onqelos freely rendered this part of the verse [44.5, RP]: "and he, moreover, carefully tests with it' (*whw'bdq 'mbdyq byh*)" '. The same fear of attributing something like this practice of divination to Joseph can be discerned in Sarna's 'It is not stated that Joseph actually believes in divination. He wants the brothers to think he does' (*Genesis*, 304).

69. Apart from the book of Genesis the verb חוה occurs 22 times in the Torah. In 20 occurrences it is used to express the bowing down before either God or (the angel of) YHWH or other gods and related elements: Before God or (the angel of) YHWH: Exod. 4.31; 12.27; 24.1; 33.10; 34.8; Num. 22.31; Deut. 26.10. Before other gods, carved images or the sun and the moon: Exod. 20.5; 23.24; 32.8 (the golden calf); 34.14; Lev. 26.1; Num. 25.2; Deut. 4.19; 5.9; 8.19; 11.16; 17.3; 29.25; 30.17. In Exod. 11.8 Moses addresses the Egyptians and says that they will come and bow down before him (which they never do), whereas in 18.7 Moses bows down before his father-in-law Jethro, who is a Midian priest. For texts outside the Torah where people bow down (חוה) before God or idols, cf. Josh. 23.7, 16; Judg. 2.12; 17.19; 1 Sam. 1.28; 2 Sam. 12.20; 1 Kgs. 9.9; 16.31; 22.54; 2 Kgs. 17.35, 36; 21.3, 21.

70. In the Hebrew Bible as well as in non-biblical texts, the common Semitic noun בעל also refers to the Canaanite deity Baal. In texts found at Ras Shamra (1350 BC) it is told—among other things—that Baal 'obtained royal rule and reigns as a king (KTU 1.2 iv.32; 1.4 vii.49-50)' (K. van der Toorn, B. Becking and P.W. van der Horst [eds.], *Dictionary of Deities and Demons in the Bible* [Leiden: E.J. Brill, 1995], 249-63 [254]). According to Hos. 2.18 בעל at one time was used to designate YHWH (257). Also cf. *NIDOTE*, V, 422-28.

71. The same notion may be present in Joseph's '[God] has made me a father to Pharaoh' (45.8)—for who in Egyptian religion is Pharaoh's father?

5. *Israel to Egypt*

It has been noticed by many that in Gen. 37–50 the narrator presents God speaking to someone only once, 46.2-4, when he addresses Jacob in a night-time vision. It has been noticed also that, contrary to the stories about Abraham, Isaac and Jacob, God is hardly ever present in Gen. 37–50. Only when Joseph is a servant (both in Potiphar's house and in prison) does the narrator mention YHWH (39.2, 3 [twice], 5 [twice], 21, 23 [twice]) –yet also in Gen. 38 does one come across YHWH (vv. 7 [twice], 10)—the final and twelfth occurrence of the divine name in the story of Gen. 37–50 is in Jacob's words, in his farewell speech (49.18).

After the brothers returned home from Egypt,[72] laden with presents and food and communicated Pharaoh's message to their father (45.17-20), Jacob departs for Egypt. On his way he passes Beer-sheba (46.1),[73] a place met several times before in Genesis. Once upon a time Abraham had journeyed there (he then planted a tamarisk-tree and called the name of YHWH the everlasting God, 21.33) and lived there (22.19). Isaac lived there as well: he built an altar and called the name of YHWH after YHWH had appeared to him (26.23-33). In the period that Israel's name was still Jacob, he also used to live in Beer-sheba—before his flight to Haran (28.10). Now, on the eve of his departure for Egypt he returns to the old family dwelling. In the course of the night God speaks to him in visions—at the same spot as when he spoke to Isaac (26.24). God's words to Israel resemble those he directed to Isaac: God identifies himself,[74] he tells his addressee not to be afraid and promises to be with him. Although God has given him his new name, 'Israel', twice, he still addresses Jacob by his old name,

> Jacob, Jacob…I am the God, the God of your father; do not be afraid to go down to Egypt, for I will make of you a great nation there. I myself will go down with you to Egypt, and I will also bring you up again; and Joseph's own hand shall close your eyes (46.2-4).

72. Although they should not be too excited (רגז) during their journey, Joseph warns them (45.24). Strangely enough several translations have 'quarrel' for רגז: 'In an unusual instance, Joseph uses this term when ordering his brothers not to argue or quarrel while travelling home' (*NIDOTE*, III, 1045-46); I can see no reason for translating 'quarrelling' or regarding this an 'unusual instance'.

73. ויסע ישראל ('And Israel set out') occurs both in 35.21 (immediately after Rachel's death) and 46.1.

74. In 26.24 he says: 'I am the God of Abraham'; in 46.3 it is: 'I am the God, the God of your father'.

In God's words to Israel[75] one can not only detect several similarities with God's earlier promise to Isaac in Beer-sheba (26.24), but also observe that it is a slightly revised version of earlier promises, both to Isaac and to Jacob (in Bethel; 35.11-12). For example, in 26.24 God stated that he was going to bless Isaac and make his offspring numerous for Abraham's sake —an element which is not present in Gen. 46. There are also some differences to be noted between this and God's appearance to Jacob (35.9-12). God orders Jacob to be fruitful and multiply, which is followed by the promise that a nation and a host of nations are to come from Israel, and also that kings will come forth from Israel (35.11). Now, in 46.3, God modifies his promise and concentrates on a situation that is imminent: 'I will make you a great nation *there*'. So, God has apparently adapted his prior promise to the recently arisen fact that Joseph has sent for his family to face the famine in Egypt.[76]

The astonishing thing about God's promise is that although Jacob will become a great nation (as appears from Exod. 1; cf. Gen. 15.13), God will never bring Jacob up again, even though he said so in 46.4 (which seems to be a repetition of his words to Jacob in Bethel: 'Know that I am with you and will keep you wherever you go, and will bring you back to this land; for I will not leave you until I have done what I have promised you', 28.15). He does bring up the sons of Israel, but in his words God addressed the patriarch as 'Jacob', not as 'Israel'. Or could the episode told in 50.7-14, where Joseph and his brothers bury their father in Machpelah, refer to God bringing Jacob back to Canaan?

God reassures Jacob to continue his way to Egypt, where the family arrive (46.28) and meet Joseph (v. 29). Gen. 46.8-27 presents a long list of Israel's descendants who are entering into Egypt. The members of this group are 70 souls (as 46.27 states, or 66 according to 46.26),[77] the foundation of the great nation which God is going to establish.

75. The last time God was speaking was 35.10-12, when Jacob for the second time received his name Israel.

76. Which could be understood to be in agreement with God's words to Abraham in 15.13-16.

77. The difference can be explained by adding 4 (Jacob, Joseph, Manasseh and Ephraim) to 66 (composed of Leah's 32 children and grandchildren; Zilpah's 16 children and grandchildren; Rachel's second son and 11 grandchildren; Bilhah's 7 children and grandchildren). Cf. Hamilton, *The Book of Genesis: 18–50*, 598.

Chapter 7

MANY FAREWELLS

After the reunion with his former favourite, Jacob spent another 17 years in Egypt, in the region of Goshen. His family did very well and they gained many possessions and were rather fruitful; they increased exceedingly (47.28-29). At the age of 147 Jacob finally died, surrounded by his sons (49.33). Before this departure there are two chapters from which it becomes clear that Jacob, despite his old age, is the one who takes decisions for the future of Israel.

1. *Jacob, Joseph, and Manasseh and Ephraim*

In Gen. 48, when Jacob is ill, Joseph goes to visit his father and takes Manasseh and Ephraim with him. During this visit Jacob adopts both of Joseph's sons: 'Now then, your two sons born to you in Egypt before I came to you here will be reckoned as mine; Ephraim and Manasseh will be mine, just as Reuben and Simeon are mine' (48.5 [NIV]).[1] He continues by saying to Joseph that 'progeny you father after them belong to you. By their brothers' name their heritage shall be recorded' (48.6).[2] The implication of these words is that if Joseph begets any more children (which according to Genesis he does not) these children will not be Jacob's but Joseph's. Their name, however, will be among the descendants of Manasseh and Ephraim. Manasseh and Ephraim have become Jacob's sons—they are no longer Joseph's, as is confirmed by Israel's words in 48.16: '(the Angel who has delivered me from all harm—may he bless these boys.) May they be called by *my* name and the names of *my* fathers Abraham and Isaac, and may they increase greatly upon the earth.'[3] Biologically Manasseh and

1. Apart from the children of Judah's unnamed Canaanite wife it is clear that also the children of an Egyptian woman become a substantial part of Israel.

2. Translation by Hamilton, *The Book of Genesis: 18–50*, 627.

3. When the land is divided among the tribes Manasseh and Ephraim each receive

Ephraim are Joseph's sons, ideologically, however, in Israel's history, as
presented in the Hebrew Bible, they are the sons of Jacob. As such, they
share in Israel's inheritance.[4] One might wonder whether Jacob's adoption
of Joseph's Egyptian sons should actually be considered a positive deed
towards Joseph.[5]

After the adoption, Jacob blesses his new sons and, despite Joseph's
protests, Jacob neglects the custom of the elder to go before the younger
by putting his right arm on Ephraim's head. Although Manasseh is to
become a great people, his brother will become even greater. Would this
reversal of positions have anything to do with Manasseh's name? Would
there be a relation between 'God has made me forget my father's house'
and the reason why Jacob places Ephraim first? And might this be an
indication why Jacob will also neglect the former apple of his eye in Gen.
49? Joseph's neglect of his father's house during the time between his
release and the famine may have had a profound influence on Jacob's decision in his farewell speech.

Therefore one might also wonder about the precise meaning of 48.22:

ואני נתתי לך שכם אחד על־אחיך
אשר לקחתי מיד האמרי בחרבי ובקשתי

Jacob does present Joseph with one שכם, 'one mountain range', על־אחיך.
However, what do these words, על־אחיך, mean? Does he give Joseph
something 'above his brothers', or 'more than his brothers'? Or, perhaps
even (as NIV), 'as one who is over your brothers'? From the remainder of
the Hebrew Bible it is clear that Joseph does not inherit any land. Therefore, שכם (moutain range)[6] here might as well refer to the place Shechem

---

a part, Joseph is not mentioned (Josh. 15.1–19.48; cf. 14.3; cf. Num. 2). In 1 Chronicles (chs. 4–8) the descendants of Jacob's sons are listed, instead of Joseph's offspring
one encounters the children of both Manasseh and Ephraim.

4. On the basis of F. Steiner's observations in his article 'Enslavement and the
Early Hebrew Lineage System: An Explanation of Genesis 47:29-31; 48:1-16', in
B. Lang (ed.), *Anthropological Approaches to the Old Testament* (Issues in Religion
and Theology, 8; Philadelphia: Fortress Press; London: SPCK, 1985), 21-25,
Wildavsky suggests that Jacob adopts Joseph's sons because Joseph is legally no
longer Jacob's son because of his sale to Egypt (*Assimilation versus Separation*, 115).

5. The common interpretation of Jacob adopting Joseph's two sons as positive for
Joseph is also seriously questioned by de Hoop, *Genesis 49*, 338. He also draws attention to the fact that both Manasseh and Ephraim are compared to Reuben and Simeon
—two of Jacob's sons who were not treated too favourably by the narrator.

6. The Hebrew שכם can both refer to Shechem and to a pair of shoulders. In 48.22

that is referred to in Josh. 24.32, the spot where Joseph will be buried when the children of Israel enter the promised land. Would it not be possible that in 48.22 Jacob gives Joseph the only piece of land he will ever get? Joseph then is presented with a kind of consolation prize—'I have given you one mountain range (שׁכם) against[7] your brothers [because they will get a larger part of the land]'—the portion that Jacob gives to Joseph is, however, taken from the Amorites by Jacob himself.

2. *Jacob's Farewell Speech*[8]

After God has spoken to him in Gen. 46, Jacob gradually takes control of the situation, or perhaps one can even say that he is entirely in charge. In the days of his youth his actions were largely determined by those of others: he did as his mother told him; he ran from his brother; he had to work for Laban; his wives told him to beget children by their maids; he did not dare to return to Canaan because of Esau and hardly did anything when Simeon and Levi murdered the whole tribe of Hamor; and so on. Now, after God has told him to go down to Egypt he finally presents himself as the head of the family: he faces and even blesses Pharaoh (47.7-10),[9] he adopts Joseph's sons (Gen. 48) and addresses all his sons in the longest speech in the book of Genesis before he breathes his last and is gathered to his forefathers.

The Hebrew text of Jacob's farewell address to his sons in Gen. 49 presents a lot of lexical, syntactic and literary-structural problems.[10] In this section I will not enter into the discussions concerning these textual problems, and the precise meaning of every verse or every word. Rather, I examine the address within its larger context and relate it—if possible—to

this is to be understood metaphorically: a shoulder of mount (KB, 970). Because of the numeral אחד ('one'), the mountain-like interpretation seems preferable.

7.   For this meaning of על, cf. KB, 704; *HALAT*, 781, Joüon and Muraoka, *A Grammar of Biblical Hebrew*, §133, 489-90, cf. 485.

8.   It is beyond the scope of this study to consider Moses' blessing of the 12 tribes in Deut. 33 extensively. I will neither delve into the further adventures of the various tribes. For a study of the genealogical lists in the Hebrew Bible, cf. Z. Kallai, 'The Twelve-Tribe Systems of Israel', *VT* 47 (1997), 53-90.

9.   On this see B.A. McKenzie, 'Jacob's Blessing on Pharaoh: An Interpretation of Gen. 46.31–47.26', *WTJ* 45 (1983), 386-99. According to McKenzie Joseph's agrarian reforms (47.13-26) are the result of Jacob blessing Pharaoh.

10.   A thorough and extensive investigation of Gen. 49 is to be found in R. de Hoop's study *Genesis 49*.

the story read so far. In this section I will restrict myself to comments on the brothers I commented upon before, namely, Reuben, Simeon, Levi, Judah, Joseph and Benjamin. The remaining six are barely of interest.[11]

Jacob's speech to his sons starts as a direct continuation of his words to Joseph in 48.21-22. Jacob has reached the end of his days, his eyes are dim (48.10). When he has delivered his speech, he asks his sons that he be buried in Canaan and passes away (49.29-33). Interestingly, Jacob (Israel) earlier posed the same question to Joseph (47.29-31). Is Jacob—after his blessings (49.1-28)—so lacking in confidence in Joseph's doing as he is asked that he repeats his question to be buried in the grave of his fathers in front of all his sons? Or does he merely mention his wish again, because Joseph is ignorant of the burial place of his ancestors?

When considering 49.1-28 within Gen. 37–50 one comes upon a number of things that are to be expected, but there are some peculiarities as well. It by no means comes as a surprise that Jacob does not devote too many of his last words to the six sons that are hardly ever mentioned in chapters 37–50.[12] To be expected, however, is the attention and space Jacob devotes to the sons who have played minor and major parts in the preceding chapters, namely, Reuben, Simeon, Levi, Judah and Joseph. Jacob's rather harsh words about Benjamin, of whom Judah in 44.20, 22, 31, said that his father loved him very much, may come as a surprise. A further element that needs some attention is the narrator's comment in 49.28: 'All these are the 12 tribes of Israel, and this is how their father spoke to them when he blessed them, each with his own blessing'. From his words it is clear that Jacob not only addresses his sons individually; the 'blessings' reach further, they go beyond the lives of each of his sons and relate to future times, as appears

11. In his 'testament' Jacob does not address his sons in the order of their birth. Sarna discerns a chiastic structure in the patriarch's last words. He first addresses Leah's sons, a son of Bilhah, followed by Zilpah's two sons, then again a son of Bilhah —the address is closed by his words to the sons of Rachel; see Sarna, *Genesis*, 331.

12. Leah's sons Zebulon (v. 13) and Issachar (vv. 14-15) receive 10 and 20 words respectively. The sons of Rachel's maid Bilhah, Dan (vv. 16-18) and Naphtali (v. 21) receive 23 and 6 words respectively, and Zilpah's sons Gad (v. 19) and Asher (v. 20) have six and seven words. The total number of words is 72—an average of 12 words each. Although Gad is the seventh born and the gematria of his name is seven (gimmel, three, plus daleth, four) and according to the list of Gen. 46 he appears to have seven sons (and in which list he is in seventh position as well; these observations are made by J.M. Sasson, 'A Genealogical "Convention" in Biblical Chronography?', *ZAW* 90 [1978], 171-85 [181]), Jacob does not devote seven words to him, nor is Gad in seventh position in Gen. 49.

from the introduction to the individual 'blessings': 'Gather around, so that I can tell you what will happen in days to come' (49.1).

In the previous sentence I wrote the word blessings between inverted commas. This was done not only because the narrator did indeed use the Hebrew word for 'blessing', ברך—a rather ambiguous word—but also because some of Jacob's words resemble anything but a blessing. And therefore, in several instances, the reverse meaning of ברך may be intended.[13] So, in his farewell address Jacob both blesses (like Judah) and curses his sons (like Simeon and Levi).[14]

Reuben

3a	Reuben, you are my firstborn,	ראובן בכרי אתה 3a
b	my power and the first of my strength	כחי וראשית אוני b
c	excelling in authority and excelling in might.	יתר שאת ויתר עז c
4a	(You are) uncontrollable[15] as water,	פחז כמים 4a
b	you shall not excel.	אל־תותר b
c	for you have ascended your father's bed;	כי עלית משכבי אביך c
d	then you profaned...	אז חללת d
e	onto my couch he has climbed.	יצועי עלה e

The first to be addressed is Reuben, since he is Jacob's firstborn (49.3a). Jacob's words to Reuben, on the one hand, refer to the present (v. 3) and are directed toward the past (vv. 4c-d-e); most finite verb forms are of the *qatal* type (vv. 4c-d-e; v. 3 has nothing but verbless clauses). The only *yiqtol* form is found in verse 4b, where it is used to express a negative imperative: 'You shall not excel'. Considering both the verb forms and the episodes told about Reuben one cannot but conclude that Jacob (at last!) lectures Reuben on his misbehaviour relayed by the narrator in 35.22, when Reuben slept[16] with Bilhah, his father's concubine.[17] The way in

13. Cf. 1 Kgs 21 where Naboth is being accused by ברך Elohim and the king (10, 13)—which can mean nothing but curse; cf. also the use of ברך in Job 1.5, 11; 2.5, 9 and the analysis of these verses in van Wolde, 'A Text-Semantic Study of the Hebrew Bible.

14. Note also the superb title of a chapter in Wildavsky's *Assimilation versus Separation*: 'If These are Jacob's Blessings, What Would his Curses be Like?'.

15. I follow Hamilton's translation of פחז (*The Book of Genesis: 18–50*, 645).

16. 'Reuben slept' in 35.22 is expressed by a *wayyiqtol* of the verb שכב ('sleep'); in 49.4c Jacob says: 'for you have ascended your father's bed' (משכב).

17. Cf. S. Gervitz, 'The Reprimand of Reuben', *JNES* 30 (1979), 87-98, who also suggests an alternative reading of Gen. 49.3-4.

which Jacob now rebukes his firstborn shows that his mind still is not at ease regarding Reuben's attempt at a coup so many years ago.[18] Thus, the anacoluthon in v. 4d ('then you profaned...') combined with the sudden shift from second (cf. אתה, v. 3a and the second person verb forms in v. 4) to third person between v. 4d and 4e ('onto my couch he has climbed') are illustrative of Jacob's indignation of his eldest's sons action regarding himself and Bilhah.

Simeon and Levi

5a	Simeon and Levi are brothers,	שמעון ולוי אחים	5a
b	instruments of violence are their swords.[19]	כלי חמס מכרתיהם	b
6a	Into their council let my soul not enter,	בסדם אל־תבא נפשי	6a
b	in their company let me not be joined,	בקהלם אל־תחד כבדי	b
c	for in their anger they have killed a man,	כי באפם הרגו איש	c
d	and at will hamstrung an ox.	וברצנם עקרו־שור	d
7a	Cursed be their fury, for it is fierce	ארור אפם כי עז	7a
b	and their rage, for it is cruel,	ועברתם כי קשתה	b
c	I will scatter them in Jacob,	אחלקם ביעקב	c
d	I will disperse them in Israel.	ואפיצם בישראל	d

Next in line are Simeon and Levi (vv. 5-7). They are the only two of Jacob's sons who are presented as a pair, which immediately reminds one of the other occasion on which they were mentioned together, that is, the killing of Hamor and his family in Gen. 34.[20] The way in which Jacob addresses them consequently sets the tone. Hamilton writes that there 'is

18. Jacob disqualifying Reuben has to do nothing whatsoever with the motif of 'the younger surpassing the elder (or: the firstborn)' that one frequently encounters in studies on Genesis. Not only is this not the case in Gen. 37–50, it is neither present in the cases of Ishmael and Isaac, and Esau and Jacob. In fact, in the book of Genesis the firstborn is never replaced by the younger—just as Israel is never replaced by another people (cf. Exod. 4.22: 'This is what YHWH says: Israel is my firstborn son'), except in the case of Manasseh and Ephraim.

19. The hapax מכרתיהם is translated by 'their swords' (from Greek μάχαιρα) both in NIV and NRSV; cf. O. Margalith, '*M^eKĒRŌTĒHEM* (Genesis XLIX 5)', *VT* 34 (1984), 101-102, in response to M. Cohen, '*M^eKĒRŌTĒHEM* (Genèse XLIX 5)', *VT* 31 (1981), 472-77. Jacob comments 'Das schwierige Wort hat die mannigfachsten Ableitungen und Deutungen erfahren' (*Das erste Buch der Tora*, 896).

20. S. Gervitz, however, does not agree: 'Exegetes have long endeavored to interpret the poem of Gen. 49:5-7 in the light of Gen. 34, the story of the rape of Dinah and the vengeance exacted by the sons of Jacob. Between the two passages, however, significant differences in detail exist' ('Simeon and Levi in "The Blessing of Jacob" (Gen. 49:5-7)', *HUCA* 52 [1981], 93-128).

little problem in connecting most of the language of vv. 5-6 with Gen. 34. The only phrase that lacks a clear reference is *at will they hamstrung an ox.*'[21] As were vv. 3-4, the opening clauses here in vv. 5-6 are clauses without verb forms, they present a state of affairs: 'Simeon and Levi are brothers; instruments of violence are their swords' (v. 5). This is followed by two negated jussives that regard Jacob himself (vv. 6a-b), and two *qatal* clauses, introduced by כִּי, that refer to the past actions of both brothers (v. 6c-d). This segment on Simeon and Levi is concluded by a curse (an imperative) that rules both vv. 7a and 7b,[22] and is followed by two *yiqtol* clauses by means of which the future comes into view (vv. 7c-d): both Simeon and Levi will be scattered in Israel. This scattering—as Benno Jacob understands—does not refer to their scattering throughout Israel (in a geographical sense); it means that they become separated from one another, '[sie] sollen von einander getrennt werden' ('they have to be separated from one another') in order to prevent them committing another crime together.[23]

Readers of the biblical accounts know about Levi that in the later history of the sons of Israel his descendants will take care of the service of the sanctuary (e.g. Num. 18.1), and are in this way scattered through Israel. Simeon, on the other hand, does share in the inheritance of the land, as is told in Josh. 19.1-9. Except for the book of Chronicles, the tribe of Simeon is only mentioned five more times in the Hebrew Bible (Josh. 21.4, 9; Ezek. 48.24, 25, 33). The almost immediate disappearance of Simeon in the history of Israel—as presented in the Bible[24]—may reflect Jacob's prediction of Simeon being scattered in Israel.[25]

---

21. Hamilton, *The Book of Genesis: 18–50*, 651. Perhaps one could see in עקרו ('they hamstrung') a reference to עכרתם ('you have brought trouble', 34.30), a pun on the verbs עקר and עכר. If, however, one understands שׁוּר (v. 6) as the same word שׁוּר in v. 22, where it is supposed to mean 'wall', it is possible to see a reference to Gen. 34 and the demolition of Hamor's city: 'at will they uprooted a wall'—this translation of עקר (piel) is closer to the qal and niphal meaning than is the piel meaning ('hamstring, lame') that is given in *HALAT* (III, 827-28).

22. Both 'their fury' (אפם) and 'their rage' (ועברתם) are cursed. The above translation is Hamilton's (*The Book of Genesis: 18–50*, 650).

23. Jacob, *Das erste Buch der Tora*, 898-99.

24. It is good to keep Thompson's words in mind: 'in reality this history existed—like the events in the land of Narnia—only within the pages of books!' (T.L. Thompson, 'How Yahweh Became God: Exodus 3 and 6 and the Heart of the Pentateuch', *JSOT* 68 (1995), 57-74 (65).

25. However, no tribal boundaries are given for Simeon: 'The list of cities included in Simeon's territory, found in Josh 19:1-9, probably reflects administrative concerns

Judah, Joseph and Benjamin

As for Judah and Joseph, both of them are allocated five verses (vv. 8-12 are devoted to Judah; vv. 22-26 to Joseph); the number of words is more or less the same: Judah receives 55 words, Joseph 61.

Judah

8a	Judah, you, your brothers shall praise you;	יהודה אתה יורוך אחיך	8a
b	your hand is on the neck of your enemies;[26]	ידך בערף איביך	b
c	your father's sons shall bow down before you.	ישתחוו לך בני אביך	c
9a	Judah is a lion's whelp;	גור אריה יהודה	9a
b	from the prey, my son, you have gone up.	מטרף בני עלית	b
c	He crouched down	כרע	c
d	he stretched out like a lion, and like a 'king's lion',[27]	רבץ כאריה וכלביא	d
e	who shall rouse him up?	מי יקימנו	e
10a	The scepter shall not depart from Judah,	לא־יסור שבט מיהודה	10a
b	nor the ruler's staff from between his feet,	ומחקק מבין רגליו	b
c	until he comes to Shiloh;[28]	עד כי־יבא שילה	c
d	and the obedience of the peoples is his.	ולו יקהת עמים	d
11a	Binding his foal to the vine	אסרי לגפן עירה	11a
b	and his donkey's colt to the choice vine,	ולשרקה בני אתנו	b
c	he washed his garments in wine	כבס ביין לבשו	c
d	and his robe in the blood of grapes;	ובדם־ענבים סותה	d
12a	his eyes are darker than wine,	חכלילי עינים מיין	12a
b	and his teeth whiter than milk.	ולבן־שנים מחלב	b

of the monarchy. These cities are found in the southernmost section of Judah's territory... Judges represents Judah and Simeon as forming a pact; both agree to cooperate in the face of threats. Simeon does assist Judah in battles against "the Canaanites and the Perizzites" at Bezek (Judg 1:4) and at Zephath (Judg 1:17), yet there are no accounts of Judah defending Simeon, reflecting Simeon's dependency on Judah. Not much else is known about the activities of Simeon' (*ABD*, VI, 26).

26. In vv. 8a-b there is a pun on Judah (יהודה), 'they shall praise you' (יודוך) and 'your hand' (ידך); moreover, in v. 8a there is a reference to Jacob's preceding statements: 'brothers' (אחים) is also in v. 5, whereas 'you' (אתה) is in v. 3 as well. There may also be a wordplay on 'your enemies' (איבך, v. 8b) and 'your father' (אביך; v. 8c)

27. I follow de Hoop's suggestion: אריה and לביא both mean 'lion'; the rendering 'king's lion' is chosen to indicate that there are two different Hebrew words (de Hoop, *Genesis 49*, 114).

28. For the numerous difficulties this clause presents, see Hamilton, *The Book of Genesis: 18–50*, 658-61, and de Hoop, *Genesis 49*, 122-35.

These words to Judah refer to a (distant) future in which Judah is going to hold the sceptre and will be ruler (v. 10), or better, a descendant of Judah is going to hold the sceptre.[29] All this might refer to the royal line that will come forth from Judah. This is prepared for in vv. 8-9, in which Jacob says that Judah's brothers shall praise him, and that they will come to bow down before him. Jacob's images of the lion also confirm Judah's special and elevated position among Jacob's sons.[30] This image of Judah painted by Jacob is a continuation of the impression Judah may have made on a reader of Gen. 37–50. Being part of the brothers' collective in ch. 37 he has detached himself gradually from his brothers—a detachment that turns out to be positive: via his emendation of Reuben's suggestion (37.26-27) to kill Joseph and his maltreatment of Tamar and his subsequent realization that Tamar was more right than he was himself (ch. 38), he did grow in order to convince his father to send Benjamin along with him (ch. 43), after which he exposes the Egyptian vizier (ch. 44). All this has prepared Judah to assume Israel's kingship in some future time (in the biblical narrative).[31] Until now, Jacob's words have made a shift from simply focussing on the present and the past (Reuben) to focussing mainly on the future (Judah)—in between is the address to Simeon and Levi in which there was a balance between present, past and future.

There is a strange phenomenon to be seen in Jacob's prediction about Judah. In his words to Judah, he uses the verbs חוה ('bow down', v. 8), טרף ('tear', v. 9), אסר ('bind', v. 11) as well as the noun גפן ('vine', v. 11). These words are encountered elsewhere, but in all of these instances they were used in connection with Joseph.[32] What might this observation imply? The following is based solely upon the verb חוה. Since Jacob was a mem-

---

29. Cf. the *yiqtol* verb forms in vv. 8ac, 9e, 10ac. Although these verb forms refer to the future, there are several *qatal* forms as well: vv. 9bcd, 11c; the remaining clauses are verbless.

30. The 'foal' and the 'donkey' in vv. 11ab do not prompt the reader to think of the brothers' journeys to Egypt. The donkeys they rode upon were חמרים; the word חמור is not in v. 11.

31. E.M. Good reads Jacob's words on Judah as ironic ('The 'Blessing' on Judah, Gen 49.8-12', *JBL* 82 (1963), 427-32; also cf. C.M. Carmichael, 'Some Sayings in Genesis 49', *JBL* 88 (1969), 435-44 (438-44).

32. חוה in 37.7, 9, 12 (cf. when the brothers come to see Joseph in Egypt and bow down before him); טרף in 37.33; 44.28; אסר (qal) in 39.20; 40.3, 5; 42.24; 46.29; גפן in 40.9, 10. I could find one reference in Jacob's oracle to Joseph that could be connected to Judah: Jacob uses the word עין ('fountain', v. 22) that is also found in 38.14 (עינים, 'fountains').

ber of the audience that heard Joseph's second dream (in Gen. 37) it is possible that by Jacob's usage of the verb חוה, the narrator depicts a scene in which Jacob (for the second time perhaps) ridicules Joseph's dream (and Joseph himself): the 'bowing down' in the dream, which he initially interpreted as bowing down before *Joseph* (37.10), is now transformed into the brothers' (including Joseph's) bowing down before *Judah*. So here Jacob may be rebuking Joseph once again—this time when Joseph is at the height of his career. This might also account for the rather odd and, at that time, difficult to explain concluding part of 37.11: 'his father kept the matter (הדבר) in mind'. Now in 49.8, it has become clear why Jacob kept Joseph's dream in mind.

In retrospect, when a reader takes the books of Samuel and Kings into account, books in which is told that a royal dynasty has come forth from Judah, the narrator's ascription of 49.8-12 to Jacob might indicate that one day Judah is to reach a position that will be equal to the position Joseph had obtained in Egypt.

Joseph

22a	The foal of a wild she-ass[33] is Joseph,	בן פרת יוסף 22a
b	the foal of a wild she-ass at a fountain;	בן פרת עלי־עין b
c	(the foal of) wild asses by a rocky rim.[34]	בנות צעדה עלי־שור c
23a	They harried with him,	וימררהו 23a
b	and have become many	ורבו b
c	and the archers pressed him hard.	וישטמהו בעלי חצים c
24a	And his bow remained taut,	ותשב באיתן קשתו 24a
b	and his arms were made agile.	ויפזו זרעי ידיו b
c	From the hands of the Mighty One of Jacob,	מידי אביר יעקב c
d	from there a shepherd, a rock of Israel,	משם רעה אבן ישראל d
25a	from the God of your father,[35]	מאל אביך 25a

33. I do not follow the translation of בן פרת as 'a young fruit tree', in which פרת is related to the verb פרה, which again might be a reference to Ephraim (cf. 41.52, 'God has made me fruitful'); see e.g. Westermann, *Genesis 37–50*, 270; de Hoop, *Genesis 49*, 181-87. De Hoop mentions several objections against the 'fruit tree', among which (1) בן is never used for plants, and (2) v. 22 would present the only plant-metaphor in Gen. 49. However, he translates בן־פרת as a 'young bullcalf'. The translation 'wild she-ass', as suggested by Hamilton, is based on Ugaritic texts (*The Book of Genesis: 18–50*, 678).

34. This translation of v. 22 (with the exception of 'rocky rim') is suggested by S. Gervitz, 'Of Patriarchs and Puns: Joseph at the Fountain, Jacob at the Ford', *HUCA* 46 (1975), 33-54 (41), and is followed by Hamilton, *The Book of Genesis: 18–50*, 678.

35. From here (till v. 26a) Jacob addresses Joseph directly—before Jacob talked

b	may he help you,	ויעזרך b
c	and with the Almighty,	ואת שדי c
d	may he bless you with blessings of heaven above,	ויברכך ברכת שמים מעל d
e	blessings of the deep that lies beneath,	ברכת תהום רבצת תחת e
f	blessings of the breasts and of the womb.	ברכת שדים ורחם f
26a	The blessings of your father were stronger than the blessings of the eternal mountains, the bounties of the everlasting hills;	ברכת אביך גברו על־ברכת הורי עד־ תאות גבעת עולם 26a
b	may they be on the head of Joseph,	תהיין לראש יוסף b
c	on the brow of the one set apart from his brothers.	ולקדקד נזיר אחיו c

Like the previous predictions about Reuben, Simeon, Levi and Judah, this one also begins with a series of verbless clauses, expressing the present state of affairs ('Joseph is…'). These are followed by both *wayyiqtol* (vv. 23ac, 24ab), *qatal* (vv. 23b, 26a) and *w^{e}yiqtol* (vv. 25bd, 26b) clauses. This prediction, in contrast to Judah's, does not have a reference to the future. For the bigger part, it focuses on the past.

A further element that is to be discerned in this blessing, is the presence of God, and which is strongly connected to Jacob's use of the *w^{e}yiqtol* forms; all these are modal forms[36]—'may he [the God of your father] help you', 'may he [the Almighty] bless you', 'may they [the blessings] be on his head'. Jacob's use of these modal forms illustrates his doubts about Joseph's interpretation of the past events. He hopes for Joseph's wellbeing that God may bless Joseph in the days to come, even though he is not certain about it. Jacob never explicitly expressed his scepticism about his son's view of the past to Joseph himself: not until 50.17 does Joseph become aware that his father did not subscribe to his view of God having turned evil into good (see the next section).

In Jacob's words to Joseph, an intriguing phenomenon may be observed. There are several words that suggest a relationship between Joseph's blessing by Jacob and the description of what happens to Ishmael by the narrator. In his commentary, Hamilton mentions some of these. To begin with, there is שור (above translated as 'rocky rim', 49.22), a place that Hagar is heading for in 16.7. Moreover, she is going to the fountain (על־העין) on

about his son; cf. v. 25b: 'so steh' er dir bei' (Jacob, *Das erste Buch der Tora*, 923).

36. Cf. A. Niccacci, 'A Neglected Point of Hebrew Syntax: Yiqtol and Position in the Sentence', *Liber Annuus* 37 (1987), 7-19.

the road to Sur (שׁוּר); which quite resembles עַל־הָעַיִן ('at a spring/foun-tain') in 49.22. Apart from the spring and the name of the place, there is also Ishmael who is called a פֶּרֶא אָדָם ('a wild ass of a man', 16.12), whereas Jacob calls Joseph 'the foal of a wild she-ass' (בֵּן פֹּרָת, 49.22).[37] There are, however, some more similarities between Joseph and Ishmael to be detected which Hamilton did not notice. In both 21.16 and 49.24 a bow is mentioned (קֶשֶׁת); and besides, both 21.16-20 and 49.23-24a are entirely dominated by the archers and shooting (cf. בַּעֲלֵי חִצִּים, 'the arch-ers', literally, 'lords of arrows', in 49.23c). Further, 49.24a says about Joseph that 'his bow (קֶשֶׁת) remained taut': Joseph is depicted as being an archer himself. This establishes a link to 21.20 where the narrator states about Ishmael that he is to become an archer (רֹבֶה קֶשֶׁת). The word רֹבֶה ('the one shooting') could be related to וָרָבּוּ (which is translated above as 'and have become many', 49.23b), which is derived from the verb רָבָה ('to become many'). There is, however, also a verb, רָבַב, which means 'to shoot', and which is attested in Gen. 21.20, Jer. 50.29 and Ps. 18.15.[38]

Apart from Jacob's blessing of Joseph in Gen. 49, there are some more resemblances between Joseph and Ishmael to be found. In Gen. 41, Phar-aoh (an Egyptian) gave Joseph an Egyptian wife (v. 45), which might remind one of Ishmael being given an Egyptian wife by Hagar, his Egyp-tian mother (21.21). From Abraham's reaction—he thought it evil to send Hagar and Ishmael into the desert (21.11)—one can infer that Abraham was attached to his son, as was Jacob to Joseph. Another element from Gen. 21 is that Sarah saw Abraham's son מְצַחֵק, 'mocking'—which is exactly the same action of which Joseph was accused by Potiphar's wife (39.14, 17, לְצַחֶק). Yet another similarity is that both Ishmael and Joseph are being cast (שָׁלַךְ): the one under a bush (21.15) and the other into a pit (37.24)—both of them בַּמִּדְבָּר, 'in the wilderness' (21.14; 37.22). And to mention a final resemblance: in Gen. 39 the narrator makes it clear several times that YHWH was with Joseph (וַיְהִי יְהוָה אֶת־יוֹסֵף, 39.2, 3, 21)—something similar was said about Ishmael in 21.20: וַיְהִי אֱלֹהִים אֶת־הַנַּעַר, 'And God was with the lad' (cf. 37.2 in which Joseph was called a נַעַר as well).

37. Hamilton, *The Book of Genesis: 18–50*, 679. Cf. Gervitz, 'Of Patriarchs and Puns', 42-43; Sarna, *Genesis*, 343.

38. Cf. Hamilton, *The Book of Genesis: 18–50*, 680; Jacob, *Das erste Buch der Tora*, 921: 'Da machten es ihm bitter und schossen, da befeindeten ihn die Leute mit den Pfeilen'; *HALAT*, IV, 1099, BDB, 914 (however, they only mention Gen. 49.23 and Ps. 18.15).

Where might these similarities take one with regard to Joseph?[39] What could the connection between Abraham's and Jacob's sons imply for Joseph? The narrator suggests a relationship between Ishmael and Joseph by words and motifs that appear in his description of Ishmael and Joseph, as well as in Jacob's blessing of Joseph. Both characters have several things in common. Could the implication be that both will follow a similar route?

After the narrator has stated that God was with Ishmael (21.20), he hardly mentions Ishmael any more (Gen. 28.9; 36.3; 1 Chron. 1.28, 29, 31). He loses sight of Ishmael—for the narrator, Ishmael is a dead end. Yet, several times Ishmael's offspring will step into the spotlight. Apart from 25.12-18, Ishmaelites—if they are Ishmael's descendants—are to be found elsewhere (Gen. 37.25, 27, 28; 39.1, Judg. 8.24; Ps. 83.6). Interestingly, those Ishmaelites make their appearance in Gen. 37 (and 39.1) to buy and sell Joseph. And in Judg. 8.24 they pay their respects to Gideon, son of Joas who is of the tribe of Manasseh (cf. 6.11, 15)—in other words, a descendant of Joseph's. As for Joseph, regarding the inheritance of the land, he will not share in it: two portions of the land will belong to his sons (or, rather, Jacob's adopted sons) Manasseh and Ephraim. And just as one sometimes comes across Ishmael's offspring, now and then Joseph's descendants are met. They are often referred to as 'the house of Joseph',[40] yet there is no 'tribe of Joseph'. Perhaps in this sense there is a link between Joseph and Ishmael. Although they are both sons of patriarchs, there will—as far as land promised to their forebears is concerned—be no region of 'Ishmael', or 'Joseph', in the land, or for that matter, anywhere.

39. For an elaboration of the similarities in a geo-political sense cf. Gervitz, 'Of Patriarchs and Puns', 41-49. To mention an example: by using the word שׁוּר in combination with 'fountain' it is Gervitz' contention that Gen. 49.22 'deliberately and explicitly alludes' to the 'geographic area which is delineated in Gen. 16.7, 14—an area in the Negeb which is said to lie between Kadesh and Bered, and in which was located the well, Beer-Lahai-roi' (42). According to Gervitz it would seem that by connecting Joseph and Ishmael, both figures and the 'house of Joseph' are linked to the region of the Negeb (cf. 43-47).

40. Joseph is certainly mentioned outside Gen. 37–50. Joseph's bones, as he orders in 50.25, are taken out of Egypt (Exod. 13.19), and are buried in Shechem (Josh. 24.32). Joseph is highly praised by Moses in Deut. 33.13-17, and there are indeed several references to 'the house of Joseph' (like Josh. 17.17; Judg. 1.22-23; 2 Sam. 19.21; 1 Kgs. 11.28) and 'the sons of Joseph' (Num. 34.23; Josh. 14.4; 16.1; 17.14-18). Joseph also frequently appears in or near lists, like Exod. 1.2-6; Num. 1.5-16, 20-43; 13.4-15; 26.20-37; 1 Chron. 2.1-2.

In this sense they differ from Esau, who—although he is no part of Israel —does not only have a land to live in, but also has a region named after him as is read in 36.1: 'Esau he is Edom'.

And there may also be a reason for the occurrence of נזיר ('the one set apart')[41] in the final clause of Jacob's blessing of Joseph: '[may the blessings be on the head of Joseph,] on the skull of the one who was set apart (נזיר) from his brothers'.[42] Contrary to his brothers, Joseph will not share in the inheritance of the land. His name is no part of the geographical area, 'Israel'—in this way he is certainly set apart. His place is taken by Manasseh and Ephraim—yet another way in which he is set apart from his brothers.

Benjamin

27a	Benjamin: a wolf that shall tear apart,	בנימין זאב יטרף	27a
	b in the morning he shall eat prey	בבקר יאכל עד	b
	c and in the evening he shall divide spoil.	ולערב יחלק שלל	c

The last son to be addressed by Jacob is Benjamin. It is rather remarkable that Jacob only directs nine words (in the Hebrew) to his youngest son— the son of whom Judah, in Gen. 44, stated that his father's soul was bound up with his (44.30). Apart from its brevity, this is actually, and virtually, the only information on Benjamin the reader ever gets. During the narrated events of the preceding chapters, the goblet-incident excepted, Benjamin was only one of the brothers who were acting anonymously.[43] Jacob's

41. According to *ThWAT*, V, 329: 'die Wurzel *nzr* bzw. *ndr* kommt in allen Zweigen des Semit. vor (ob akk. *Nazāru* 'beschimpfen' hierher gehört, ist fraglich). Grundbedeutung ist "dem üblichen Gebrauch entziehen, aussondern"'. In the same vein is *HALAT*, III, 646. According to BDB, 634, the root means 'dedicate, consecrate, separate'. Interpretations like 'the one singled out, the one of high rank, the one consecrated', are derived from this root. In Moses' farewell speech (Deut. 33.16) נזיר is once again used to depict Joseph. The remaining places in the Torah where the noun is found are Lev. 25.5, 11, and Num. 6.2, 13, 18, 21. The verb occurs in Lev. 15.31 (hiphil), 22.2 (niphal) and Num. 6.2, 5, 6, 12 (hiphil). All occurrences in Numbers deal with being a Nazirite. I cannot see any relationship with the occurrence of נזיר in Gen. 49.

42. Cf. de Hoop, *Genesis 49*, 217: 'So we do not follow the suggestions to render נזיר here with "prince" or "leader" as is sometimes suggested on the basis of the meaning נזר "crown"'.

43. In 45.14 the narrator says that Benjamin was weeping upon Joseph's neck. In the list of Jacob's offspring who come to Egypt Benjamin is said to have ten sons (46.21).

portrayal of Benjamin (in three *yiqtol* clauses) sheds a rather awkward
light on his youngest son.

Two out of the nine words that Jacob spoke to Benjamin are present
earlier in Gen. 37–50 as well: חיה רעה אכלתהו טרף טרף יוסף ('an evil
beast has eaten him; Joseph certainly has been torn apart', 37.33). Both the
verb טרף ('tear apart') and the verb אכל ('eat') are used in 37.33 and
49.27. Is Jacob implying that 'the evil beast' that had torn Joseph apart
might have been Benjamin? It is almost too absurd to think, yet, by having
Jacob use the same words in both utterances, could not the narrator be
insinuating that Jacob thought Benjamin to be one of the major protagonists who, in Gen. 37, got rid of Joseph? If this assumption is correct, the
conclusion reached by Jacob concerning Benjamin's behaviour would also
help explain another riddle of Gen. 37–50—that is, Joseph's insistence on
seeing Benjamin and his placing of the goblet in the latter's sack. Joseph
struck hard at Benjamin in Gen. 44 because Benjamin let him down back
in Dothan. And perhaps it was not only Benjamin who played a major part
in the pit-incident, he may have had assistance from Simeon: for, of all
brothers, it was he who was to remain incarcerated in Egypt.[44]

However, if Joseph had a grudge against Benjamin, why would he have
given his younger brother more presents (45.22) than he gave the other
brothers?[45] And why was the size of Benjamin's portion at dinner with the
Egyptian (43.34) five times larger than that of the brothers? To understand
these gestures, one has to take a look at a few preceding narratives in which
people are sent or given presents.

The first story that comes to mind is Gen. 32–33, an episode in which
Joseph and his brothers were present as well, and during which Jacob is on
his way back to Canaan to meet his brother Esau, of whom he is scared to
death. To put Esau in the right mood and be reconciled with him, Jacob
sends lots of presents to appease him (32.13-21a; 33.10). Another text
which shows the bringing of presents is Gen. 43. When the brothers are
about to leave for Egypt a second time their father Israel orders them to
take both presents and money (43.11-15). Again, the one sending presents

---

44. Westermann does not regard Jacob's comparison of Benjamin to a wolf to be
negative: 'Benjamin wird mit einem reißenden Wolf verglichen. Sonst wird im AT
nie mehr so positiv vom Wolf gesprochen; später ist er nur noch der "böse Wolf",
besonders in der prophetischen Gerichtsankündigung Jer 5, 6; Ezek. 22, 27; Hab. 1,
8; Zeph 3, 3' (*Genesis 37–50*, 275).

45. Not to mention the 300 pieces of silver.

is doing so out of fear (in this case the fear to lose Benjamin).[46] Sending presents has the look of appeasement. So, when Joseph presents Benjamin (and also his brothers) with gifts, could not the implication be that he still fears his brothers? Even though he is more powerful than they are, could he not still be afraid of them? And might this fear not be another reason why he delayed revealing himself to his family for so long?

3. *Final Conversations*

When Jacob has died and after the brothers have taken his body to Canaan and buried him in the cave in the field of Machpelah, the narrator records the first conversation between the brothers and Joseph after their settling in Egypt (50.18-21). Before, however, the brothers discuss the matter among themselves. They make a statement about their deeds toward Joseph in 50.15-17: 'What if Joseph bears a grudge (יִשְׂטְמֵנוּ)[47] against us? He will certainly pay us back all the wrong (הָרָעָה [literally 'evil']) with which we treated him'. After which they inform Joseph, 'Your father has given this instruction before he died, "Say to Joseph, please, forgive the crime (פֶּשַׁע)[48] of your brothers and their wrong (חַטָּאתָם) because they treated you badly (רָעָה)".[49] Now therefore please forgive the crime (פֶּשַׁע) of the servants of the God of your father.'[50]

---

46. Also cf. Gen. 20, in which Abraham is laden with gifts by Abimelech, even though Abraham had brought Abimelech's country into jeopardy by saying that his wife was his sister.

47. The activity the brothers here ascribe to Joseph is in Gen. 49.23 ascribed to Joseph's enemies by Jacob.

48. 'Crime' (פֶּשַׁע), according to Hamilton, 'is a word whose use originated in the political sphere, where it referred to the rebellion of a vassal against an overlord' (*The Book of Genesis: 18–50*, 702)—the brothers' usage of it here could refer to their rebellion against their father by not accepting Joseph as their father's favourite. Also cf. *NIDOTE*, II, 88.

49. After 42.36 another indication that Jacob knew about what had happened in Dothan.

50. I do not understand why commentators doubt the truth of the brothers' message to Joseph: '[A]mong modern commentators this interpretation [viz. thinking favourably of the truthfulness of the message] is rare' (Hamilton, *The Book of Genesis: 18–50*, 703) since 'such an instruction from Jacob is nowhere earlier recorded' (703). This is awkward because when Jacob reports about God speaking to him (31.10-13) this 'is nowhere earlier recorded' either, yet Hamilton believes it to have happened just like that (cf. 289); see also Sternberg, *The Poetics of Biblical Narrative*, 379, who considers the message 'a desperate fabrication'. Vawter also states: 'They [namely, the brothers]

These texts show that the brothers feel guilty about their past behaviour toward Joseph. That is an obvious fact. Yet, the brothers' last words also reveal something else: they do not share Joseph's view of God having turned evil into good—a notion that, by the way, is not until here present in Genesis.[51] This makes it understandable that 'Joseph wept when they spoke to him' (50.17).[52] The brothers (and Jacob), however, picked up the importance that Joseph attributed to God in 45.5-8, so they do mention God in their request (50.15-17) to their brother.

But it is not only the brothers who do not share Joseph's view. In the words of Jacob's instruction to his sons, one can clearly see that Jacob did not share his son's view all the time either.[53] As Judah did in 44.18-34, the brothers collectively emphasize their father's role when they address Joseph, and in their words they make clear that their father has the same point of view with regard to the relationship between Joseph and the

must invent—for surely it was an invention—a safe conduct uttered in their favor by a dying father' and Joseph 'does not even remark on the brothers' thin story' (B. Vawter, *Genesis: A New Reading* [London: Geoffrey Chapman, 1977], 474).

51. White also remarks that the brothers did not share their brother's 'theory of a cosmic plot' (*Narration and Discourse*, 274).

52. In this respect Westermann's 'Aber der neue Einsatz mit 50, 15 ist unmotiviert und eigentlich unbegreiflich' (*Genesis 37–50*, 231) is actually 'unbegreiflich'.

53. A possible reason why Jacob and the brothers do not share Joseph's view can be found in the stories related in the book of Genesis in which Jacob's ancestors play a part. In a number of stories YHWH punishes people who commit evil deeds. Gen. 6.5, e.g., says that God saw the רעה ('wickedness') of humankind; therefore humankind is swept away by the flood. Or take Gen. 18.20, where YHWH states that the חטאת ('sin') of Sodom and Gomorrah is grave (cf. the use of the word רע, 13.13, and the verb רעע, 19.7, 9, with regard to Sodom and Gomorrah); consequently both cities are destroyed by sulphur and fire from heaven. Or, on a much smaller scale, in the eyes of YHWH both Er and Onan acted wickedly (רעע, 38.7, 10), and therefore they had to die. As said above, these examples serve to illustrate that the notion of God (YHWH) turning evil into good is not (yet) present in Genesis. In Jacob's saying to Rachel and Leah that 'your father has cheated me and changed my wages ten times, but God did not permit him to רעע (harm) me' (31.7), Jacob expresses that God has averted the evil to happen, which is of course different from turning evil into good. Consequently, I disagree with the first part of Soggin's statement that 'one could summarize the main thesis of the story [Gen. 37–50] with the words of the Nicene fathers: things happened *hominum confusione, sed Dei providentiā*, a rather unusual thesis, by the way, in the Hebrew Bible' (J.A. Soggin, 'Notes on the Joseph Story', in A. Graeme Auld [ed.], *Understanding Poets and Prophets: Essays in Honour of George Wishart Anderson* [JSOTSup, 152; Sheffield: JSOT Press, 1993], 336-49 [344]).

brothers as the brothers have themselves. By using the expression חטאתם ('their wrong') it is obvious that Jacob (as well as the brothers) is by no means convinced of Joseph's interpretation of his Egyptian adventure. On חטאת, *ThWAT* states that:

> Gemäß dem für das Hebr. selbstverständlichen Tun-Ergehen-Zusammenhang bedeutet *ḥāttā't* nicht nur die böse Tat, sondern auch eine entsprechende Tatfolge. Die Untat stellt man sich als eine Sphäre vor, die unsichtbar am Täter haften bzw. in seiner Nähe bleibt, so daß sie im Laufe der Zeit sich unheilbringend an ihm auswirkt.[54]

This is, of course, also expressed by the brothers themselves when they say that 'he will certainly pay us back with all the wrong with which we treated him' (50.15). Beyond the grave there now seems to be another separation (or rather, a great chasm) between Joseph and his father. Small wonder he weeps once again.[55]

One thing, at least, is clear from the brothers' words: they are not too confident about their future now their father has passed away. They appear to feel guilty about what they did to Joseph (which is by now over 39 years ago); they are full of fear[56] and apparently do not trust their brother. Therefore, they now approach Joseph to make their interpretation of Joseph's first dream come true and subject themselves to Joseph: 'And his brothers also came, fell down[57] before him, and said, "Here, we are to be your slaves"' (50.18; cf. 47.13-26). Although Joseph tries to comfort his brothers ('do not fear', 50.19, 21) and promises to sustain his family (50.21), he nevertheless appears to share in his brothers' distrust, because when he is about to die he does not ask his brothers to bring his bones up out of Egypt on that future day when God will take care of the sons of Israel, but he makes them swear (שבע; 50.25) to do so.[58]

---

54. *ThWAT*, II, 860.

55. So, he does not weep because he finds out that the brothers' distrust has once more arisen, or because of his memories of the past (Westermann, *Genesis 37–50*, 232), but because he has not been able to convince his father of his 'divine mission'.

56. In the same vein G. Josipivici, *The Book of God: A Response to the Bible* (New Haven: Yale University Press, 1988), 79-82. Cf. 50.15: 'and they saw' (ויראו) is from the root ראה, the consonants could also be read as 'and they feared', from the verb ירא (as in 1 Sam. 4.7; 7.7); see Hamilton, *The Book of Genesis: 18–50*, 699.

57. The verb is נפל instead of חוה (as in 37.7). As I showed before, חוה does not indicate submission. Cf. Brueggemann, 'Genesis L 15-21', 46.

58. Just like Israel made Joseph swear to bury him in the grave of his fathers (47.31).

Something else that needs attention here, and which is closely connected to what was said above, is Joseph's statement to his brothers in 45.5-11 as well as his words in 50.20. Joseph appears to be of the opinion that the evil that his brothers schemed against him was turned into good by God. It is by all means possible that Joseph has gradually developed this view on the basis of what happened to him in Egypt, but he did not express this view before 45.5-11, and it did not appear to be his view when he was in prison and asked the cup-bearer to remember him to Pharaoh (40.14-15). I do not doubt that Joseph's interpretation of his past is sincere; however, his sincerity is not the issue here. Nevertheless, it should be noted that it is *his* interpretation of the events; the narrator nowhere denies nor confirms it.[59] There is another element that also occurs in Joseph's words to his brothers: he does not only try to reassure his brothers, but his reassuring words function to prove his own status and position in Egypt as well. Both elements are divided equally in 45.5-11. Three times Joseph claims that it was not the brothers but God who sent him to Egypt (45.5, 7, 8), and three times he says that God has put him in a special position: as a father to Pharaoh; as a lord over Pharaoh's house; and as a ruler over all the land of Egypt (45.8). For Joseph himself, however, it appears that his rise to power—by divine consent—is the most important, since, in 45.9, he mentions this a fourth time by saying his brothers to tell his father that 'God has established me as lord over all of Egypt' (whereas this was actually done by Pharaoh, 41.40-45).

The first time Joseph expressed his opinion that God sent him 'ahead of you', the reason was that God had sent him ahead of his brothers 'for preservation of life' (45.5). This element returns a few times. He elaborates upon it in 45.7, where he comments that God has sent him ahead 'to ensure for you a remnant on earth and keep alive for you many survivors'.[60] In 50.20 Joseph picks up this theme once more: 'You have done

59. 'The speech tells much of Joseph's character and his development in theological awareness, but it does not necessarily say that God did actually intervene in past events. Joseph certainly believes it; the reader can, but does not have to. The narrator does not affirm Joseph's interpretation nor does God himself appear in the narrative to confirm it' (P.D. Miscall, 'The Jacob and Joseph Stories as Analogies', *JSOT* 6 [1978], 28-40 [31]).

60. The translation is Hamilton's (*The Book of Genesis: 18–50*, 572). What could this mean, one wonders. Would the family die if they were unwilling to go down to Egypt? Is Canaan completely bereaved of its inhabitants? It indicates that Joseph's image of God is still a long way from the image of a universal God. It appears to be a god who takes care of one group of people only; cf. Deut. 7.

something malicious against me; God has done something beneficial in order that he might do what has now happened—the survival of many people'.[61] In this latter utterance Joseph modifies his statements from Gen. 45. He now reduces his own activity in the 'survival of many people'—all of it was God's doing.

4. *The Departure of Joseph*

In 49.26 Jacob called Joseph נְזִיר, the one set apart from his brothers. He is set apart from them because he will not—as they do—acquire a region in the promised land. Despite the fact that he used to be his father's favourite and notwithstanding his elevated position in Egypt, Joseph will disappear from the tales about the children of Israel. In this section I summarize some important points that have come to the surface in this study—taken together they may account for Joseph's disappearance, for his situation of being set apart from his brothers.

In the preceding chapters I have indicated two important issues regarding Joseph. The first is concerned with Joseph's position within his family. The beginning of the tale of the brothers depicts Joseph as his father's dearest son, of which the robe is the material proof. When the story continues, Joseph literally and figuratively leaves his father's house. After being sent on a mission to see how his brothers are faring, he is sold to Egypt (Gen. 37) and enters into the service of several Egyptians: Potiphar, the captain of the guard, and finally Pharaoh (chs. 39–41). During his time in Egypt, he forgets about his father's house, as is most prominently indicated by the naming of his firstborn son 'Manasseh' (41.51). Despite this forgetfulness of his father's house, the notion of his father's house gradually returns when his brothers come to buy food during the period of the famine (chs. 42–44).

Within this scope there are also a few more things to be mentioned. There is, for example, the awkward circumstance that Joseph did not try to contact his father when he had reached a powerful position in Egypt. Another thing that needs to be mentioned concerns Joseph's unjust and false accusations—both to his brothers in Gen. 42 and to Benjamin in ch. 44. Apart from this he has imprisoned his brother Simeon for a year, despite the fact that Simeon was innocent. This might have been caused by Joseph's fear of his brothers. From the reaction of the brothers it becomes

---

61. Translation by Hamilton (*The Book of Genesis: 18–50*, 701).

clear that in their view the relationship with Joseph is far from being restored. Their message to Joseph in Gen. 50 showed that they did not endorse Joseph's interpretation of the past events—the same holds for Jacob. Another matter that cannot be avoided here is the fact that Jacob deprived Joseph of his sons (ch. 48) which results in his absence from the land. And finally, would Joseph's enslavement of the Egyptians (ch. 47) have had any repercussions on the enslavement of the Israelites that is recounted in the book of Exodus?

All this is of importance when evaluating Joseph's role in Gen. 37–50 and trying to solve the mystery of Joseph's disappearance from the later biblical books. Yet, there is also another issue that is of major significance.

This second matter touches upon the relationship between Joseph and God as well as Joseph and the divine. A first example here is the contention about YHWH being with Joseph when Joseph was in Potiphar's service (ch. 39). During his stay at Potiphar's house Joseph also mentions God while refusing to sleep with Potiphar's wife: 'How could I do such a wicked thing and sin against God?' (39.9). Once he is in prison YHWH is again with Joseph. In prison he also makes his acquaintance with the chief of the bakers and the chief of the cupbearers. It is to them that Joseph says that the explanation of dreams comes from God (40.8), whereas he himself subsequently explains both the baker's and the cupbearer's dreams. So, during his stay at Potiphar's house, as well as in prison, Joseph introduces God. The very same strategy is applied by Joseph when he interprets Pharaoh's dreams. Joseph talks about God once more when he names his sons. And it is especially the naming of Manasseh that raises questions: 'God has made me forget all my hardship and my father's house' (41.51)— Joseph appears to ascribe his own neglect of his father's house to God. However, when he is confronted by his brothers, his father's house comes to the fore again. This is illustrated by the words he used to enforce his statements: he no longer says 'As Pharaoh lives'—this has changed into 'I fear God' (42.15-18). One more example is Joseph's divination by means of the goblet that is forbidden—according to several biblical laws.

Apart from these facts, there is also the episode in which Joseph makes himself known to his brothers (ch. 45) and in which he mentions God several times: God sent me here, God has made me a ruler of Egypt, God has made me a father to Pharaoh,[62] and so on. Furthermore, there are the

---

62. This might in fact be another instance where Joseph enters the realm of the divine. If in Egyptian belief Pharaoh was the son of the deity, it is clear that Joseph's utterance equals him to this deity.

passages in which Joseph makes other people think that God has done something to them, whereas it was actually Joseph himself who had done so. This is to be seen in the texts in which the brothers discover the money in their bags (42.28). The same happens when Joseph's servant tells the brothers that their God has given them a treasure in their sacks (43.28). A little further Judah exclaims: 'God has uncovered your servant's guilt' (44.16). Something similar could be seen after Joseph had interpreted Pharaoh's dreams, for then Pharaoh said: 'Can we find any one like this man, one in whom is the spirit of God?' (41.38).

Taken together these texts might indicate Joseph's striving to acquire a position for himself that borders on the realm of the divine. This more or less divine status he did acquire when he became Egypt's second in command.[63] And here may be another reason why Joseph did not contact his family. Once he had established this elevated position, he wanted to keep things this way. If he informed his father about this, he might come into conflict with Jacob. Because in Jacob's view it is crystal clear that there is only one who is elevated: the one who once appeared to him in Bethel.

So, both Joseph's neglect of his family and his divine aspirations[64] may have led to his absence in the promised land and to the circumstance that there was to be no tribe of Joseph in Israel.[65]

Before his death at the age of 110, Joseph summoned his brothers and repeated the words Jacob had told him: the promise that God would bring

63. See the previous note.

64. Despite his different approach and evaluation of Gen. 37–50, I partly agree with Wildavsky's conclusion with regard to the disappearance of Joseph from the Torah: 'Chief among his moral lapses is Joseph's too great service to the wrong master, for Joseph comes close to idolatry, whether this be defined as self-worship or bowing down to the false god, Pharaoh. For this reason, Joseph is virtually expunged from the rest of the Torah' (*Assimilation versus Separation*, 7). Wildavsky goes into the possible idolatrous character of Joseph's dreams in his chapter 'The Dreamer is the Dream' (69-92).

65. When, in the book of Joshua, the land is finally conquered it appears that two of Jacob's sons have no land of their own to live in: these are Levi and Joseph. In future times, however, the sons of Levi shall be responsible for the 'offences connected with the priesthood' (Num. 18.1). They are set apart to carry the ark of the covenant, to stand before YHWH to minister to him, and to bless in his name (Deut. 10.8; cf. 18.1; Josh. 14.3). If, now, Levi is denied a part of the land it is because of his tribe's future service to the sanctuary, to the tent of the covenant, could it not be that Joseph is denied a part of the land for a more or less opposite reason? His strive to obtain a divine position approached the regions of idolatry—an element not very much appreciated in the land promised to Abraham, Isaac and Jacob.

them back to the land promised to Abraham, Isaac and Jacob. He also made his brothers swear to take his body to the promised land (50.22-26), And this happened when the children of Israel finally left Egypt, guided by Moses, on their way to a land flowing with milk and honey (Exod. 13.19).

At the end of this study I would like to finish by making one or two tentative remarks concerning the origin and development of the tale presented in Gen. 37–50.

The image of Joseph as a paragon of virtue and righteousness is predominant in Jewish and Christian writings, both in early and later interpretations of the story of Gen. 37–50. This rather positive evaluation of Joseph is for the bigger part based on his adventure with the wife of Potiphar. By refusing to get himself entangled by her desires, he shows his virtue and his obeisance to God's commandments.[1]

This is especially illustrated in texts like *The Testaments of the Twelve Patriarchs* and also in the Hellenistic novel *Joseph and Aseneth* or the *Midrash Tanuma*[2]—texts that have had a major influence on later traditions. Yet, there are also several—be it less influential—traditions in which Joseph does not look like Jacob's wise and righteous son at all. Earle Hilgert called this Joseph's 'Dual Image': besides the positive image, he 'also appears as a wily, ambitious and vain politician, ruled by passions and attachment to the things of this world, and is even presented as the cause of his nation's downfall'.[3] One of the texts in which this picture is presented is the Hebrew *Testament of Naphtali*, in which Naphtali addresses his sons:

> Because I know that one day the children of Joseph will depart from the Lord, the God of their fathers, and cause the children of Israel to sin, and to be banished from the good land into another that is not ours, as we have been exiled through his being a bond-servant in Egypt (*T. Naph.* 1.10).[4]

1. See J.L. Kugel, *In Potiphar's House: The Interpretive Life of Biblical Texts* (Cambridge, MA: Harvard University Press, 1994 [1990]), 11-155.

2. Kugel, *In Potiphar's House*, 29.

3. E. Hilgert, 'The Dual Image of Joseph in Hebrew and Early Jewish Literature', *Papers of the Chicago Society of Biblical Research* 30 (1985), 5-21 (5).

4. In R.H. Charles (ed.), *The Apocrypha and Pseudepigrapha of the Old Testament in English with Introductions and Critical and Explanatory Notes to the Several Books*, II (Oxford: Clarendon Press, 1969 [1913]), 361.

A little further in the *Testament*, Naphtali relates two visions to his sons. In the second of these Jacob's sons are on a ship while Joseph refuses to heed Judah's instructions—he does not steer the ship 'according to the words of his father and the teaching of Judah; and the ship went on a wrong course, and the waves of the sea dashed it on a rock, so that the ship was broken up' (*T. Naph.* 5.5). After the brothers have abandoned the ship to save their lives, they come onto a shore and meet Jacob who reproves Joseph. Naphtali then continues to tell his sons about Jacob's reaction to his vision:

> And when I recounted this vision to my father, he smote his hands together and sighed, and his eyes shed tears. And I waited till I was ashamed, but he spake no word to me. So I took the hand of my father to embrace it and to kiss it, and I said to him, 'O servant of the Lord! Why do thine eyes shed tears?' He said unto me, 'my son, because of the repetition of thy vision my heart has sunk within me, and my body is confounded by reason of Joseph my son, for I loved him above you all; and for the wickedness of my son Joseph you will be sent into captivity, and you will be scattered among the nations. For thy first and second visions are both one and the same vision. Therefore I command you not to unite with the sons of Joseph, but only with Levi and Judah' (*T. Naph.* 7.1-6).[5]

So, from early interpretations and elaborations of Gen. 37–50 it is obvious that Joseph really has a dual image. The positive reading of Joseph is probably based on his refusal to sleep with Potiphar's wife, and perhaps also because he was thought to have been sold by his brothers. However, in Chapter 3 of this study I have shown that there are some serious doubts with regard to this sale by the brothers. Another thing that has emerged in the previous chapters is that there are quite a few things in Gen. 37–50 that might support a more critical evaluation of Joseph—both with regard to God and his family—and these could account for the characteristics attributed to Joseph in a text like the Hebrew *Testament of Naphtali*. The seeds of Joseph's negative depiction are definitely present in the Hebrew texts themselves.

In the Hebrew Bible this more negative view is present as well. Not only —as mentioned before—is Joseph hardly to be found from Genesis onwards, but one might also think of a text like Ps. 78.67-68 (NIV).[6]

> Then he rejected the tents of Joseph, he did not choose the tribe of Ephraim but he chose the tribe of Judah, Mount Zion, which he loved.

5.   Charles (ed.), *The Apocrypha and Pseudepigrapha*, 362-63.
6.   Cf. Hilgert, 'The Dual Image of Joseph', 6.

This text appears to agree with the evaluations given in this study: Joseph is depicted negatively whereas Judah is praised. On the other hand, there is an unmistakable positive attitude towards Joseph as well, as can be seen in Psalm 105.16-22 (NIV):

> [16]He called down famine on the land and destroyed all their supplies of food; [17]and he sent a man before them—Joseph, sold as a slave. [18]They bruised his feet with shackles, his neck was put in irons, [19]till what he fore-told came to pass, till the word of the LORD proved him true. [20]The king sent and released him, the ruler of peoples set him free. [21]He made him master of his household, ruler over all he possessed, [22]to instruct his princes as he pleased and teach his elders wisdom.

The interesting thing now is that both the positive and the negative picture of Joseph are present within and outside the Hebrew Bible. As is clear from the analyses in this study, the story told in Gen. 37–50 results in Judah's rise and Joseph's decline—even though Joseph is presented favourable in several episodes (like ch. 39).

Which of both traditions regarding Joseph is the older one, the positive or the negative image or the one presented in Psalm 78 or in Psalm 105, cannot be established with certainty. Yet, phenomena like these in the Hebrew Bible itself and in the literature of the so-called Second Temple Period may give impulses to reconsider the origin and development of Gen. 37–50, or perhaps I should in this respect rather speak of the 'Joseph Story'. As Redford comments:

> For, as has long been realized, the Joseph story is in fact a novella or short story. It shares with other Egyptian and Near Eastern stories of the same genre a number of specific characteristics. As in folktales and wisdom there is a preference for the generic 'god' as opposed to the name of the deity, and proper nouns are likewise avoided. Terms of relationship ('father', 'older brother', 'younger brother') and titles are preferred to names; and toponyms, while a few are present, are generally suppressed. This all con-tributes to an atmosphere of timelessness and placelessness in the setting of the story: admittedly, as the story is now placed, it takes place in Egypt, but the basic shape of the plot does not demand a Nilotic setting.[7]

It is not impossible that not before it took its present form and position in Genesis the 'Joseph Story' may have become the story of Jacob's sons; as

7.   Redford, *Egypt, Canaan, and Israel in Ancient Times*, 423. In *A Study of the Biblical Story of Joseph* Redford wrote: 'the original Joseph Story seems to be nothing more than the Hebrew version of the common motif of the boy who dreamed great things' (251).

37.2 indicates: 'This is the story of Jacob's *toledot*' (אלה תלדות יעקב).
Moreover, if the tale of Gen. 37–50 is considered from a diachronic view
one might with the majority of historical-critic scholars opt for an original
'Joseph Story' in which Joseph was the praiseworthy leading character.[8]
This story was later situated (in several stages?[9]) in the larger framework
of the patriarchal narratives and expanded by parts in which Joseph's role
is reduced or presented less favourably[10] and Judah's role enlarged and
given more prominence. Perhaps the character of Judah or Judah's prede-
cessor (if any) was not even a part of the story as it was originally conceived?[11] This 'new' story may have co-existed for a while with the original
'Joseph Story',[12] hence the presence of positive and negative evaluations
of Joseph in some of the Second Temple Period writings and in the Hebrew
Bible itself. The tale was not as fixed as was the case in later tradition.

According to Soggin, some parts of Gen. 37–50, such as Joseph's accusation against the brothers that they are spies (42.8-17, which presents not
a favourable picture of Joseph) can refer only to the second century BCE.[13]

8. According to Redford, as he inferred from comparing Gen. 37–50 to Egyptian
sources from the first millennium BC, the story has to be composed somewhere between
the middle of the seventh and fifth centuries BC (*A Study of the Biblical Story of
Joseph*, 187-243, 252-53). This, however, only holds if part of the original 'Joseph
Story' was situated in Egypt.

9. Cf. Davies: 'between these two ends of the process, the initial composition and
the final canonization, there is much to be investigated' (*In Search of 'Ancient Israel'*,
113; cf. 131). Furthermore, if Gen. 39 is inspired by or based on the Egyptian tale of
the Two Brothers, then it is clear that the author/redactor considers himself free to
rework and revise the material he uses extensively.

10. Like the episode in which Joseph enslaves the Egyptians (47.13-26), which
'could have been added to the Joseph Story by the same hand which effected the
Judah-expansion; but this is not certain' (Redford, *A Study of the Biblical Story of
Joseph*, 182).

11. According to Dietrich the 'Josephs-Novelle' runs from Gen. 37–45, excluding
chs. 38 and 39, as well as Judah's speech in 44.18-34. The tale ends when the brothers
are reconciled in Gen. 45 and Jacob is reported that his son is still alive (*Die Josephsgeschichte*, 53-66). Of course, more 'original' Joseph-stories have been detected; see,
e.g., the studies of Coats, Westermann and Scharbert.

12. That is, *if* its main character was named 'Joseph'.

13. Soggin, 'Notes on the Joseph Story', 340. Lemche also prefers a late dating of
the Pentateuch, and consequently of Gen. 37–50: 'Endlich wären durch eine Datierung
des Pentateuch in 5., 4. oder sogar 3. Jahrhundert die Anknüpfungspunkte zwischen
der alttestamentlichen und der griechischen Geschichtsschreibung unendlich viel ein-
facher zu erklären' (N.P. Lemche, *Die Vorgeschichte Israels: Von den Anfängen bis*

With regard to the narrator's remark in 43.32 about the Egyptians not being able to eat with Hebrews, he writes that:

> nothing of the kind appears in ancient Egyptian sources, while it is attested by later Greek authors. Therefore one is at least entitled to ask the question whether the whole reasoning should not be reversed, in the sense that the reference is to the later Israelite custom, with its severe dietary laws that made it practically impossible to share meals with foreigners.[14]

The tale of the brethren as it is now in the Hebrew Bible is not a historical record of the far past, about how and why Israel's forebears entered into Egypt—although it is exactly this on a *narrative level*. Gen. 37–50 is woven into a larger story in which the inhabitants of the province of Judah (hence Judah's rising star in Gen. 37–50) are given a history of their own,[15] a national identity; or, in Philip Davies' words:

> To explain the existence of the biblical literature, we must conclude that the creation of what was in truth a *new society*, marking a definitive break with what had preceded, was accompanied by—or at least soon generated—an ideological superstructure which denied its more recent origins, its imperial basis, and instead indigenized itself.[16]

As for Gen. 37–50, Davies writes that Ben Sira

> omits Joseph from his survey until he introduces him at the end [49.15], in a final strophe, which reverses the chronological order and alludes to Enoch, Joseph, Shem, Seth and Adam. But Joseph is out of sequence, and is remembered only for his bones being 'cared for': there is no allusion to his success in Egypt, or his ability to decipher dreams, which one might expect from Ben Sira. The allusion is certainly suspicious, and it makes one wonder whether it is primary or secondary, and, even if it is primary, what Ben Sira knew about Joseph at all.[17]

It would be a worthwhile project to correlate the conclusions that the

---

zum Ausgang des 13. Jahrhunderts v. Chr. [Biblische Enzyklopädie, 1; Stuttgart: Verlag W. Kohlhammer 1996], 217).

14. Soggin, 'Notes on the Joseph Story', 341.

15. Cf. Lemche, *Die Vorgeschichte Israels*, 218.

16. Davies, *In Search of 'Ancient Israel'*, 87.

17. Davies, *In Search of 'Ancient Israel'*, 142. Thompson opts for a still later dating: the biblical texts 'are first known from Qumran in the second century, BCE, in contexts which clearly show that the formation of biblical books is still in process: hence my chronology of 165 BCE to 135 CE' (T.L. Thompson, 'Defining History and Ethnicity in the South Levant', in L.L. Grabbe [ed.], *Can a 'History of Israel' Be Written?* [JSOTSup, 245; Sheffield: Sheffield Academic Press, 1997], 166-87 [187]).

present study has ventured—Judah being brought into prominence and Joseph's example not to be imitated—with Davies' views about the development of the biblical writings, their gradual formation and final redaction during the third and second centuries BCE.[18]

All remarks in this epilogue, as said, ought to be considered tentative suggestions and are in need of much further elaboration in future studies on Gen. 37–50.

18. The 'classical' sources J, E and P will not do, neither can the development be described by a Judah- and Reuben-version. The relation between the original 'Joseph Story' and the present tale in Genesis could perhaps be described in terms such as the relation between the gospels of Mark and Matthew: a fundamental revision of an older work that has resulted in an entirely novel writing. In the case of the gospels, Mark did survive, the 'original' Joseph-Story (if it ever existed) did not.

BIBLIOGRAPHY

Ackerman, J.S., 'Joseph, Judah, and Jacob', in K.R.R. Gros Louis and J.S. Ackerman (eds.), *Literary Interpretations of Biblical Narratives* (2 vols.; Nashville: Abingdon Press, 1982), II, 85-113.

Ages, A., 'Why Didn't Joseph Call Home?', *BR* 9 (1993), 42-46.

Alter, R., *The Art of Biblical Narrative* (New York: Basic Books, 1981).

Alter, R., and F. Kermode (eds.), *The Literary Guide to the Bible* (London: Collins, 1987).

Anbar, M., 'Changement des noms des tribus nomades dans la relation d'un même événement', *Bib* 49 (1968), 221-32.

Armstrong, P.B., *Conflicting Readings: Variety and Validity in Interpretation* (Chapel Hill: The University of North Carolina Press, 1990).

Bae, E.-J., *A Multiple Approach to the Joseph Story: With a Detailed Reading of Genesis 46,31–47, 31; 50,1-11,14* (Rome: Pontificia Universitas Gregoriana, 1995).

Barr, J., 'Did Isaiah Know about Hebrew "Root Meanings"?', *ExpTim* 75 (1964), 242.

—'Semitic Philology and the Interpretation of the Old Testament', in G.W. Anderson (ed.), *Tradition and Interpretation: Essays by Members of the Society for Old Testament Study* (Oxford: Clarendon Press, 1979), 31-64.

—'Three Interrelated Factors in the Semantic Study of Ancient Hebrew', *ZAH* 7 (1994), 33-44.

Bechtel, L.M., 'What if Dinah is not Raped? (Genesis 34)', *JSOT* 62 (1994), 19-36.

Becking, B., ' "They hated him even more": Literary Technique in Genesis 37.1-11', *BN* 60 (1991), 40-47.

Berlin, A., *Poetics and Interpretation of Biblical Narrative* (Bible and Literature Series, 9; Sheffield: Almond Press, 1983).

Boecker, H.-J., 'Überlegungen zur Josephsgeschichte', in J. Hausmann and H.-J. Zobel (eds.), *Alttestamentlicher Glaube und Biblische Theologie: Festschrift für Horst Dietrich Preuss* (Stuttgart: W. Kohlhammer, 1992), 35-45.

Bos, J.W.H., 'Out of the Shadows Genesis 38; Judges 4.17-22; Ruth 3', *Semeia* 42 (1988), 37-67.

Branson, R.D., *A Study of the Hebrew Term* נשא (Boston: Boston University Graduate School, 1976).

Bromiley, G.W. (ed.), *The International Standard Bible Encyclopedia* (4 vols.; Grand Rapids: Eerdmans, 1979–1988).

Brueggemann, W., *Genesis* (Interpretation: A Bible Commentary for Teaching and Preaching; Atlanta: John Knox Press, 1982).

—'Genesis L 15-21: A Theological Exploration', in J.A. Emerton (ed.), *Congress Volume, Salamanca 1983* (VTSup, 36; Leiden: E.J. Brill, 1985), 40-53.

Caine, I., 'Numbers in the Joseph Narrative', in R. Brauner (ed.), *Jewish Civilization: Essays and Studies* (Philadelphia: Reconstructionist Rabbinical College, 1979), 3-17.

Carmichael, C.M., 'Some Sayings in Genesis 49', *JBL* 88 (1969), 435-44.

Cassuto, U., 'The Story of Judah and Tamar', in U. Cassuto, *Biblical and Oriental Studies*. I. *Bible* (Jerusalem: Magnes Press/Hebrew University, 1973), 29-40.

Charles, R.H. (ed.), *The Apocrypha and Pseudepigrapha of the Old Testament in English with Introductions and Critical and Explanatory Notes to the Several Books*, II (2 vols.; Oxford: Clarendon Press, 2nd edn, 1969).

Christensen, D.L., 'Anticipatory Paronomasia in Jonah 3.7-8 and Genesis 37.2', *RB* 90 (1983), 261-63.

Clines, D.J.A., *The Theme of the Pentateuch* (JSOTSup, 10; Sheffield: JSOT Press, 1978).

—*What Does Eve Do to Help? and Other Readerly Questions to the Old Testament* (JSOTSup, 94; Sheffield: JSOT Press, 1990).

Clines, D.J.A. (ed.), *The Dictionary of Classical Hebrew* (Sheffield: Sheffield Academic Press, 1993–).

Coats, G.W., 'The Joseph Story and Ancient Wisdom: A Reappraisal', *CBQ* 35 (1973), 285-97.

—'Redactional Unity in Genesis 37–50', *JBL* 93 (1974), 15-21.

—*From Canaan to Egypt: Structural and Theological Context for the Joseph Story* (CBQMS, 4; Washington: Catholic Biblical Association, 1976).

Cohen, M., '*M^{e}KĒRŌTĒHEM* (Genèse XLIX 5)', *VT* 31 (1981), 472-77.

Cohn, R.L., 'Narrative Structure and Canonical Perspective in Genesis', *JSOT* 25 (1983), 3-16.

Cotterell, P., and M. Turner, *Linguistics and Biblical Interpretation* (London: SPCK, 1989).

Davies, P.R., *In Search of Ancient Israel* (JSOTSup, 148; Sheffield: Sheffield Academic Press, 1992).

Deist, F., 'A Note on the Narrator's Voice in Gen 37, 20-22', *ZAW* 108 (1996), 621-22.

Dietrich, W., *Die Josepherzählung als Novelle und Geschichtsschreibung: zugleich ein Beitrag zur Pentateuchfrage* (Biblisch-Theologische Studien, 14; Neukirchen–Vluyn: Neukirchener Verlag, 1989).

Donner, H., *Die literarische Gestalt der alttestamentlichen Josephsgeschichte* (Heidelberg: Carl Winter/Universitätsverlag, 1976).

Douglas, J.D. (ed.), *New Bible Dictionary* (Leicester: Inter-Varsity Press; Wheaton, IL: Tyndale House, 1982).

Eben-Soshan, A., *New Concordance to the Tora, the Prophets and the Writings* (קונקורדנציה חדשה לתורה לנביאים ולכתובים, א. אבן־שושן) (Jerusalem: Kiryath Sepher Ltd, 1993).

Ehrlich, E.L., *Der Traum im alten Testament* (BZAW, 73; Berlin: Alfred Töpelmann, 1953).

Emerton, J.A., 'The Etymology of *HIŠTAḤ^{A}WĀH*', in H.A. Brongers *et al.* (eds.), *Instruction and Interpretation: Studies in Hebrew Language, Palestinian Archeology and Biblical Exegesis; Papers Read at the Joint British–Dutch Old Testament Conference held at Louvain, 1976* (OTS, 20; Leiden: E.J. Brill, 1977), 41-55.

Endo, Y., *The Verbal System in Classical Hebrew in the Joseph Story: An Approach from Discourse Analysis* (Studia Semitica Neerlandica, 32; Assen: Van Gorcum, 1996).

Exum, J.C., *Fragmented Women: Feminist (Sub)versions of Biblical Narratives* (JSOTSup, 163; Sheffield: JSOT Press, 1993).

Fewell, D.N., and D.M. Gunn, 'Tipping the Balance: Sternberg's Reader and the Rape of Dinah', *JBL* 110 (1991), 193-211.

Fokkelman, J.P., 'Genesis', in R. Alter and F. Kermode (eds.), *The Literary Guide to the Bible* (London: Collins, 1987).

—'Genesis 37 and 38 at the Interface of Structural Analysis and Hermeneutics', in L.J. de

Regt *et al.* (eds.), *Literary Structure and Rhetorical Strategies in the Hebrew Bible* (Assen: Van Gorcum; Winona Lake, IN: Eisenbrauns, 1996), 152-87.

Fox, M.V., 'Wisdom in the Joseph Story', *VT* 15 (2001), 26-41.

Fretheim, T.E., *The Pentateuch* (Interpreting Biblical Texts; Nashville: Abingdon Press, 1996).

Fritsch, C.T., ' "God was with him": A Theological Study of the Joseph Narrative', *Int* 9 (1955), 21-34.

Fung, Y.-W., *Victim and Victimizer: Joseph's Interpretation of his Destiny* (JSOTSup, 308; Sheffield: Sheffield Academic Press, 2000).

Gervitz, S., 'The Reprimand of Reuben', *JNES* 30 (1971), 87-98.

—'Of Patriarchs and Puns: Joseph at the Fountain, Jacob at the Ford', *HUCA 46* (1975), 33-54.

—'The Life Spans of Joseph and Enoch and the Parallellism *šib 'ātayim–šib 'îm wĕšib 'āh*', *JBL* 96 (1977), 570-71.

—'Simeon and Levi in "The Blessing of Jacob" (Gen. 49.5-7)', *HUCA* 52 (1981), 93-128.

Gesenius, W., *Hebräisches und aramäisches Handwörterbuch über das alte Testament* (Berlin: Springer Verlag, 1987; [18th edn; 1810]).

Gibson, J.C.L., *Genesis*, II (2 vols.; The Daily Study Bible; Edinburgh: The Saint Andrew Press; Philadelphia: Westminster Press, 1982).

Gibson, J.C.L., *Davidson's Introductory Hebrew Grammar—Syntax* (Edinburgh: T. & T. Clark, 1994).

Goldin, J., 'The Youngest Son or Where Does Genesis 38 Belong?', *JBL* 96 (1977), 27-44.

Good, E.M., 'The Blessing on Judah, Gen 49 8-12', *JBL* 82 (1963), 427-32.

Görg, M., *Die Beziehungen zwischen dem alten Israel und Ägypten von den Anfängen bis zum Exil* (Erträge der Forschung, 290; Darmstadt: Wissenschaftliche Buchgesellschaft, 1997).

Gorp, H. van (ed.), *Lexicon voor literaire termen* (Groningen: Wolters-Noordhof, 1993).

Green, B., *'What Profit for Us?' Remembering in the Story of Joseph* (Lanham: University Press of America, 1996).

Greenstein, E.L., 'An Equivocal Reading of the Sale of Joseph' in K.R.R. Gros Louis and J.S. Ackerman (eds.), *Literary Interpretations of Biblical Narratives* (2 vols.; Nashville: Abingdon Press, 1982), II, 114-25.

Gunn, D.M., and D.N. Fewell, *Narrative in the Hebrew Bible* (Oxford Bible Series; Oxford: Oxford University Press, 1993).

Hadda, J., 'Joseph: Ancestor of Psychoanalysis', *Conservative Judaism* 37 (1984), 17-21.

Halpern, B., 'The Exodus from Egypt: Myth or Reality', in H. Shanks (ed.), *The Rise of Ancient Israel* (Washington, DC: Biblical Archeological Society, 1992), 86-113.

Hamilton, V.P., *The Book of Genesis: Chapters 18–50* (NICOT; Grand Rapids: Eerdmans, 1995).

Hawking, S., *A Brief History of Time: From the Big Bang to Black Holes* (Toronto: Bantam Books, 1988).

—*Black Holes and Baby Universes and Other Essays* (New York: Bantam Books, 1993).

Hettema, T.L., *Reading for Good: Narrative Theology and Ethics in the Joseph Story from the Perspective of Ricoeur's Hermeneutics* (Kampen: Kok, 1996).

Hilgert, E., 'The Dual Image of Joseph in Hebrew and Early Jewish Literature', *Papers of the Chicago Society of Biblical Research* 30 (1985), 5-21.

Hoop, R. de, *Genesis 49 in its Literary and Historical Context* (Leiden: E.J. Brill, 1998).

Hospers, J.H., 'Polysemy and Homonymy', *ZAH* 6 (1993), 114-22.

Humphreys, W.L., *Joseph and his Family: A Literary Study* (Studies on the Personalities of the Old Testament; Columbia: University of South Carolina Press, 1988).

Jacob, B., *Das erste Buch der Tora: Genesis* (repr., New York: Ktav, 1968 [1934]).

Jeffers, A., 'Divination by Dreams in Ugaritic Literature and in the Old Testament', *IBS* 12 (1990), 167-83.

Josipivici, G., *The Book of God: A Response to the Bible* (New Haven: Yale University Press, 1988).

Joüon, P., and T. Muraoka, *A Grammar of Biblical Hebrew* (Subsidia Biblica 14.1-2; Rome: Pontificio Istituto Biblico, 1993).

Kallai, Z., 'The Twelve-Tribe Systems of Israel', *VT* 47 (1997), 53-90.

Kekebus, N., *Die Josepherzählung: Literarkritische und redaktionsgeschichtliche Untersuchungen zu Genesis 37–50* (Internationale Hochschulschriften; Münster: Waxmann, 1990).

Knauf, E.A., 'Midianites and Ishmaelites', in J.F.A. Sawyer and D.J.A. Clines (eds.), *Midian, Moab and Edom: The History and Archaeology of Late Bronze and Iron Age Jordan and North-West Arabia* (JSOTSup, 24; Sheffield: JSOT Press, 1983), 147-62.

Kugel, J.L., *In Potiphar's House: The Interpretive Life of Biblical Texts* (Cambridge, MA: Harvard University Press, 1994 [1990]).

Kunin, S.D., *The Logic of Incest: A Structuralist Analysis of Hebrew Mythology* (JSOTSup, 185; Sheffield: Sheffield Academic Press, 1995).

Krauss, L.M., *The Physics of Star Trek* (New York: Basic Books, 1995).

Lambe, A.J., 'Genesis 38: Structure and Literary Design', in P.R. Davies and D.J.A. Clines, *The World of Genesis. Persons, Places, Perspectives* (JSOTSup, 257; Sheffield: Sheffield Academic Press, 1998), 102-120.

—'Judah's Development: The Pattern of Departure–Transition–Departure', *JSOT* 83 (1999), 53-68.

Lamprecht, J.J., 'Karakterisering in Gen. 37–50' (unpublished PhD dissertation, University of Stellenbosch, South Africa, 1990).

Lehming, S., 'Zur Erzählung von der Geburt der Jakobsöhne', *VT* 13 (1963), 74-81.

Lemche, N.P., *Die Vorgeschichte Israels: Von den Anfängen bis zum Ausgang des 13. Jahrhunderts v. Chr.* (Biblische Enzyklopädie, 1; Stuttgart: W. Kohlhammer, 1996).

Lerner, B.D., 'Joseph the Unrighteous', *Judaism* 38 (1989), 278-81.

Licht, J., *Storytelling in the Bible* (Jerusalem: Magnes Press/Hebrew University, 1978).

Long, V.P., *The Reign and Rejection of King Saul: A Case for Literary and Theological Coherence* (SBLDS, 118; Atlanta, GA: Scholars Press, 1989).

—*The Art of Biblical History* (Foundations of Contemporary Interpretation, 5; Grand Rapids: Zondervan, 1994).

Longacre, R., 'Who Sold Joseph into Egypt?', R.L. Harris *et al.* (eds.), *Interpretation and History: Essays in Honour of Allan A. MacRea* (Singapore: Christian Life Publishers, 1986), 75-92.

—*Joseph: A Story of Divine Providence* (Winona Lake, IN: Eisenbrauns, 1989).

Longman, T., III, 'Literary Approaches and Interpretation', in *NIDOTE*, I, 103-24.

Lowenthal, E.I., *The Joseph Narrative in Genesis: An Interpretation* (New York: Ktav, 1973).

Lyons, J., *Linguistic Semantics: An Introduction* (Cambridge: Cambridge University Press, 1995).

Mann, T., *Joseph and his Brothers* (London: Minerva, 1997).

Margalith, O., '*MᵉKĒRŌTĒHEM* (Genesis XLIX 5)', *VT* 34 (1984), 101-102.

Matthews, V.H., 'The Anthropology of Clothing in the Joseph Narrative', *JSOT* 65 (1995), 25-36.

McKenzie, B.A., 'Jacob's Blessing on Pharaoh: An Interpretation of Gen 46.31–47.26', *WTJ* 45 (1983), 386-99.

Miller, J.M., and J.H. Hayes, *A History of Ancient Israel and Judah* (Philadelphia: Westminster Press, 1986).

Miscall, P.D., 'The Jacob and Joseph Stories as Analogies', *JSOT* 6 (1978), 28-40.

Morimura, N., 'Tamar and Judah—A Feminist Reading of Gen 38', in T. Schneider and H. Schüngel-Straumann (eds.), *Theologie zwischen Zeiten und Kontinenten: Für Elisabeth Gössman* (Freiburg: Herder, 1993), 2-18.

Morris, G., 'Convention and Character in the Joseph Narrative', *Proceedings of the Eastern Great Lakes and Midwest Bible Societies* 14 (1994), 69-85.

Muilenberg, J., 'The Birth of Benjamin', *JBL* 75 (1956), 195-201.

Muraoka, T., 'On Verb Complementation in Biblical Hebrew', *VT* 29 (1979), 424-35.

Negenman, J., *Geografische gids bij de bijbel* (Boxtel: Katholieke Bijbelstichting, 1981).

Negev, A. (ed.), *Archäologisches Lexikon zur Bibel* (Munich: Kunstverlag Edition Praeger, 1972).

Niccacci, A., 'A Neglected Point of Hebrew Syntax: Yiqtol and Position in the Sentence', *Liber Annuus* 37 (1987), 7-19.

—*The Syntax of the Verb in Classical Hebrew Prose* (JSOTSup, 86; Sheffield: JSOT Press, 1990).

—'On The Hebrew Verbal System', in R.D. Bergen (ed.), *Biblical Hebrew and Discourse Linguistics* (Dallas, TX: Summer Institute of Linguistics, 1995), 117-37.

Nicholson, G.C., *Death as Departure: The Johannine Descent-Ascent Schema* (SBLDS, 63; Chico, CA: Scholars Press, 1983).

Niditch, S., 'The Wronged Woman Righted: An Analysis of Genesis 38', *HTR* 72 (1979), 143-49.

O'Brien, M.A., 'The Contribution of Judah's Speech, Genesis 44.18-34, to the Characterization of Joseph', *CBQ* 59 (1997), 429-47.

Oppenheim, A.L., *The Interpretation of Dreams in the Ancient Near East: With a Translation of an Assyrian Dream-Book* (Transactions of the American Philosophical Society, 46; Philadelphia: The American Philosophical Society, 1956).

Paap, C., *Die Josephsgeschichte, Genesis 37–50: Bestimmungen ihrer literarischen Gattung in der zweiten Hälfte des 20. Jahrhunderts* (Europäische Hochschulschriften, 23, Theologie 534; Frankfurt: Peter Lang, 1995).

Peck, J., 'Note on Genesis 37.2 and Joseph's Character', *ExpTim* 82 (1970–71), 342-43.

Pirson, R., 'What is Joseph Supposed to Be? On the Interpretation of נער in Genesis 37.2', in A. Brenner and J.W. van Henten (eds.), *Recycling Biblical Figures: Papers Read at a NOSTER Colloquium in Amsterdam 12–13 May 1997* (Studies in Theology and Religion, 1; Leiden: Deo, 1999), 81-92.

—'The Sun, the Moon and Eleven Stars. An Interpretation of Joseph's Second Dream', in A. Wénin (ed.), *Studies in the Book of Genesis: Literature, Redaction and History* (Bibliotheca Ephemeridum Theologicarum Lovaniensium, 155; Leuven: Peeters, 2001), 561-68.

Poulssen, N., *Brood en spelen: Over de werking van het Jozefverhaal (Genesis 37–50)* (Tilburg: Tilburg University Press, 1992).

Prewitt, T.J., *The Elusive Covenant: A Structural-Semiotic Reading of Genesis* (Advances in Semiotics; Bloomington: Indiana University Press, 1990).

Rad, G. von, 'Josephsgeschichte und ältere Chokma', in G. von Rad, *Gesammelte Studien zum Alten Testament* (TBü, 8; Munich: Chr. Kaiser Verlag, 1965), 272-80.

—*Genesis. A Commentary* (OTL; London: SCM Press, 3rd edn, 1970).

Radday, Y.T., 'Humour in Names', in Y.T. Radday and A. Brenner (eds.), *On Humour and the Comic in the Hebrew Bible* (Bible and Literature Series, 23; Sheffield: Almond Press, 1990), 59-97.

Redford, D.B., 'The "Land of the Hebrews" in Gen. XL 15', *VT* 15 (1965) 529-32.

—*A Study of the Biblical Story of Joseph (Genesis 37–50)* (VTSup, 20; Leiden: E.J. Brill, 1970).

—*Egypt, Canaan and Israel in Ancient Times* (Princeton, NJ: Princeton University Press, 1992).

Richter, W., 'Traum und Traumdeutung im AT: Ihre Form und Verwendung', *BZ* 7 (1963), 202-20.

Rudolph, W., 'Die Josefsgeschichte', in P. Volz and W. Rudolph, *Der Elohist als Erzähler: Ein Irrweg der Pentateuchkritik? An der Genesis erläutert* (BZAW, 63; Giessen: Alfred Töpelmann, 1933), 145-83.

Ruppert, L., *Die Josephserzählung der Genesis: Ein Beitrag zur Theologie der Pentateuchquellen* (SANT, 11; Munich: Kösel-Verlag, 1965).

—'Die Aporie der gegenwärtigen Pentateuchdiskussion und die Josefserzählung der Genesis', *BZ* 29 (1985), 31-48.

—'Zur neueren Diskussion um die Josefsgeschichte der Genesis', *BZ* 33 (1989), 92-97.

Salm, E., *Juda und Tamar: Eine exegetische Studie zu Gen 38* (Forschung zur Bibel, 76; Würzburg: Echter Verlag, 1996).

Saeed, J.I., *Semantics* (Oxford: Basil Blackwell, 1997).

Samuel, M., 'The True Character of the Biblical Joseph: Joseph—the Brilliant Failure', *BR* 2 (1986), 38-51.

Sarna, N.M., *The JPS Torah Commentary: Genesis—*בראשית (Philadelphia: The Jewish Publication Society of America, 5749/1989).

Sasson, J.M., 'A Genealogical "Convention" in Biblical Chronography?', *ZAW* 90 (1978), 171-85.

Savran, G.W., 'The Character as Narrator in Biblical Narrative', *Prooftexts* 5 (1985), 1-17.

—*Telling and Retelling. Quotation in Biblical Narrative* (Indiana Studies in Biblical Literature; Bloomington: Indiana University Press, 1988).

Sawyer, J.F.A., 'Root-Meanings in Hebrew', *JSS* 12 (1967), 37-50.600.

Sawyer, J.F.A., and D.J.A. Clines, *Midian, Moab and Edom: The History and Archaeology of Late Bronze and Iron Age Jordan and North-West Arabia* (JSOTSup, 24; Sheffield: JSOT Press, 1983), 147-61.

Saydon, P., 'The Conative Imperfect in Hebew', *VT* 12 (1962), 124-26.

Scharbert, J., *Ich bin Joseph euer Bruder: Die Erzählung von Joseph und seinen Brüdern wie sie nicht in der Bibel steht* (St Ottilien: EOS Verlag Erzabtei, 1988).

Schmidt, L., *Literarische Studien zur Josephsgeschichte* (BZAW, 167; Berlin: de Gruyter, 1986).

Schmitt, H.-C., 'Die Hintergründe der "neuesten Pentateuchkritik" und der literarische Befund der Josephsgeschichte Gen 37-50', *ZAW* 97 (1985), 161-79.

Schneider, W., *Grammatik des biblischen Hebräisch: Völlig neue Bearbeitung der "Hebräischen Grammatik für den akademischen Unterricht" von Oskar Grether. Ein Lehrbuch* (Munich: Claudius Verlag, 8th edn, 1993 [1974]).

Seebass, H., *Geschichtliche Zeit und theonome Tradition in der Joseph- Erzählung* (Gütersloh: Gütersloher Verlagshaus/Gerd Mohn, 1978).

Seybold, D.A., 'Paradox and Symmetry in the Joseph Narrative', in K.R.R. Gros Louis,

J.S. Ackerman and T.S. Warshaw (eds.), *Literary Interpretations of Biblical Narratives* (Nashville: Abingdon Press, 1974), 59-73.

Shippey, T., *The Road to Middle-Earth* (London: George Allen & Unwin, 1982).

Silva, A., *La symbolique des rêves et des vêtements dans l'histoire de Joseph et de ses frères* (Heritage et project, 52; Quebec: Fides, 1994).

Skinner, J., *A Critical and Exegetical Commentary on Genesis* (ICC; Edinburgh: T. & T. Clark, 2nd edn, 1930).

Soggin, J.A., 'Notes on the Joseph Story', in A. Graeme Auld (ed.), *Understanding Poets and Prophets: Essays in Honour of George Wishart Anderson* (JSOTSup, 152; Sheffield: JSOT Press, 1993), 336-49.

Speiser, E.A., *Genesis* (AB, 1; Garden City, NY: Doubleday, 1964).

Sperber, A. (ed.), *The Bible in Aramaic*. I. *The Pentateuch According to Targum Onkelos* (5 vols.; Leiden: E.J. Brill, 1992, 2nd impression [1959-1973]).

Steiner, F., 'Enslavement and the Early Hebrew Lineage System: An Explanation of Genesis 47:29-31; 48:1-16', in B. Lang (ed.), *Anthropological Approaches to the Old Testament* (Issues in Religion and Theology, 8; Philadelphia: Fortress Press; London: SPCK, 1985), 21-25.

Steinmetz, D., *From Father to Son: Kinship, Conflict and Continuity in Genesis* (Literary Currents in Biblical Interpretation; Louisville, KY: Westminster/John Knox Press, 1991).

Stern, E. (ed.), *The New Encyclopedia of Archeological Excavations in the Holy Land* (4 vols.; Jerusalem: Israel Exploration Society, 1993).

Sternberg, M., *The Poetics of Biblical Narrative: Ideological Literature and the Drama of Reading* (Bloomington: Indiana University Press, 1985).

—'Time and Space in Biblical (Hi)story Telling: The Grand Chronology', in R.M. Schwartz (ed.), *The Book and the Text: The Bible and Literary Theory* (Oxford: Basil Blackwell, 1990), 81-145.

Sykes, S., 'Time and Space in Haggai–Zechariah 1–8: A Bakhtinian Analysis of a Prophetic Chronicle', *JSOT* 76 (1997), 97-124.

Syrén, R., *The Forsaken Firstborn: A Study of a Recurrent Motif in the Patriarchal Narratives* (JSOTSup, 133; Sheffield: JSOT Press, 1993).

Talstra, E. 'Clause Types and Textual Structure: An Experiment in Narrative Syntax', in *idem* (ed.), *Narrative and Comment: Contributions to Discourse Grammar and Hebrew Bible Presented to Wolfgang Schneider* (Amsterdam: Societas Hebraica Amstelodamensis, 1995), 166-80.

—'A Hierarchy of Clauses in Biblical Hebrew Narrative', in E. van Wolde (ed.), *Narrative Syntax & the Hebrew Bible: Papers of the Tilburg Conference 1996* (Biblical Interpretation Series, 29; Leiden: E.J. Brill, 1997), 85-118.

Thompson, T.L., 'The Joseph and Moses Narratives', in J.H. Hayes and J.M. Miller (eds.), *Israelite and Judean History* (OTL; London: SCM Press, 1977), 149-212.

—*The Origin Tradition of Ancient Israel*. I. *The Literary Formation of Genesis and Exodus 1-23* (JSOTSup, 55; Sheffield: JSOT Press, 1987).

—'How Yahweh Became God: Exodus 3 and 6 and the Heart of the Pentateuch', *JSOT* 68 (1995), 57-74.

—'Defining History and Ethnicity in the South Levant', in L.L. Grabbe, *Can a 'History of Israel' Be Written?* (JSOTSup, 245; Sheffield: Sheffield Academic Press, 1997), 166-87.

Toorn, K, van der, B. Becking and P.W. van der Horst (eds.), *Dictionary of Deities and Demons in the Bible* (Leiden: E.J. Brill, 1995).

Turner, L.A., *Announcements of Plot in Genesis* (JSOTSup, 96; Sheffield:JSOT Press, 1990).
VanGemeren, W.A., 'Introduction', in *NIDOTE*, I, 5-13.
VanGemeren, W.A. (ed.), *The New International Dictionary of Old Testament Theology and Exegesis* (5 vols; Carlisle: Paternoster, 1997).
Vanhoozer, K., 'Introduction: Hermeneutics, Text, and Biblical Theology', in *NIDOTE*, I, 14-50.
Vawter, B., *Genesis: A New Reading* (London: Geoffrey Chapman, 1977).
Vergote, J., *Joseph en Egypte: Genèse chap. 37–50 à la lumière des études Egyptologiques récentes* (Orientalia et Biblica Lovaniensia 3; Leuven: Publications Universitaires/ Instituut voor Oriëntalisme, 1959).
Waltke, B.K., and M. O'Connor, *An Introduction to Biblical Hebrew Syntax* (Winona Lake, IN: Eisenbrauns, 1990).
Walton, J.H., 'Principles for Productive Word Study', in *NIDOTE*, I, 161-71.
Weinrich, H., *Tempus: Besprochene und erzählte Welt* (Sprache und Literatur, 16; Stuttgart: W. Kohlhammer, 4th edn, 1985 [1964]).
Wenham, G.J., *Genesis 16–50* (WBC, 2; Dallas, TX: Word Books, 1994).
Weren, W., 'Mozes, Jezus en het manna: Een intertextuele studie van Johannes 6', in *idem*, *Intertextualiteit en Bijbel* (Kampen: Kok, 1993), 93-132.
—*Windows on Jesus: Methods in Gospel Exegesis* (London: SCM Press, 1999).
Westermann, C., *Genesis 12–36* (BKAT, 1.2; Neukirchen–Vluyn: Neukirchener Verlag, 1981).
—*Genesis 37–50* (BKAT, 1.3; Neukirchen–Vluyn: Neukirchener Verlag, 1982).
White, H.C., 'The Joseph Story: A Narrative which "Consumes" its Content', *Semeia* 31 (1985), 49-69.
—'Rueben and Judah: Duplicates or Complements?', in J.T. Butler *et al.* (eds.), *Understanding the Word: Essays in Honor of Bernard W. Anderson* (JSOTSup, 37; Sheffield: JSOT Press, 1985), 73-97.
—*Narration and Discourse in the Book of Genesis* (Cambridge: Cambridge University Press, 1991).
Wildavsky, A., *Assimilation versus Separation: Joseph the Administrator and the Politics of Religion in Biblical Israel* (New Brunswick, NJ: Transaction Publishers, 1993).
—'Survival Must not be Gained through Sin: The Moral of the Joseph Stories Prefigured through Judah and Tamar', *JSOT* 62 (1994), 37-48.
Willi-Plein, I., 'Historiografische Aspekte der Josephsgeschichte', *Henoch* 1 (1979), 305-31.
Williams, J.G., 'Number Symbolism and Joseph as Symbol of Completion', *JBL* 98 (1979), 86-87.
Wolde, E. van, *Aan de hand van Ruth* (Kampen: Kok, 1993).
—'Semantics and (Ana)Logic', in E. van Wolde, *Words become Worlds. Semantic Studies of Genesis 1–11* (Leiden: E.J. Brill, 1994), 149-59.
—'A Text-Semantic Study of the Hebrew Bible, Illustrated with Noah and Job', *JBL* 113 (1994), 19-35.
—*Words become Worlds. Semantic Studies of Genesis 1–11* (Leiden: E.J. Brill, 1994), 149-59.
—'Who Guides Whom? Embeddedness and Perspective in Biblical Hebrew and in 1 Kings 3.16-28', *JBL* 114 (1995), 623-42.
—'The Text as an Eloquent Guide: Rhetorical, Linguistic and Literary Features in Genesis 1', in L.J. de Regt, J. de Waard and J.P. Fokkelman (eds.), *Literary Structure and Rhetorical Strategies in the Hebrew Bible* (Assen: Van Gorcum, 1996), 134-51.
—'Linguistic Motivation and Biblical Exegesis', in E. van Wolde (ed.), *Narrative Syntax & the Hebrew Bible: Papers of the Tilburg Conference 1996* (Biblical Interpretation Series, 29; Leiden: E.J. Brill, 1997), 21-50.

—'Texts in Dialogue with Texts: Intertextuality in the Ruth and Tamar Narratives', *BibInt* 5 (1997), 1-28.

—'Textsemantics: A Bridge between Linguistics and Literary Theory', in I. Rauch and G.F. Carr (eds.), *Semiotics around the World: Synthesis in Diversity. Proceedings of the Fifth Congress of the International Association for Semiotic Studies, Berkeley 1994* (Berlin: Mouton de Gruyter, 1997), 267-70.

Yoseph, A. Ben, 'Joseph and his Brothers', *Jewish Bible Quarterly* 21 (1993), 153-58.

Zenger, E., 'Die Bücher der Tora/des Pentateuch', in E. Zenger *et al.*, *Einleitung in das Alte Testament* (Kohlhammer Studienbücher Theologie, 1, 1; Stuttgart: W. Kohlhammer, 1995), 34-75.

INDEX

INDEX OF REFERENCES

OLD TESTAMENT

160 *The Lord of the Dreams*

Genesis (cont.)

37.23	33, 62, 64, 65, 68	38.23	109
37.24	64, 65, 83, 131	38.26	85, 100
37.25	68-70, 72, 74, 75, 83, 108, 132	39–41	85, 139
37.26-27	62, 70, 80, 128	39	76, 83, 85, 86, 131, 140, 145, 146
37.26	61, 62, 66, 67	39.1	75, 76, 85, 86, 132
37.27	62, 67, 68, 70, 75, 80, 132	39.2-21	86
37.28	65, 69-76, 80, 132	39.2-20	85
37.29-30	70	39.2-6	86
37.29	37, 62, 72, 80, 81, 98	39.2	118, 131
37.30	72, 73, 80, 81	39.3	86, 89, 92, 118, 131
37.31	33	39.5	118
37.32	38	39.7	86
37.33	33, 81, 82, 106, 128, 134	39.9	86, 116, 140
37.34-35	79	39.14	131
37.34	38, 80, 82	39.17	131
37.35	82, 98, 106	39.20	128
37.36	74-77, 80, 85, 86	39.21–40.23	86
38	2, 24, 83, 85, 99, 104, 109, 113, 146	39.21-23	86
		39.21	92, 118, 131
38.1	83	39.23	86, 118
38.2	22, 83	40	52, 53, 59, 83, 86, 90, 114, 117
38.7	84, 118, 136	40.1	86
38.10	118, 136	40.3-4	86
38.11	84	40.3	128
38.14	128	40.5	52, 128
38.17-18	109	40.8	45, 52, 87-89, 114, 117, 140
38.17	104	40.9-11	52
38.18	83, 104	40.9	45, 52, 53, 128
38.20	104, 109	40.10	52, 53, 128
		40.11	52, 53
		40.12	87
		40.14-15	138
		40.14	107
		40.15	70, 73, 77, 78, 83

40.16-17	53		
40.16	53		
40.17	53		
40.18	87		
40.20	56, 87		
40.22	87		
40.23	107		
41	24, 54, 59, 83, 86, 87, 89, 90, 114, 117, 131		
41.1-7	54, 87		
41.1	86		
41.3	54		
41.4	59		
41.7	59		
41.8	45, 58, 87, 88		
41.9-13	88		
41.10	86		
41.11	52		
41.12	45, 86		
41.14	83, 88		
41.15	52, 58, 88		
41.16	37, 88		
41.17-24	54, 55, 88		
41.17	54		
41.18	54		
41.19	54		
41.20	54, 59		
41.21	54, 55		
41.22	55		
41.23	55		
41.24	44, 55, 59, 88		
41.25	44, 58, 59, 88-90, 112		
41.28	88, 89, 112		
41.32	88-90, 112		
41.33-36	88		
41.33	90		
41.34-36	91		
41.37	88, 89		
41.38	89, 90, 114, 141		

INDEX OF AUTHORS

JOURNAL FOR THE STUDY OF THE OLD TESTAMENT
SUPPLEMENT SERIES